PHP Reactive Programming

Leverage the power of reactive programming with PHP

Martin Sikora

BIRMINGHAM - MUMBAI

PHP Reactive Programming

First published: March 2017

Production reference: 1230317

Published by Packt Publishing Ltd.
Livery Place
35 Livery Street
Birmingham
B3 2PB, UK.

ISBN 978-1-78646-287-9

www.packtpub.com

Credits

Author

Martin Sikora

Reviewer

Alexandru-Emil Lupu

Commissioning Editor

Kunal Parikh

Acquisition Editor

Chaitanya Nair

Content Development Editor

Zeeyan Pinheiro

Technical Editor

Vivek Pala

Copy Editor

Safis Editing

Project Coordinator

Vaidehi Sawant

Proofreader

Safis Editing

Indexer

Francy Puthiry

Graphics

Abhinash Sahu

Production Coordinator

Aparna Bhagat

About the Author

Martin Sikora has been professionally programming since 2006 for companies such as Miton CZ, Symbio Digital, and PRIA in various languages, mostly PHP and TypeScript. Since 2017, he's freelancing, trying to work on open source projects in TypeScript, PHP, Dart, C, and Python. He's been actively contributing to RxPHP and RxJS 5 on both Github and StackOverflow. He is a Zend certified engineer and was a member of the winning team during Google Dart Hackathon 2012 in Prague. His first publication was *Dart Essentials*, by Packt, published in May 2015. Occasionally, Martin writes articles for `https://www.smashi ngmagazine.com/`. You can connect with him on LinkedIn at `https://cz.linkedin.com/in /martin-sikora-a63b9a30` or GitHub at `https://github.com/martinsik`.

About the Reviewer

Alexandru-Emil Lupu has about 10 years of experience in the web development area, during which he has developed a range of skills, from the implementation of e-commerce platforms and presentation sites to writing code for online games. He is one of those developers who is constantly learning new programming languages, and he has no problem understanding Ruby, PHP, Python, JavaScript, and Java code.

He is passionate about programming and computer science. When he was a teenager, he did not own a computer or have an Internet connection and would constantly go to an Internet cafe to read all about his programming problems, then go home and struggle to implement what he read. He gladly recounts those days and likes to believe that he's the same guy he was 10 years ago, but with much more experience. For him, "passion" is the word that describes the challenge he had when he was a youngster willing to learn new stuff, getting home at 2 or 3 AM determined to install Linux just to learn something new- this too when he had a Pentium I at 133 MHz in the Pentium IV at 1800 MHz era!

Alexandru-Emil is learning all the time and likes to stay close to well-trained and passionate people who better motivate him. He also likes teams that work intelligently and are energetic, which is why he joined the eJobs team--to face a challenge.

As a proof of his perseverance, Alexandru-Emil Lupu is a certified Scrum Master who is passionate about Agile Development. His resume also includes 3 years as a Ruby on Rails developer and a CTO at 2Performant Network (2Parale); 4 years at eRepublik.com, an online game, during which he was responsible for a long list of tasks, including feature development, performance optimization, and a Tech Lead for an internal project. He has learned the hard way the necessary skills to fulfill his day-to-day tasks at 2Performant.com and, later, all the experience he's got, he is using at eJobs.ro to face new kinds of challenges.

In his little free time, he develops small personal projects. And if he still has any spare time, he reads some technical or project management books or articles. When he's relaxing, he watches thriller movies and likes playing shooter or strategy games.

He doesn't talk too much, but he's willing to teach others programming. If you meet him for a coffee, prepare yourself to be entertained, he likes to tell a lot of contextual jokes.

You can connect with him on LinkedIn at `https://www.linkedin.com/in/alecslupu` and interact with him on `http://github.com/alecslupu`.

www.PacktPub.com

For support files and downloads related to your book, please visit www.PacktPub.com.

Did you know that Packt offers eBook versions of every book published, with PDF and ePub files available? You can upgrade to the eBook version at www.PacktPub.com and as a print book customer, you are entitled to a discount on the eBook copy. Get in touch with us at service@packtpub.com for more details.

At www.PacktPub.com, you can also read a collection of free technical articles, sign up for a range of free newsletters and receive exclusive discounts and offers on Packt books and eBooks.

https://www.packtpub.com/mapt

Get the most in-demand software skills with Mapt. Mapt gives you full access to all Packt books and video courses, as well as industry-leading tools to help you plan your personal development and advance your career.

Why subscribe?

- Fully searchable across every book published by Packt
- Copy and paste, print, and bookmark content
- On demand and accessible via a web browser

Customer Feedback

Thanks for purchasing this Packt book. At Packt, quality is at the heart of our editorial process. To help us improve, please leave us an honest review on this book's Amazon page at https://goo.gl/5qqL4V.

If you'd like to join our team of regular reviewers, you can e-mail us at customerreviews@packtpub.com. We award our regular reviewers with free eBooks and videos in exchange for their valuable feedback. Help us be relentless in improving our products!

Table of Contents

Preface

Reactive programming has gained distinct popularity in recent years. This is partly thanks to JavaScript web frameworks such as Angular2 or React, but also because of the increasing popularity of functional and asynchronous programming in languages that support multiple programming paradigms, such as JavaScript, Java, Python, or PHP.

Nowadays, reactive programming is closely associated with Reactive Extensions (also called ReactiveX or just Rx); the most popular library to leverage reactive programming. Notably, RxJS 5, the JavaScript implementation of Rx, is very likely to be the first encounter with reactive programming for many developers. In this book, we will mostly focus on using the PHP port of Rx, called RxPHP (`https://github.com/ReactiveX/RxPHP`).

Asynchronous programming is not what PHP developers typically deal with. In fact, it's kind of an uncharted territory because there aren't many resources available on this topic in PHP. Since reactive programming goes hand in hand with asynchronous programming, we'll work a lot with event loops, blocking and non-blocking code, subprocesses, threads, and IPC.

Our primary intention, however, will be learning Reactive Extensions and reactive programming with RxPHP. This book includes both RxPHP 1 and RxPHP 2. All examples are written for RxPHP 1 because the API is almost the same, and at the time of writing this book, RxPHP 2 is still in development. Also, RxPHP 1 requires just PHP 5.6+, while RxPHP 2 requires PHP 7+. Nonetheless, we'll properly emphasize and explain whenever the APIs of RxPHP 1 and RxPHP 2 differ.

What this book covers

Chapter 1, *Introduction to Reactive Programming*, explains definitions of typical programming paradigms such as imperative, asynchronous, functional, parallel, and reactive programming. We'll see what are the prerequisites to use functional programming in PHP and how all this is related to Reactive Extensions. At the end, we'll introduce the RxPHP library as a tool of choice for this entire book.

Chapter 2, *Reactive Programming with RxPHP*, presents the basic concepts and common terminology used in reactive programming with RxPHP. It introduces Observables, observers, operators, Subjects, and disposables as the building blocks of any Rx application.

Chapter 3, *Writing a Reddit Reader with RxPHP*, builds on the knowledge from the previous chapter to write a Reddit reader application internally based on RxPHP. This will require downloading data via cURL and handling user input, and comparing the difference between blocking and non-blocking code in PHP in relation to RxPHP. We'll also have a sneak peak into using event loops in PHP.

Chapter 4, *Reactive versus a Typical Event-Driven Approach*, shows that in order to use Rx in practice, we need to know how can we combine RxPHP code with some already existing code that isn't based on Rx. For this reason, we'll take the Event Dispatcher component that comes with the Symfony3 framework and extend it with Rx functionality.

Chapter 5, *Testing RxPHP Code*, covers testing, which is a crucial part of every development process. Apart from PHPUnit, we'll also use the special testing classes that come with RxPHP out of the box. We'll also take a look at testing asynchronous code in general and what caveats we need to be aware of.

Chapter 6, *PHP Streams API and Higher-Order Observables*, introduces the PHP Streams API and event loops. These two concepts are tightly coupled in RxPHP and we'll learn why and how. We'll talk about the issues we can encounter when using multiple event loops in the same application and how the PHP community is trying to solve them. We'll also introduce the concept of higher-order Observables as a more advanced functionality of Rx.

Chapter 7, *Implementing Socket IPC and WebSocket Server/Client*, demonstrates how in order to write a more complicated asynchronous application, we'll build a chat manager, server, and client as three separate processes that communicate with each other via Unix sockets and WebSockets. We'll also use in practice the higher-order Observables from the previous chapter.

Chapter 8, *Multicasting in RxPHP and PHP7 pthreads Extension*, introduces us to the concept of multicasting in Rx and all the components that RxPHP provides for this purpose. We'll also start using the pthreads extension for PHP7. This will let us run our code in parallel in multiple threads.

Chapter 9, *Multithreaded and Distributed Computing with pthreads and Gearman*, wraps the knowledge of pthreads from the previous chapter into reusable components that can be used together with RxPHP. We also introduce the Gearman framework as a way to distribute work among multiple processes. In the end, we'll compare the pros and cons of using multiple threads and processes to run tasks in parallel.

Chapter 10, *Using Advanced Operators and Techniques in RxPHP*, will focus on not-so-common principles in Rx. These are mostly advanced operators for very specific tasks, but also implementation details of RxPHP components and their behavior in specific use cases that we should be aware of.

Appendix, *Reusing RxPP Techniques in RxJS*, demonstrates with practical examples how to deal with typical use cases where either RxPHP or RxJS come in handy. We'll see how asynchronous programming is used in a JavaScript environment and compare it to PHP. This final chapter also goes into more detail about what RxJS 5 is and how it differs from RxPHP.

What you need for this book

The main prerequisites for most of this book are a PHP 5.6+ interpreter and any text editor.

We'll use the Composer (https://getcomposer.org/) tool to install all external dependencies in our examples. Some basic knowledge of Composer and PHPUnit is helpful but not absolutely necessary.

In later chapters, we'll also use the pthreads PHP extension, which requires PHP 7 or above and the Gearman job server; both should be available for all platforms.

Also, some basic knowledge of the Unix environment (sockets, processes, signals, and so on) is helpful.

Who this book is for

This book is intended for intermediate developers with at least average knowledge of PHP who want to learn about asynchronous and reactive programming in PHP and Reactive Extensions in particular.

Apart from the RxPHP library, this book is framework agnostic, so you don't need knowledge of any web framework.

All the topics regarding RxPHP are generally applicable to any Rx implementation, so switching from RxPHP to RxJS, for example, will be very easy.

Conventions

In this book, you will find a number of text styles that distinguish between different kinds of information. Here are some examples of these styles and an explanation of their meaning.

Code words in text, database table names, folder names, filenames, file extensions, pathnames, dummy URLs, user input, and Twitter handles are shown as follows: "Every time we write an Observable, we'll extend the base Rx\Observable class."

A block of code is set as follows:

```
Rx\Observable::just('{"value":42}')
    ->lift(function() {
        return new JSONDecodeOperator();
    })
    ->subscribe(new DebugSubject());
```

When we wish to draw your attention to a particular part of a code block, the relevant lines or items are set in bold:

```
use Rx\Observable\IntervalObservable;
class RedditCommand extends Command {
    /** @var \Rx\Subject\Subject */
    private $subject;
    private $interval;
```

Any command-line input or output is written as follows:

```
$ sleep.php proc1 3
proc1: 1
proc1: 2
proc1: 3
```

New terms and **important words** are shown in bold. Words that you see on the screen, for example, in menus or dialog boxes, appear in the text like this: "PHP has to be compiled with the **Thread Safety** option enabled."

Warnings or important notes appear in a box like this.

Tips and tricks appear like this.

Reader feedback

Feedback from our readers is always welcome. Let us know what you think about this book-what you liked or disliked. Reader feedback is important for us as it helps us develop titles that you will really get the most out of. To send us general feedback, simply e-mail `feedback@packtpub.com`, and mention the book's title in the subject of your message. If there is a topic that you have expertise in and you are interested in either writing or contributing to a book, see our author guide at `www.packtpub.com/authors`.

Customer support

Now that you are the proud owner of a Packt book, we have a number of things to help you to get the most from your purchase.

Downloading the example code

You can download the example code files for this book from your account at `http://www.packtpub.com`. If you purchased this book elsewhere, you can visit `http://www.packtpub.com/support` and register to have the files e-mailed directly to you.

You can download the code files by following these steps:

1. Log in or register to our website using your e-mail address and password.
2. Hover the mouse pointer on the **SUPPORT** tab at the top.
3. Click on **Code Downloads & Errata**.
4. Enter the name of the book in the **Search** box.
5. Select the book for which you're looking to download the code files.
6. Choose from the drop-down menu where you purchased this book from.
7. Click on **Code Download**.

Once the file is downloaded, please make sure that you unzip or extract the folder using the latest version of:

- WinRAR / 7-Zip for Windows
- Zipeg / iZip / UnRarX for Mac
- 7-Zip / PeaZip for Linux

The code bundle for the book is also hosted on GitHub at `https://github.com/PacktPubl ishing/PHP-Reactive-Programming`. We also have other code bundles from our rich catalog of books and videos available at `https://github.com/PacktPublishing/`. Check them out!

Errata

Although we have taken every care to ensure the accuracy of our content, mistakes do happen. If you find a mistake in one of our books-maybe a mistake in the text or the code-we would be grateful if you could report this to us. By doing so, you can save other readers from frustration and help us improve subsequent versions of this book. If you find any errata, please report them by visiting `http://www.packtpub.com/submit-errata`, selecting your book, clicking on the **Errata Submission Form** link, and entering the details of your errata. Once your errata are verified, your submission will be accepted and the errata will be uploaded to our website or added to any list of existing errata under the Errata section of that title.

To view the previously submitted errata, go to `https://www.packtpub.com/books/conten t/support` and enter the name of the book in the search field. The required information will appear under the **Errata** section.

Piracy

Piracy of copyrighted material on the Internet is an ongoing problem across all media. At Packt, we take the protection of our copyright and licenses very seriously. If you come across any illegal copies of our works in any form on the Internet, please provide us with the location address or website name immediately so that we can pursue a remedy.

Please contact us at `copyright@packtpub.com` with a link to the suspected pirated material.

We appreciate your help in protecting our authors and our ability to bring you valuable content.

Questions

If you have a problem with any aspect of this book, you can contact us at `questions@packtpub.com`, and we will do our best to address the problem.

1
Introduction to Reactive Programming

Reactive programming has become a very popular and in demand topic over the last few years, and even though the ideas behind it aren't new, it takes the good parts from multiple different programming paradigms. This book's purpose is to teach you how to start writing PHP applications with principles of reactive programming in mind and in combination with pre-existing libraries.

In this chapter, we'll learn the most important principles that will guide us throughout this entire book:

- Recap well-known programming paradigms and quickly explain their meaning for humans.
- We'll see how we can use functional PHP programming, even today, using practical examples. We pay special attention to how we can use anonymous functions.
- Explain what reactive programing is and what good parts it takes from other programming paradigms.
- We'll have a look at some examples of widely spread JavaScript and PHP libraries that already use very similar principles to reactive programming.
- Introduce Reactive Extensions and see how these fit into the world of reactive programming.
- Show what using Reactive Extensions looks like using RxJS and how it fits into the grand scheme of things.
- Create a first simple demo with RxPHP library.

Since reactive programming is a programming paradigm, we'll take a quick look at other common paradigms that all of us have probably already heard of and that you'll see mentioned every time you read or hear about reactive programming.

Imperative programming

Imperative programming is a programming paradigm around executing statements that change the program's state.

What this means in human language:

- **Programming paradigm**: This is a set of concepts defining a style of building and structuring programs. Most programming languages, such as PHP, support multiple paradigms. We can also think of it as a mindset and a way we approach problems when using such paradigms.

- **Statements**: Units of action with side effects in imperative programming evaluated in sequences usually containing expressions. Statements are executed for their side effects and expressions for their return value. Consider this example:

  ```
  $a = 2 + 5
  ```

  This line of code is a statement where `2 + 5` is an expression. The expected side effect is assigning the value `7` to the `$a` variable. This leads to changing the program's current state. Another statement could be, for instance:

  ```
  if ($a > 5) { }
  ```

  This statement has one expression and no return value.

- **State**: Values of program variables in memory at any given time. In imperative programming, we define a series of statements that control the program's flow and, therefore, change its state.

Declarative programming

Declarative programming is a paradigm focused on describing a program's logic instead of particular executional steps. In other words, in declarative programming, we define what we want instead of how we want it. In contrast to imperative programming, programs in declarative programming are defined with expressions instead of statements.

Very common examples could be SQL and HTML languages. Consider the following database query:

```
SELECT * FROM user WHERE id = 42
```

In SQL, we define what data from what table we want to query, but the implementation details are completely hidden for us. We don't even want to worry about how the database engine stores or indexes the data.

In HTML, we define the structure of elements; what's behind the browser's rendering process isn't important for us. We just want to see the page on the screen.

Sequential and parallel programming

We can think of sequential and parallel programming as counterparts.

In sequential programming, we're executing processes in order. This means that a process is started when the preceding process has finished. In other words, there is always only one process being executed. The following figure illustrates this principle:

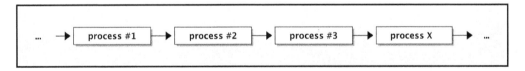

In parallel programming, multiple processes can be executed concurrently:

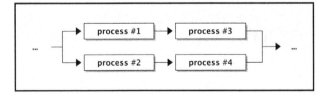

To make this easier to understand and more relevant to PHP, we can, instead of processes, think of lines of code. PHP interpreter is always sequential and it never executes code in parallel.

In Chapter 9, *Multithreaded and Distributed Computing with pthreads and Gearman*, we'll use PHP module pthreads that makes it possible to run PHP code in multiple threads, but we'll see that it's not as simple as it seems. Module pthreads, in fact, creates multiple independent PHP interpreters, each running in a separate thread.

Asynchronous programming

The term asynchronous programming is very common in languages such as JavaScript. A very general definition is that, in asynchronous programming, we're executing code in a different order than it was defined. This is typical for any event based application.

For example, in JavaScript, we first define an event listener with its handler, which is executed some time later, when an appropriate event occurs.

In PHP, this could be, for example, a web application that needs to send an e-mail when we create a new blog article. Just, instead of lines of code, we're considering tasks. The following figure demonstrates an asynchronously triggered event:

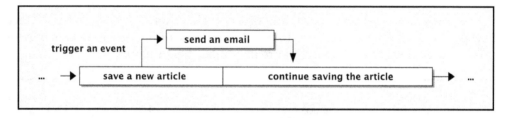

While the web application was saving an article (processing a task), it triggered an event that sent an e-mail and then carried on with the original task. The event handler had to be defined somewhere before we started this task.

Asynchronous versus parallel programming

A very common misconception is that asynchronous and parallel programming are the same, or that one is an implication of the other. This is very common in JavaScript where, from the user's perspective, it looks like things are running in parallel.

This isn't true, but many programming languages (in fact, just their interpreters), create the illusion of running in parallel while they're still sequential. They appear to be parallel due to it's event-based nature (JavaScript), or because of their interpreter internals.

For example, Python simulates threads by switching the execution context between different parts of the application. The Python interpreter is still single threaded and executes instructions sequentially, but creates the illusion of running code in parallel.

Functional programming

The functional programming paradigm treats program flow as an evaluation of functions. It utilizes several concepts, where the most important for us are eliminating side effects, avoiding mutable data, functions as first-class citizens and higher-order functions. The output of each function is dependent only on its input argument values, therefore, calling the same function twice has to always return the same value. It's based on declarative programming, in the sense of using expressions instead of statements.

Let's have a deeper look what this means:

- **Eliminating side effects**: While in imperative programming side-effects were desired during program execution, in functional programming it's the exact opposite. Each function is supposed to be an individual building block whose return value is based only on its input values. Note that, in functional programming, it almost never makes sense to define a function that takes no arguments and returns no value. Assuming that functions have no side effects, this means that this function can't do anything (or at least anything observable from the outside). This is in contrast to imperative programming, where using such functions makes sense because they can modify some internal state (of an object for instance). Eliminating side effects leads to more independent and better testable code.
- **Avoiding mutable data**: The concept of not modifying any input values and working with their copies works well with not creating any side effects. Executing the same function with the same input parameters will always return the same value.
- **First-class citizens and higher-order functions**: In programming languages, stating that type/object/function is a first-class citizen (or first-class element) means that this entity supports operations generally available to all other entities. Usually, this includes:
  - It can be passed as a parameter to functions
  - It can be returned from a function

- It can be assigned to a variable

Higher-order functions have a very similar meaning and have to do at least one of these:

- Take a function as an argument
- Return a function as a result

In functional programming, this concept of higher-order function is often used in connection with methods on collections such as `map()`, `filter()`, `reduce()`, `concat()`, and `zip()`

Functional programming in PHP

Let's step aside for a moment and see how the three concepts mentioned above are related to PHP.

Eliminating side effects

This is mostly a matter of a good programming style and self-discipline. Of course, PHP doesn't restrict us from violating this rule. Note that, by side effects, we also mean use cases like the following:

```php
function sum($array) {
    $sum = 0;
    foreach ($array as $value) {
        $sum += $value;
    }
    saveToDatabase($sum);
    return $sum;
}
sum([5, 1, 3, 7, 9]);
```

Even though we have not defined the function `saveToDatabase()` ourselves (for example, it comes from a framework we are using), it's still a side effect. If we execute the same function again, it will return the same value, but the end state is different. For example, it will create the record in the database twice.

Avoiding mutable data

This concept is simple with primitive data types, for example:

```
function add($first, $second) {
    return $first + $second;
}
add(5, 2);
```

However, when working with collections, this principle requires the creation of a new collection and copying values from the old collection to the new one:

```
function greaterThan($collection, $threshold) {
    $out = [];
    foreach ($collection as $val) {
        if ($val > $threshold) {
            $out[] = $val;
        }
    }
    return $out;
}
greaterThan([5, 12, 8, 9, 42], 8);
// will return: [12, 9, 42]
```

The preceding example shows this principle in practice.

In PHP, arrays are passed by reference for performance reasons until the first attempt to modify them. Then the interpreter will create a copy of the original array behind the scene (so called copy-on-write). However, objects are always passed as references, so we'll have to be very careful when working with them.

This concept of immutable collections (or objects in general) became very popular in JavaScript with libraries such as `Immutable.js`, made by Facebook (`https://facebook.github.io/immutable-js/`), or the so-called `onPush` change detection mechanism in Angular2.

Apart from making our code more predictable, when it's used appropriately, it will simplify checking for changes in large collections because, if any of its items have changed, then the entire collection is replaced by a new instance.

In order to check if two collections contain the same data, we can use the identity operator (=== three equal signs) instead of comparing the collections' items one by one.

In PHP, there are already libraries that make this task easier, for instance, `Immutable.php` (`https://github.com/jkoudys/immutable.php`). Also, for example, PHP 5.5+ comes with an immutable version of `DateTime` class called `DateTimeImmutable` by default.

First-class citizens and higher-order functions

Now it starts to get interesting. Functions in PHP have been first-class citizens for a very long time already. Moreover, since PHP 5.3+, we can use anonymous functions, which greatly simplifies the usage of higher-order functions.

Consider a very trivial example that applies a function on every item in a collection with the built-in `array_map()` function:

```
$input = ['apple', 'banana', 'orange', 'raspberry'];
$lengths = array_map(function($item) {
    return strlen($item);
}, $input);
// $lengths = [5, 6, 6, 9];
```

We have used PHP's `array_map()` function to iterate the array and return the length of each string. If we consider just this function call, it uses many of the concepts from multiple paradigms that we have explained above:

```
array_map(function($item) {
    return strlen($item);
}, $input);
```

What this means in particular:

- Single expression `strlen($item)` and no assignments (declarative programming).
- Implementation details on how the array is actually iterated are hidden from us (declarative programming).
- First-class citizens and higher-order functions (functional programming).
- Immutable data – this function call doesn't change the original, but creates a new array (functional programming).
- No side effects – everything happens inside the inner closure. If we used any variables, they would exist only inside this closure (functional programming).

Just for comparison, if we wanted to write the same example in imperative programming, it would be just one line longer:

```
$result = [];
foreach ($input as $value) {
    $result[] = strlen($value);
}
```

Let's take this a little further, and say we want to get the sum of all lengths greater than 5. First, we'll start with the most obvious imperative approach:

```
$input = ['apple', 'banana', 'orange', 'raspberry'];
$sum = 0;
foreach ($input as $fruit) {
    $length = strlen($fruit);
    if ($length > 5) {
        $sum += $length;
    }
}
// $sum = 21
printf("sum: %d\n", $sum);
```

Now, we can write the same thing using functional programming, utilizing three methods we mentioned earlier: map, filter and reduce. In PHP, these are called `array_map()`, `array_filter()`, and `array_reduce()` respectively:

```
$lengths = array_map(function($fruit) {
    return strlen($fruit);
}, $input);
$filtered = array_filter($lengths, function($length) {
    return $length > 5;
});
$sum = array_reduce($filtered, function($a, $b) {
    return $a + $b;
});
```

We got rid of all statements and used only expressions. The resulting code isn't short, and we had to also create three variables to hold partially processed arrays. So let's transform this into one large nested call:

```
$sum = array_reduce(array_filter(array_map(function($fruit) {
    return strlen($fruit);
}, $input), function($length) {
    return $length > 5;
}), function($a, $b) {
    return $a + $b;
});
```

This is a little shorter; we can see the sequence of functions applied and their respective expressions in the same order. We've already encountered inconsistency in function declarations in PHP, as shown in the following code, which has been highly criticized:

```
array array_map(callable $callback, array $array1 [, $... ])
array array_filter(array $array, callable $callback)
mixed array_reduce(array $array, callable $callback)
```

These are shortened function definitions from PHP documentation. We can see that, sometimes the first argument is the iterated collection; sometimes it's the callback function. The same problem exists with string functions and their haystack-needle arguments. We can try to improve the readability a little with functional-PHP library (https://github.com/lstrojny/functional-php) – a collection of functions for functional programming in PHP.

The following code represents the same example as above, but uses lstrojny/functional-php library:

```
use function Functional\map;
use function Functional\filter;
use function Functional\reduce_left;

$sum = reduce_left(filter(map($input, function($fruit) {
    return strlen($fruit);
}), function($length) {
    return $length > 5;
}), function($val, $i, $col, $reduction) {
    return $val + $reduction;
});
```

It definitely looks better, but this is probably the best we can get when using standard PHP arrays.

Let's have a look at how the same problem could be solved in a language where arrays are objects and map, filter and reduce are its methods. Javascript, for example, is such a language, so we can rewrite the same example from above one more time:

```
var sum = inputs
    .map(fruit => fruit.length)
    .filter(len => len > 5)
    .reduce((a, b) => a + b);
```

We'll use the new ES6 standard whenever we show any JavaScript code throughout this entire book.

Well, this was quite easy and it meets all our expectations from functional programming much better than PHP. This might be the reason why we almost never use higher-order functions in PHP. They are just too hard to write, read and maintain.

Before we move on, we should look at another topic related to functional programming in PHP that is worth mentioning.

Anonymous functions in PHP

Every anonymous function is internally represented as an instance of a Closure class, shown as follows (we'll also refer to anonymous functions as closures or callables):

```
$count = function() {
    printf("%d ", count($this->fruits));
};
var_dump(get_class($count));
// string(7) "Closure"
```

What's unusual is that we can bind custom $this object when calling a closure, a concept that is very common in JavaScript but very rarely used in PHP.

Let's define a simple class that we'll use for demonstration:

```
class MyClass {
    public $fruits;
    public function __construct($arr) {
        $this->fruits = $arr;
    }
}
```

Then, test the function stored in $count variable on two objects:

```
// closures_01.php
// ... the class definition goes here
$count = function() {
    printf("%d ", count($this->fruits));
};

$obj1 = new MyClass(['apple', 'banana', 'orange']);
$obj2 = new MyClass(['raspberry', 'melon']);

$count->call($obj1);
$count->call($obj2);
```

This example prints to console the following output:

```
$ php closures_01.php
3
2
```

In PHP, we can specify what variables we want to pass from the parent scope to the closure with the use keyword. Variables can be also passed by reference, similar to passing variables by reference on function calls. Consider the following example that demonstrates both principles:

```php
// closures_03.php
$str = 'Hello, World';

$func = function() use ($str) {
    $str .= '!!!';
    echo $str . "\n";
};
$func();
echo $str . "\n";

$func2 = function() use (&$str) {
    $str .= '???';
    echo $str . "\n";
};
$func2();
echo $str . "\n";
```

We have two closures $func and $func2. The first one works with a copy of $str so, when we print it outside of the function, it's unmodified. However, the second closure, $func2 works with a reference to the original variable. The output for this demo is as follows:

```
$ php closures_03.php
Hello, World!!!
Hello, World
Hello, World???
Hello, World???
```

We'll be passing objects to closures a lot in this book.

There's also a `bindTo($newThis)` method with a similar purpose. Instead of evaluating the closure, it returns a new Closure object with `$this` binded to `$newThis`, which can be later called with for example, `call_user_func()` method. When using closures inside objects, the context `$this` is bind automatically, so we don't need to worry about it.

 Anonymous functions and the Closure class are very well explained in the official documentation, so head over there if you have any hesitations: `http://php.net/manual/en/functions.anonymous.php`

PHP magic methods

PHP defines a set of names that can be used as class methods with a special effect. These are all prefixed with two underscores __. For our purposes, we'll be particularly interested in two of them, called `__invoke()` and `__call()`.

The `__invoke()` method is used when we try to use an object as if it were a regular function. This is useful when we use higher-order functions because we can treat objects and functions exactly the same way.

The second `__call()` method is used when we attempt to call an object method that doesn't exist (to be precise, a method that is inaccessible). It receives as arguments the original method name and an array of its arguments that was used when trying to call it.

We'll use both of these magic methods in `Chapter 2`, *Reactive Programming with RxPHP*.

The principles shown here aren't very common in PHP, but we'll meet them on several occasions when using functional programming.

 Throughout this entire book, we'll try to follow PSR-1 and PSR-2 coding standards (`http://www.php-fig.org/psr/`). However, we'll often violate them on purpose to keep the source codes as short as possible.

Now, we'll finally grasp reactive programming.

Reactive programming

Reactive programming is yet another programming paradigm. It is based around the ability to easily express data flows and the automatic propagation of changes.

Let's explore this in more depth:

- **Data flows** (or data streams): In reactive programming, we want to think about variables as "values that change over time". For example, this could be a mouse position, user click or data coming via WebSockets. Basically, any event-based system can be considered a data stream.
- **Propagation of change**: A very nice example is a spreadsheet editor. If we set the value of a single cell to A1 = A2 + A3, this means that every change to cells A2 and A3 will be propagated to A1. In programmers' speech, this corresponds to the observer design pattern where A2 and A3 are observables and A1 is an observer. We'll talk about the observer pattern again later in this chapter.
- **Easily express data flows**: This is related mostly to libraries we use rather than to the language itself. It means that, if we want to use reactive programming effectively, we need to be able to manipulate data streams easily. This principle also suggests that reactive programming falls under the category of declarative paradigms.

As we can see, the definition is very broad.

The first part about data flows and propagation of change looks like the observer design pattern with iterables. Expressing data flows with ease could be done with functional programming. This all basically describes what we've already seen in this chapter.

The main differences to the observer pattern are how we think and manipulate with data streams. In previous examples, we always worked with arrays as inputs, which are synchronous, while data streams can be both synchronous and asynchronous. From our point of view, it doesn't matter.

Let's see what a typical implementation of the observer pattern might look like in PHP:

```php
// observer_01.php
class Observable {
    /** @var Observer[] */
    private $observers = [];
    private $id;
    static private $total = 0;

    public function __construct() {
        $this->id = ++self::$total;
```

```
    }

    public function registerObserver(Observer $observer) {
        $this->observers[] = $observer;
    }

    public function notifyObservers() {
        foreach ($this->observers as $observer) {
            $observer->notify($this, func_get_args());
        }
    }

    public function __toString() {
        return sprintf('Observable #%d', $this->id);
    }
}
```

In order to be notified about any changes made by the Observable, we need another class called Observer that subscribes to an Observable:

```
// observer_01.php
class Observer {
    static private $total = 0;
    private $id;

    public function __construct(Observable $observable) {
        $this->id = ++self::$total;
        $observable->registerObserver($this);
    }

    public function notify($obsr, $args) {
        $format = "Observer #%d got \"%s\" from %s\n";
        printf($format, $this->id, implode(', ', $args), $obsr);
    }
}
```

Then, a typical usage might look like the following:

```
$observer1 = new Observer($subject);
$observer2 = new Observer($subject);
$subject->notifyObservers('test');
```

This example will print two messages to the console:

```
$ php observer_01.php
// Observer #1 got "test" from Observable #1
// Observer #2 got "test" from Observable #1
```

This almost follows how we defined the reactive programming paradigm. A data stream is a sequence of events coming from an Observable, and changes are propagated to all listening observers. The last point we mentioned above – being able to easily express data flows – isn't really there. What if we wanted to filter out all events that don't match a particular condition, just like we did in the examples with `array_filter()` and functional programming? This logic would have to go into each `Observer` class implementation.

The principles of reactive programming are actually very common in some libraries. We'll have a look at three of them and see how these relate to what we've just learned about reactive and functional programming.

jQuery Promises

Probably every web developer has used jQuery at some point. A very handy way of avoiding so-called **callback hell** is using Promises when dealing with asynchronous calls. For example, calling `jQuery.ajax()` returns a `Promise` object that is resolved or rejected when the AJAX call has finished:

```
$.get('/foo/bar').done(response => {
    // ...
}).fail(response => {
    // ...
}).complete(response => {
    // ...
});
```

A `Promise` object represents a value in the future. It's non-blocking (asynchronous), but lets us handle it in a declarative approach.

Another useful use case is chaining callbacks, forming a chain, where each callback can modify the value before propagating it further:

```
// promises_01.js
function functionReturningAPromise() {
    var d = $.Deferred();
    setTimeout(() => d.resolve(42), 0);
    return d.promise();
}

functionReturningAPromise()
    .then(value => value + 1)
    .then(value => 'result: ' + value)
    .then(value => console.log(value));
```

In this example, we have a single source which is the `functionReturningAPromise()` call, and three callbacks where only the last one prints the value that resolved the Promise. We can see that the number `42` was modified twice when going through the chain of callbacks:

```
$ node promises_01.js
result: 43
```

 In reactive programming, we'll use a very similar approach to Promises, but while a `Promise` object is always resolved only once (it carries just one value); data streams can generate multiple or even an infinite number of values.

Gulp streaming build system

The Gulp build system has become the most popular build system in JavaScript. It's completely based on streams and manipulating them. Consider the following example:

```
gulp.src('src/*.js')
   .pipe(concat('all.min.js'))
   .pipe(gulp.dest('build'));
```

This creates a stream of files that match the predicate `src/*.js`, concats all of them together and finally writes one single file to `build/all.min.js`. Does this remind you of anything?

This is the same declarative and functional approach we used above, when talking about functional programming in PHP. In particular, this `concat()` function could be replaced with PHP's `array_reduce()`.

Streams in gulp (aka vinyl-source-stream) can be modified in any way we want. We can, for example, split a stream into two new streams:

```
var filter = require('gulp-filter');
var stream = gulp.src('src/*.js');
var substream1 = stream.pipe(filter(['*.min.js']));
var substream2 = stream.pipe(filter(['!/app/*']));
```

Or, we can merge two streams and uglify (minify and obfuscate the source code) into one stream:

```
var merge = require('merge2');
merge(gulp.src('src/*.js'), gulp.src('vendor/*'))
    .pipe(uglify());
```

```
    .pipe(gulp.dest('build'));
```

This stream manipulation corresponds very well to the last concept we used to define the reactive programming paradigm – express data flows with ease – while it's both functional and declarative.

EventDispatcher component in PHP

Probably every PHP framework comes with some type of event-driven component to notify various different parts of an application using events.

One such component comes with the Symfony framework out-of-the-box (https://github.com/symfony/event-dispatcher). It's an independent component that allows subscribing and listening to events (the observer pattern).

Event listeners can be later grouped by the events they subscribe to and can also be assigned custom tags, as shown in the following code:

```
use Symfony\Component\EventDispatcher\EventDispatcher;
$dispatcher = new EventDispatcher();
$listener = new AcmeListener();
$dispatcher->addListener('event_name', [$listener, 'action']);
```

This principle is very similar to Zend\EventManager used in Zend Framework. It is just another variation of the Observable – observer combination.

We'll come back to Symfony EventDispatcher component in Chapter 4, *Reactive vs a Typical Event-Driven approach*, where we'll explore how to apply the reactive programming approach to event-based systems, which should lead to simplification and better-organized code.

Reactive Extensions

Now that we've seen that the principles in the reactive programming paradigm aren't completely new for us, we can start thinking about how to put all this together. In other words, what libraries or frameworks do we really need in order to start writing reactive code.

Reactive Extensions (ReactiveX or just Rx in short) are a set of libraries in various languages that make reactive programming easy even in languages where concepts of asynchronous and functional programming are clumsy, such as PHP. However, there's a very important distinction:

Reactive programming doesn't equal Reactive Extensions.

A Reactive Extension is a library that introduces certain principles as one of the possible ways to approach reactive programming. Very often, when somebody tells you they're using reactive programming to do something in their applications, they're in fact talking about a particular Reactive Extension library in their favorite language.

Reactive Extensions were originally made by Microsoft for .NET and called **Rx.NET**. Later, it was ported by Netflix to Java as **RxJava**. Now, there are over a dozen supported languages, the most popular probably being **RxJS** – the JavaScript implementation.

All ports follow a very similar API design, however, differences occur and we'll talk about them a couple of times. We'll be mostly interested in differences between RxPHP and RxJS.

RxPHP is mostly uncharted territory. A more typical environment where we encounter asynchronous events is JavaScript, so we'll first demonstrate examples in JavaScript (and RxJS 5), and afterwards we will have a look at RxPHP.

Autocomplete with RxJS

Imagine we want to implement an autocomplete feature that downloads suggestions from Wikipedia (this example comes from the official collection of demos on RxJS's GitHub page):

```
function searchAndReturnPromise(term) {
    // perform an AJAX request and return a Promise
}

var keyup = Rx.Observable.fromEvent($('#textInput'), 'keyup')
    .map(e => e.target.value)
    .filter(text => text.length > 2)
    .debounceTime(750)
    .distinctUntilChanged();
var searcher = keyup.switchMap(searchAndReturnPromise);
```

Let's take a closer look at how this works:

1. We create an Observable from the form input's `keyup` event. This function is built into RxJS to simplify creating Observables. We can, of course, create our own Observables as well.

2. Apply the `map()` function. This is exactly what we have already seen above. Note that this `map()` function, is in fact, not `Array.map()`, but `Observable.map()` instead, because we're not working with arrays here.

3. Chain with `filter()` method. Exactly the same case as with `map()`.

4. Method `debounceTime()` is used to limit propagating an event down the stream only once after a period of time. In this case, we're using 750ms, which means that, when the user starts typing, it won't download data from Wikipedia on every `keyup` event, but only after at least a 750ms delay between two events.

5. The `distinctUntilChanged()` method makes sure we're calling the AJAX request only when the value has really changed from the last time, because it makes no sense to download the same suggestions twice.

6. The last statement with `keyup.switchMap()` guarantees that when making multiple asynchronous calls, only the last one in the stream gets processed. All the others are dismissed. This is important because, when dealing with AJAX calls, we have absolutely no control over which Promise resolves first.

If we didn't use RxJS, this feature would require multiple state variables. At least to keep the last value from the input, the last time the event occurred, and the last request value for the AJAX call. With RxJS, we can focus on what we want to do and not worry about its implementation details (declarative approach).

With Reactive Extensions, this approach fulfills all we described above about reactive programming, functional programming and also, mostly, declarative programming.

Mouse position on drag and drop

Let's have a look at a slightly more complicated example in RxJS. We want to track the relative mouse position from where we start dragging an HTML element, until we release it (`mouseup` event).

Pay attention to how this example combines multiple Observables (this example also comes from the official collection of demos on RxJS's GitHub page):

```
var mouseup   = Rx.Observable.fromEvent(dragTarget, 'mouseup');
var mousemove = Rx.Observable.fromEvent(document, 'mousemove');
var mousedown = Rx.Observable.fromEvent(dragTarget, 'mousedown');
```

```
var mousedrag = mousedown.mergeMap(md => {
    var sX = md.offsetX, sY = md.offsetY;
    return mousemove.map(mm => {
        mm.preventDefault();
        return {left: mm.clientX - sX, top: mm.clientY - sY};
    }).takeUntil(mouseup);
});

var subscription = mousedrag.subscribe(pos => {
    dragTarget.style.top = pos.top + 'px';
    dragTarget.style.left = pos.left + 'px';
});
```

Notice that `mousedrag` is an Observable created by calling `return mousemove(...)` and that it emits events only until a `mouseup` event is emitted thanks to `takeUntil(mouseup)`.

Normally, without RxJS and with a typical imperative approach, this would be even more complicated than the previous example, with more state variables.

Of course, this requires some basic knowledge of what functions are available for Observables, but even without any previous experience, the code should be reasonably easy to understand. Yet again, the implementation details are completely hidden for us.

Introducing RxPHP

RxPHP (`https://github.com/ReactiveX/RxPHP`) is a port of RxJS. We're going to be using Composer to handle all dependencies in our PHP projects. It has become a state of the art tool, so if you haven't used it before, download it first and check out some basic usage at `https://getcomposer.org/`.

Then, create a new directory and initialize a composer project:

```
$ mkdir rxphp_01
$ cd rxphp_01
$ php composer.phar init
```

Fill in the required fields by the interactive wizard and then add RxPHP as a dependency:

```
$ php composer.phar require reactivex/rxphp
```

When the library successfully downloads, composer will also create `autoload.php` file to handle all class auto-loading on demand.

Then, our code will print string lengths of different types of fruit:

```php
// rxphp_01.php
require __DIR__ . '/vendor/autoload.php';

$fruits = ['apple', 'banana', 'orange', 'raspberry'];
$observer = new \Rx\Observer\CallbackObserver(
    function($value) {
        printf("%s\n", $value);
    }, null, function() {
        print("Complete\n");
    });

\Rx\Observable::fromArray($fruits)
    ->map(function($value) {
        return strlen($value);
    })
    ->subscribe($observer);
```

In all future examples, we won't include the `autoload.php` file, to keep the examples as short as possible. However, it's obviously required in order to run the examples. If you're unsure, have a look at the source codes provided for each chapter.

We first created an observer – `CallbackObserver` to be precise – which takes three functions as arguments. These are called on the next item in the stream, on error and when the input stream is complete and won't emit any more items.

The advantage of the `CallbackObserver` class is that we don't need to write a custom observer class every time we want to handle incoming items in some special and not very reusable way. With `CallbackObserver`, we can just write the callables for signals we want to handle.

When we run this example, we'll see:

```
$ php rxphp_01.php
5
6
6
9
Complete
```

This example was very easy, but compared to the JavaScript environment, it's not very common to use asynchronous operations in PHP and, in case we do have to work asynchronously, it's probably something non-trivial. In Chapter 3, *Writing a Reddit reader with RxPHP*, we'll use **Symfony Console component** to handle all user input from the command line and, where we can, use similar principles to handling mouse events as we saw in the two RxJS examples above.

The JavaScript examples work very well as examples of what reactive programming using Reactive Extensions looks like and what its benefits are.

 If you want to know more about Reactive Extensions, head over to http://reactivex.io/. Also, before continuing to the next chapter, you can have a look at how many different operators Rx supports http://reactivex.io/documentation/operators.html and how these can be used in different languages.

RxPHP 1.x and RxPHP 2

As of April 2017, there're two versions of RxPHP.

The RxPHP 1.x is stable and requires PHP 5.5+. All examples in this book are made for RxPHP 1.x, more specifically, RxPHP 1.5+. It's API is based mostly on RxJS 4, but it takes some features from RxJS 5 as well.

There's also RxPHP 2 in development, which requires PHP 7.0+. RxPHP 2 API from the user's perspective is almost the same as 1.x, it just makes some things easier (for example working with even loops, as we'll see in Chapter 6, *PHP Streams API and Higher-Order Observables*). When we encounter any differences worth mentioning, we'll give them extra space.

 The newer RxPHP 2 was meant to be based to the PHP loop interoperability specification (https://github.com/async-interop/event-loop). However, the specification is still in pre-release stage and it won't be stable in the nearest future. For this reason, the RxPHP team decided to leave the async-interop support for future releases. For more information visit https://github.com/ReactiveX/RxPHP/pull/150.

Summary

In this chapter, we tried to explain the common programming paradigms used in most programming languages. These were: imperative, declarative and functional programming. We also compared the meanings of asynchronous and parallel code.

We spent some time on practical examples of functional programming in PHP and its downsides, and we went through examples of some not very common features, such as the Closure class.

Then, we examined the definition of reactive programming and how it's related to all we saw previously in this chapter.

We introduced Reactive Extensions (Rx) as a library for one of the possible approaches to reactive programming.

In two examples of RxJS, we saw what working with Reactive Extensions looks like in practice and how this matches our definition of reactive programming.

Finally, we introduced RxPHP, which we'll use throughout this entire book. We also quickly talked about differences between RxPHP 1.x and RxPHP 2.

In the next chapter, we'll have a closer look at various parts of the RxPHP library and talk more about the principles used in Reactive Extensions.

2
Reactive Programming with RxPHP

In this chapter, we're going to have a better look at how we can use PHP's reactive extension library RxPHP. We'll mostly build on what we saw in the previous chapter, but going into greater detail.

In particular, we'll go through the following:

- Various components of RxPHP that we'll use in this and all further chapters.
- We'll quickly have a look at how to read and understand the Rx documentation. In particular, we'll have a look at marble diagrams that explain the functionality of Rx operators.
- List a few basic operators that we'll use throughout the entire book and explain their functionality.
- Write custom operator that decodes JSON strings into their appropriate array representations while properly handling errors.
- Implement a simple script that downloads an HTML page via cURL. Then compare the same approach when utilizing RxPHP.
- How to write a custom Observable for our cURL example.
- We'll dig into RxPHP's source code and see what happens when we use built-in Observables and operators.

Before we look into each part of RxPHP separately, we'll quickly mention some very common terms that we'll use when talking about various aspects of Reactive Extensions.

Basic principles of Reactive Extensions

Let's have a look at a very simple example of RxPHP, similar to what we did in the previous chapter, and use it to demonstrate some of the basic principles behind Reactive Extensions.

We won't bother with defining an observer right now and will focus only on Observables and operators:

```
// rxphp_basics_01.php
use Rx\Observable;
$fruits = ['apple', 'banana', 'orange', 'raspberry'];

Observable::fromArray($fruits) // Observable
    ->map(function($value) { // operator
        return strlen($value);
    })
    ->filter(function($len) { // operator
        return $len > 5;
    })
    ->subscribe($observer); // observer
```

In this example, we have one Observable, two operators and one observer.

An Observable can be chained with operators. In this example, the operators are `map()` and `filter()`.

Observables have the `subscribe()` method that is used by observers to start receiving values at the end of the chain.

We can represent this chain by the following diagram:

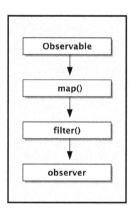

Each arrow shows the direction of propagation of items and notifications

We should probably explain the difference between using Observables and just iterating the array.

Observables are like a push model, where a value is pushed down the operator chain when it's ready. This is very important because it's the Observable that decides when it should emit the next value. The internal logic of Observables can do whatever it needs to (for example, it can run some asynchronous task) and still remain completely hidden.

A similar concept to Observables are Promises. However, while a Promise represents a single value that will exist in the future, an Observable represents a stream of values.

On the other hand, iterating the array is like a pull model. We'd be pulling one item after another. The important consequence is that we'd have to have the array prepared beforehand (that's before we start iterating it).

Another important difference is that Observables behave like a data stream (or data flow). We talked about streams in Chapter 1, *Introduction to Reactive Programming*. In practice, this means that an Observable knows when it has emitted all its items, or when an error has occurred and is able to send proper notification down the chain.

For this reason, Observables can call three different methods on their observers (we'll see how this is implemented later in this chapter when we write a custom operator and a custom Observable):

- onNext: This method is called when the next item is ready to be emitted. We typically say that "an Observable emits an item".
- onError: Notification called when an error has occurred. This could be any type of error represented by an instance of the Exception class.
- onComplete: Notification called when there're no more items to be emitted.

Each Observable can emit zero or more items.

Each Observable can send one error, or one complete notification; but never both.

This is why the CallbackObserver class we used in Chapter 1, *Introduction to Reactive Programming*, takes three callables as arguments. These callables are called when the observer receives a next item, on error notification or on complete notification, respectively. All three callables are optional parameters and we can decide to ignore any of them.

For example, we can make an observer like the following:

```php
use Rx\Observer\Callback\Observer;

$observer = new CallbackObserver(
    function($value) {
        echo "Next: $value\n";
    },
    function(Exception $err) {
        $msg = $err->getMessage();
        echo "Error: $msg\n";
    },
    function() {
        echo "Complete\n";
    }
);
```

This observer defines all three callables. We can test it on the Observable we defined above and have a look at its output:

```
$ php rxphp_basics_01.php
Next: 6
Next: 6
Next: 9
Complete
```

We can see that only three values passed the `filter()` operator, followed by a proper complete notification at the end.

In RxPHP, every operator that takes a callable as an argument wraps its call internally with `try...catch` block. If the callable throws `Exception`, then this `Exception` is sent as `onError` notification. Consider the following example:

```php
// rxphp_basics_02.php
$fruits = ['apple', 'banana', 'orange', 'raspberry'];
Observable::fromArray($fruits)
    ->map(function($value) {
        if ($value[0] == 'o') {
            throw new Exception("It's broken.");
        }
        return strlen($value);
    })
    ->filter(function($len) {
        return $len > 5;
    })
    ->subscribe($observer);
```

With the same observer that we defined previously, this example will have the following output:

```
$ php rxphp_basics_02.php
Next: 6
Error: It's broken.
```

It's important to see that, when an error occurred, no more items were emitted, there's also no complete notification. This is because, when the observer received an error, it automatically unsubscribed.

We'll talk more about the process behind subscribing and unsubscribing in Chapter 3, *Writing a Reddit Reader with RxPHP*, and in Chapter 10, *Using Advanced Operators and Techniques in RxPHP*.

In Chapter 8, *Multicasting in RxPHP and PHP7 pthreads Extension*, we'll look more in-depth into what happens inside observers when they receive an error or complete notification.

One last thing before we move on. We said that Observables represent data streams. The great advantage of this is that we can easily combine or split streams, similar to what we saw in Chapter 1, *Introduction to Reactive Programming*, when talking about the gulp build tool.

Let's have a look at a slightly more advanced example of merging two Observables:

```
// rxphp_basics_03.php
$fruits = ['apple', 'banana', 'orange', 'raspberry'];
$vegetables = ['potato', 'carrot'];

Observable::fromArray($fruits)
    ->map(function($value) {
        return strlen($value);
    })
    ->filter(function($len) {
        return $len > 5;
    })
    ->merge(Observable::fromArray($vegetables))
    ->subscribe($observer);
```

We used the merge() operator to combine the existing Observable with another Observable. Notice that we can add the operator anywhere we want. Since we added it after the filter() operator and before the subscribe() call, the items from the second Observable are going to be emitted right into the observer and will skip the preceding operator chain.

We can represent this chain by the following diagram:

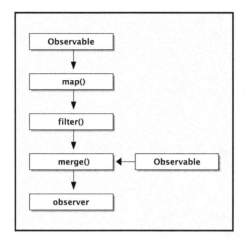

The output for this example looks like the following:

```
$ php rxphp_basics_03.php
Next: 6
Next: 6
Next: 9
Next: potato
Next: carrot
Complete
```

These principles apply to all Rx implementations. Now, we should have a basic idea of what working with Observables, observers and operators in Rx looks like and we can talk more about each of them separately.

Naming conventions in Reactive Extensions

When talking about Observables, we use terms such as **emit/send value/item**. Commonly, we say that **an Observable emits an item**, but we understand the same from **an Observable sends a value** as well.

By **emit/send** we mean that an Observable is calling the onNext method on an observer.

When talking about Observables, we use terms such as **send error/complete notification/signal**. We also often mention that **an Observable completes**, which means that an Observable has sent a complete notification.

By **notification/signal** we mean that an Observable is calling the `onError` or `onComplete` method on an observer.

In the preceding paragraph, we worked with a simple RxPHP demo that had one Observable, two operators and one observer.

This structure formed an **operator/Observable chain**. We'll understand the same thing from both of the terms **operator chain** and **Observable chain** (sometimes also referred to as a **chain of Observable operators**). This is because, from our perspective, we're chaining operators; but under the hood, each operator returns another instance of the `Observable` class, so, in fact, we're chaining Observables. In practice, this doesn't matter, so we'll just remember that these have the same meaning.

When talking about Observable chains, we sometimes use the term **source Observable**. This is the source of items in the chain. In other words, it's the first Observable in the chain. In the preceding example, the source Observable was `Observable::fromArray($fruits)`.

When talking about operators, we use the term source Observable to also describe the Observable directly preceding this particular operator (because it's the source of items for this operator).

Sometimes instead of the `onNext`, `onError` and `onComplete` terms and method names, you'll encounter just `next`, `error` and `complete`. This comes from RxJS 5, which follows the ES7 Observable specification (`https://github.com/tc39/proposal-observable`), but their meaning is exactly the same. Most Rx implementations use the names `onNext, onError` and `onComplete`.

All these terms are used in various literature and articles regarding Rx, so we'll tolerate all of them.

Components of RxPHP

Since this chapter is going to be mostly about Observables, observers and operators, we're going to start with them.

We've already seen a sneak peak in this chapter, and now we'll go into more detail.

Observables

Observables emit items. In other words, Observables are sources of values. Observers can subscribe to Observables in order to be notified when the next item is ready, all items have been emitted, or an error has occurred.

The main difference between an Observable (in the sense of reactive programming) and the observer pattern is that an Observable can tell you when all of the data has been emitted and when an error occurs. All three types of events are consumed by observers.

RxPHP comes with several basic types of Observables for general usage. Here are a few that are easy to use:

- `ArrayObservable`: This creates an Observable from an array and emits all values right after the first observer subscribes.
- `RangeObservable`: This generates a sequence of numbers from a predefined range.
- `IteratorObservable`: This iterates and emits each item in the iterable. This can be any array wrapped as Iterator. Consider the following example, where we iterate an array instead of using `ArrayObservable`:

  ```
  $fruits = ['apple', 'banana', 'orange', 'raspberry'];
  new IteratorObservable(new ArrayIterator($fruits));
  ```

  Note that this also includes generators. Consider another example with an anonymous function and `yield` keyword.

  ```
  $iterator = function() use ($fruits) {
      foreach ($fruits as $fruit) {
          yield $fruit;
      }
  };
  new IteratorObservable($iterator())
      ->subscribe(new DebugSubject());
  ```

Calling the `$iterator()` function returns an instance of a `Generator` class that implements the Iterator interface. However, these basic Observables are good mostly for demonstration purposes and are not very practical in real-world usage. In a PHP environment, we can't create Observables from mouse events as in JavaScript and RxJS, so we'll have to learn how to write custom Observables very soon in this chapter in order to create some real-world examples. In `Chapter 3`, *Writing a Reddit Reader with RxPHP*, we'll learn about the `Observable::create()` static method to create Observables with some basic custom logic. But, more on that later.

Observables can be divided into two groups based on when they start emitting values:

- **Hot**: In this group, values are emitted even when there are no observers subscribed. This is, for example, `Rx.Observable.fromEvent` from RxJS that we used in `Chapter 1`, *Introduction to Reactive Programming*. This creates an Observable from any JavaScript event. Values are emitted immediately, so when you subscribe to this Observable some time later, you receive only new values and no previously emitted values.
- **Cold**: In this group, values are emitted when at least one observer has been subscribed. This is, for example, RxPHP's `ArrayObservable`. It creates an Observable and, every time we subscribe, we receive all values passed as an input to the `fromArray()` method.

All built-in Observables in RxPHP can be instantiated easily by calling static methods from the `Rx\Observable` namespace. The following list represents the three Observables mentioned above:

- The `RxObservable::fromArray()` method returns `Rx\Observable\ArrayObservable`
- The `RxObservable::range()` method returns `Rx\Observable\RangeObservable`
- The `RxObservable::fromIterator()` method returns `Rx\Observable\IteratorObservable`

Don't be surprised that static method names don't necessarily match returned class names. Also, it's usually easier to use static calls than to instantiate Observables directly.

Observers

Observers are consumers of Observables. In other words, observers react to Observables. We've already seen the `CallbackObserver` class, which takes three optional arguments representing callables for each type of signal.

Consider a similar example that we used at the end of `Chapter 1`, *Introduction to Reactive Programming*, where we defined our observer:

```
$observer = new Rx\Observer\CallbackObserver(function($value) {
    printf("%s\n", $value);
}, function() {
    print("onError\n");
}, function() {
```

```
        print("onCompleted\n");
});
```

The `CallbackObserver` class lets us create a custom observer without necessarily extending the base class. Its constructor takes three optional arguments:

- `onNext`: This callable is called when a new item from the source Observable is emitted. This is the most common callback we'll use.
- `onComplete`: This callable is called when there are no items left and the Observable is done emitting items. Some Observables produce an infinite number of items and this callback is never called.
- `onError`: This callable is called when an error has occurred somewhere in the chain.

We can write the same example in a more reusable form to quickly test what's going on inside Observable chains:

```php
// rxphp_03.php
$fruits = ['apple', 'banana', 'orange', 'raspberry'];

class PrintObserver extends Rx\Observer\AbstractObserver {
    protected function completed() {
        print("Completed\n");
    }
    protected function next($item) {
        printf("Next: %s\n", $item);
    }
    protected function error(Exception $err) {
        $msg = $err->getMessage();
        printf("Error: %s\n", $msg);
    }
}

$source = Rx\Observable::fromArray($fruits);
$source->subscribe(new PrintObserver());
```

When extending `AbstractObserver`, the methods we need to implement are `completed()`, `next()`, and `error()`, with the same functionality as described previously.

We're using the `subscribe()` method to subscribe an observer to an Observable.

There's also the `subscribeCallback()` method that takes just three callables as arguments. Since RxPHP 2, the `subscribeCallback()` method is deprecated and its functionality has been merged with `subscribe()`.

This means that, in RxPHP 2, we can also write the following code:

```
$source->subscribe(function($item) {
    printf("Next: %sn", $item);
});
```

We made a single callable instead of subscribing with an observer. This handles only `onNext` signals.

Singles

Singles are like Observables; the only difference is that they always emit just one value. In RxPHP, we don't distinguish any difference between Observables and Singles, so we can use the `Observable::just()` static method:

```
// single_01.php/
require __DIR__ . '/PrintObserver.php';

RxObservable::just(42)
    ->subscribe(new PrintObserver());
```

This creates a new Observable that calls `onNext()` with the value `42`, and immediately after that `onComplete()`. The output for this very simple example is the following:

```
$ php single_01.php
Next: 42
Completed
```

Similar to the preceding explanation, calling `RxObservable::just()` static method returns an instance of `Rx\Observable\ReturnObservable`.

 The term "Single" was used mostly in RxJS 4. Since RxPHP was originally ported from RxJS 4, and later also took things from RxJS 5, you might encounter this term sometimes. If you're familiar only with RxJS 5, then you've probably never heard of it. Nonetheless, we'll always refer to all sources of values as Observables, even when they emit just a single, or no value at all.

Subject

The `Subject` is a class that acts as an Observable and observer at the same time. This means that it can subscribe to an Observable just like an observer, and also emit values like an Observable does. Eventually, it can also emit its own values independently of its source Observable.

In order to see how the `Subject` class can be used in different situations, we'll work through three examples based on the same example we used at the beginning of this chapter.

We can use a `Subject` class instead of an Observable. However, we need to emit items manually by calling `onNext()` on the `Subject` instance:

```php
// subject_01.php
use Rx\Subject\Subject;

$subject = new Subject();
$subject
    ->map(function($value) {
        return strlen($value);
    })
    ->filter(function($len) {
        return $len > 5;
    })
    ->subscribe(new PrintObserver());

$subject->onNext('apple');
$subject->onNext('banana');
$subject->onNext('orange');
$subject->onNext('raspberry');
```

This code produces the same output as the original example with Observable:

```
$ php subject_01.php
Next: 6
Next: 6
Next: 9
```

Another use case could be using `Subject` to subscribe to an Observable. We'll reuse the `PrintObserver` class we made a moment ago to print all of the items and notifications that went through the `Subject` instance:

```php
// subject_02.php
use Rx\Subject\Subject;
use Rx\Observable;
```

```
$subject = new Subject();
$subject->subscribe(new PrintObserver());

$fruits = ['apple', 'banana', 'orange', 'raspberry'];
Observable::fromArray($fruits)
    ->map(function($value) {
        return strlen($value);
    })
    ->filter(function($len) {
        return $len > 5;
    })
    ->subscribe($subject);
```

Notice that we subscribed `PrintObserver` to the `Subject` and then subscribed
the `Subject` at the end of the operator chain. As we can see, by default the `Subject` class
just passes through both items and notifications. The output is the same as in the previous
example.

The final situation we want to demonstrate is using an instance of Subject in the middle of
an operator chain:

```
// subject_03.php
use Rx\Subject\Subject;
use Rx\Observable;

$fruits = ['apple', 'banana', 'orange', 'raspberry'];

$subject = new Subject();
$subject
    ->filter(function($len) {
        return $len > 5;
    })
    ->subscribe(new PrintObserver());

Observable::fromArray($fruits)
    ->map(function($value) {
        return strlen($value);
    })
    ->subscribe($subject);
```

Yet again, the console output is the same.

Later in this chapter, we'll write the `DebugSubject` class, that we'll use many times
throughout this book, to quickly see what's going on in our Observable chains.

Disposable

All Rx implementations internally use the Dispose pattern. This design decision has two reasons:

- To be able to unsubscribe from an Observable
- To be able to release all data used by that Observable

For example, if we had an Observable that downloads a large file from the Internet and saves it to a temporary location until it's completely downloaded, we'd like to remove the temporary file if its observer unsubscribed, or any error occurred.

There're already a couple of classes available out-of-the-box with RxPHP, each with a different purpose. We don't need to worry about Disposables right now. We'll have a look at how they are used inside built-in Observables and operators in the next Chapter 3, *Writing a Reddit Reader with RxPHP*.

You can read more about the dispose pattern on Wikipedia https://en.wikipedia.org/wiki/Dispose_pattern or, more specifically, why it's used in reactive extensions on StackOverflow http://stackoverflow.com/a/7707768/310726.

However, it's good to know that something like releasing resources in Rx is important and we need to aware of it.

Scheduler

Observables and operators usually don't execute their work directly, but use an instance of the Scheduler class to decide how and when it should be executed.

In practice, a Scheduler receives an action as an anonymous function and schedules its execution according to its internal logic. This is particularly relevant to all Observables and operators that need to work with time. For example, all delayed or periodical emissions need to schedule via a Scheduler.

In languages such as JavaScript, this is relatively simple with, for example, the setTimeout() function and the event-based nature of JavaScript interpreters. However, in PHP, where all code is executed strictly sequentially, we'll have to use an event loop.

In most situations in RxPHP, we don't have to even worry about Schedulers because, if not set differently, all Observables and operators internally use the `ImmediateScheduler` class, which executes all actions immediately without any further logic.

We'll encounter Schedulers once more at the end of this chapter, when talking about event loops.

In `Chapter 6`, *PHP Streams API and Higher-Order Observables*, we'll go into much more detail about event loops in PHP. We'll also talk about the Event Loop Interopability specification (`https://github.com/async-interop/event-loop`) and how it's related to RxPHP.

> In RxPHP 2, using Schedulers has been significantly simplified and, most of the time, we don't need to worry about event loops at all, as we'll see in `Chapter 6`, *PHP Streams API and Higher-Order Observables*.

Operators

We've used operators already without any further explanation, but now that we know how to use Observables, observers, and Subjects, it's time to see how operators glue this all together.

The core principle of Rx is using various operators to modify data flow. Typically, an operator returns another Observable and therefore allows the chaining of operator calls.

In Rx, there are tons of operators, and in RxPHP in particular, there are about 40 already. Other implementations such as RxJS have even more. Those include all we saw in the previous chapter when talking about functional programming, such as `map()`, `filter()`, and a lot more. This also includes operators for very specific use cases, such as `merge()`, `buffer()`, or `retry()`, just to name a few.

The process of creating operator chains is a little more complicated under the hood than it seems. We don't need to worry about it for now because we'll talk about it again in `Chapter 3`, *Writing a Reddit Reader with RxPHP*. Before we start using more advanced operators in practice, we should have a look at how each operator is described in the documentation. This is mostly because some functionality isn't obvious at first sight and, when it comes to asynchronous events, it's sometimes hard to understand what each operator does.

Understanding the operator diagrams

Each operator is described in the documentation using a diagram called the **marble diagram**, where each marble represents an emitted value.

The filter() operator

First, we'll have a look at how the `filter()` operator is defined. We used the PHP function `array_filter()` in the previous chapter, so we know that it takes values and a predicate function as input. Then it evaluates each value with the predicate and, based on whether it returns true or false, it adds or skips the value in its response array. The behavior of the `filter()` operator is the same, it just works with data flows instead of arrays. This means it receives items from its source (the preceding Observable) and propagates them to its consequent observer (or chained operator).

Using a marble diagram, it will look like the following figure:

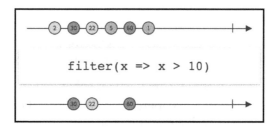

Marble diagram representing the filter() Operator from http://reactivex.io/documentation/operators/filter.html

Let's exaplain this diagram in more detail:

- At the top and bottom, we have two timelines that represent Observables. The arrow in the top right corner suggests that time goes from left to right.
- We can think of everything above the rectangle as input Observable and everything below the rectangle as output Observable. There're usually one or more input and only one output.
- Each circle (marble) represents a single value in time emitted by its respective Observable. The number inside each circle stands for its value. All values are ordered by the time they were emitted, which goes from left to right. Different colors are used to make it obvious that values at the top and bottom are the same (for example the blue "30" at the top is the same value as the bottom "30").

- The rectangle in the middle represents the transformation between the top and bottom Observables. Its functionality is usually described in words or pseudocode. In this case, we have an expression that looks like ES6 syntax, which says that it returns `true` if x is greater than `10`. Rewritten to PHP, it's equal to the following:

```
function($x) {
    return $x > 10;
}
```

- The bottom line, therefore, only contains circles with a value greater than `10`.
- Vertical lines on the right side of each line mark the point where these Observables complete. This means they have emitted all values and sent an `onComplete` notification. The `filter()` operator has no effect on the `onComplete` notification, so both Observables end at the same time.

This was pretty simple. Marble diagrams are a very comfortable way of representing data flows without worrying about implementation details (this reminds us of declarative programming, as we defined it in the first chapter, doesn't it?).

In some diagrams, you can also see a cross sign on the timeline, which represents an error (an `onError` notification to be precise). We'll see further on in this chapter that we can work with `onComplete` and `onError` notifications just as with `onNext`.

The debounceTime() operator

Let's have a look at another diagram. This time we have a `debounceTime()` operator from RxJS 5, which we saw in the first chapter, in the *Autocomplete with RxJS* example:

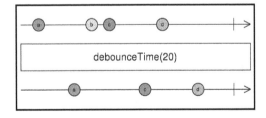

Marble diagram representing the debounceTime() operator from http://reactivex.io/documentation/operators/debounce.html

In the rectangle in the middle, we don't have any pseudocode this time; just a single expression `debounceTime(20)`. Well, in order to figure out what it does, we need to look at the documentation, or try to analyze the diagram.

When the `debounceTime()` operator receives a value, it waits a certain interval before reemitting it. If any other values arrive before the interval expires, the original value is discarded and the later value is used instead; the interval is restarted as well. This can go on for an infinite number of values.

The diagram exactly describes the previous paragraph:

- First, value **a** arrives. The transformation function waits until 20ms interval expires, and after that, the operator reemits the value further. The interval is represented by shifting the bottom values on the timeline slightly to the right. As we said previously, the horizontal lines represent values in time. When the bottom circle, labeled **a**, is shifted to the right, it means this event happened after the top **a** circle.
- Then, two more values arrive, both of them in a very short time. The first one is discarded, but after the second one, there's another longer time gap, so only the second value gets reemitted.
- The process with the last value **d** is analogous to the first one.

This operator is useful when we know we can ignore some events that occur quickly after one another. A prime example is using `debounceTime()` for autocomplete features when we want to start searching after a user has stopped typing a keyword.

The concat operator

Now we can have a look at a slightly more complicated operator, which is `concat()`. Look at the following diagram and try to guess what it does:

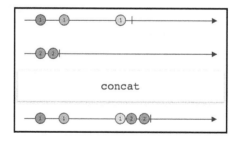

Marble diagram representing the concat() operator from http://reactivex.io/documentation/operators/concat.html

Let's analyze this together before looking to the documentation:

- At the top, we have two Observables as inputs to the operator.
- Both Observables should emit a value at the same time, but only the value from the first Observable is passed through. The same applies for the second and third values as well.
- Then the first Observable reaches the end and sends an `onComplete` notification.
- Right after that, the operator starts emitting values from the second Observable.

The `concat()` operator merges multiple Observables into one. It internally subscribes to each input Observable in order, one after another. This means that, when the first Observable completes, it subscribes to the next one. It's important to know that there's only ever one source Observable subscribed at a time (we'll work with `concat()` and a similar `merge()` operator in `Chapter 4`, *Reactive versus a typical Event-Driven Approach*).

In other words, the `concat()` operator concatenates multiple data streams into a single stream.

In the first chapter, we talked about functional programming and how most principles are the same in reactive programming. Implementing such a feature would be rather complicated because there's no built-in PHP function designed to deal with such a use case.

If we go back to the first chapter once more, we said that one key concept of reactive programming is to "express data flows with ease". This operator shows what that means in action.

Other common operators

These were only three operators out of more than 40 available in RxPHP. Apart from very simple ones like `filter()` and `map()`, there're also more sophisticated ones. We've seen `concat()` already, but here are a few interesting ones that we'll use in further chapters:

- `buffer()`: This operator has multiple variants, but all of them collect received values and reemits them in groups of a predefined size. For example, we can create groups of three items as follows:

```
Rx\Observable::range(1, 4)
    ->bufferWithCount(3)
    ->subscribe(new DebugSubject());
```

Which prints the following output:

```
13:58:13 [] onNext: [1, 2, 3] (array)
13:58:13 [] onNext: [4] (array)
13:58:13 onCompleted
```

 Note that the last array contains just one value because the Observable sent an `onComplete` notification.

- `merge()`: This operator merges all input Observables into a single output Observable, reemitting all values immediately (in contrast to `concat()`).
- `distinct()`: This operator reemits only those values that haven't passed this operator before.
- `take()`: This operator reemits only a set number of values that arrive to the operator first, then sends an `onComplete` notification.
- `retry()`: When source Observable sends `onError`, this operator tries to resubscribe automatically. You can also tell it to retry only a limited number of times until signaling `onError` (we'll use this operator in Chapter 4, *Reactive versus a Typical Event-Driven Approach*).
- `catchError()`: This operator lets us continue by subscribing to another Observable returned from its callback when an `onError` notification occurs.
- `toArray()`: This operator collects all items from its source Observable and reemits them as a single array when the source Observable completes.
- `timeout()`: This operator sends an `onError` notification if no values arrived within a certain time span.

Enough theory; let's start writing our first custom class, which we'll utilize a few times throughout this book.

Writing the DebugSubject class

One common use case for `Subject` class is proxying all values and notifications from its source Observable.

In one of the preceding paragraphs, we wrote the `PrintObserver` class, which prints all values it receives. However, a more common situation is where we want to output values from an Observable while being able to chain it with another operator or observer. The `Subject` class exactly fits this use case, so we'll rewrite the preceding `PrintObserver` class and inherit `Subject` instead of `AbstractObserver`:

```
class DebugSubject extends Rx\Subject\Subject {
  public function __construct($identifier=null, $maxLen=64){
    $this->identifier = $identifier;
    $this->maxLen = $maxLen;
  }
  public function onCompleted() {
    printf("%s%s onCompleted\n", $this->getTime(), $this->id());
    parent::onCompleted();
  }
  public function onNext($val) {
    $type = is_object($val) ? get_class($val) : gettype($val);

    if (is_object($val) && method_exists($val, '__toString')) {
      $str = (string)$val;
    } elseif (is_object($val)) {
      $str = get_class($val);
    } elseif (is_array($val)) {
      $str = json_encode($val);
    } else {
      $str = $val;
    }

    if (is_string($str) && strlen($str) > $this->maxLen) {
      $str = substr($str, 0, $this->maxLen) . '...';
    }
    printf("%s%s onNext: %s (%s)\n",
        $this->getTime(), $this->id(), $str, $type);
    parent::onNext($value);
  }
  public function onError(Exception $error) {
    $msg = $error->getMessage();
    printf("%s%s onError (%s): %s\n", $this->getTime(),$this->>
        $this->id(), get_class($error), $msg);
    parent::onError($error);
  }
  private function getTime() {
    return date('H:i:s');
  }
  private function id() {
    return ' [' . $this->identifier . ']';
  }
```

```
}
```

This `DebugSubject` class prints all values, their types, and the time they were received by the `DebugSubject`. It also allows us to set a unique identifier for each `DebugSubject` instance to be able to distinguish their output. We're going to use this class a couple of times throughout this book to quickly see what's going on inside our Observable chains.

Then, using this class is just like using any other observer:

```php
// rxphp_04.php
$fruits = ['apple', 'banana', 'orange', 'raspberry'];
$observer = Rx\Observable::fromArray($fruits)
    ->subscribe(new DebugSubject());
```

The output in the console is as follows:

```
$ php rxphp_04.php
17:15:21 [] onNext: apple (string)
17:15:21 [] onNext: banana (string)
17:15:21 [] onNext: orange (string)
17:15:21 [] onNext: raspberry (string)
17:15:21 [] onCompleted
```

Chaining Subjects and operators works just as with Observables:

```php
// rxphp_05.php
$subject = new DebugSubject(1);
$subject
    ->map(function($item) {
        return strlen($item);
    })
    ->subscribe(new DebugSubject(2));

$observable = Rx\Observable::fromArray($fruits);
$observable->subscribe($subject);
```

In this example, we first created an instance of `DebugSubject`, then we chained it with the `map()` operator, which returns the lengths of each item. Finally, we subscribed another `DebugSubject` that will print only numbers because it's placed after `map()`. Then we created an Observable from an array (we've seen this static method previously), which is going to be the source emitting all items. The result is as follows:

```
17:33:36 [1] onNext: apple (string)
17:33:36 [2] onNext: 5 (integer)
17:33:36 [1] onNext: banana (string)
17:33:36 [2] onNext: 6 (integer)
17:33:36 [1] onNext: orange (string)
```

```
17:33:36 [2] onNext: 6 (integer)
17:33:36 [1] onNext: raspberry (string)
17:33:36 [2] onNext: 9 (integer)
17:33:36 [1] onCompleted
17:33:36 [2] onCompleted
```

Note that the order of messages matches our assumption that the source Observable emits one value at a time, which is propagated through the entire chain.

 There's one important side effect of using Subjects as we did that isn't very obvious. Since we subscribe it to the preceding Observable, it turns it from "cold" into "hot", which might be unwanted in some use cases.

RxPHP provides a series of operators all starting with the "doOn" prefix that are intended to be placed inside the operator chain to execute side effects without subscribing to an Observable. We'll have a better look at them in Chapter 5, *Testing RxPHP Code*.

Writing JSONDecodeOperator

We're going to work with calls to remote API's a few times throughout this book, so it would be very handy to have an operator that transforms JSON string responses into their PHP array representations.

This example looks like something that could be easily done with just the map() operator:

```
// rxphp_06.php
Rx\Observable::just('{"value":42}')
    ->map(function($value) {
        return json_decode($value, true);
    })
    ->subscribe(new DebugSubject());
```

This prints the correct result for sure, as we can see in the following output:

```
$ php rxphp_06.php
16:39:50 [] onNext: {"value": 42} (array)
16:39:50 [] onCompleted
```

Well, but what about malformed JSON strings? What happens if we try to decode the following:

```
Rx\Observable::just('NA')
    ->map(function($value) {
        return json_decode($value, true);
    })
    ->subscribe(new DebugSubject());
```

The function `json_decode()` doesn't throw an exception when trying to process an invalid JSON string; it just returns `null`:

```
15:51:06 [] onNext:   (NULL)
```

This is probably not what we want. If the JSON string is invalid, then something is wrong because this situation should never happen and we want to send an `onError` notification.

If we wanted to know any further information about which error occurred, we'd have to call `json_last_error()`. So, this is a perfect opportunity to write a custom operator that decodes JSON strings that, if any error occurs, will send an `onError`.

All operators implement the `OperatorInterface` and `__invoke()` method. This so-called "magic" method is supported from PHP 5.3+ and allows the use of objects as functions:

```
// __invoke.php
class InvokeExampleClass {
    public function __invoke($x) {
        echo strlen($x);
    }
}
$obj = new InvokeExampleClass();
$obj('apple');
var_dump(is_callable($obj));
```

When class implements `__invoke()`, it's automatically considered as callable as well:

```
$ php __invoke.php
int(5)
bool(true)
```

Writing operators is very similar. A stub for our class will look like the following:

```
// JSONDecodeOperator.php
use Rx\ObservableInterface as ObservableI;
use Rx\ObserverInterface as ObserverI;
use Rx\SchedulerInterface as SchedulerI;
use Rx\Operator\OperatorInterface as OperatorI;
```

```
class JSONDecodeOperator implements OperatorI {
    public function __invoke(ObservableI $observable,
            ObserverI $observer, SchedulerI $scheduler = null) {
        // ...
    }
}
```

Method __invoke() takes three arguments and returns a Disposable object. Right now, we'll use just the first two and not worry about the $scheduler:

- ObservableInterface $observable: This is our input Observable that we'll subscribe to
- ObserverInterface $observer: This is where we'll emit all output values from this operator

We'll follow almost the same principle as when writing a custom Subject class. We're going to use CallbackObserver to subscribe to the Observable and perform all of our logic:

```
class JSONDecodeOperator implements OperatorI {
  public function __invoke(ObservableI $observable,
      ObserverI $observer, SchedulerI $scheduler = null) {

    $obs = new CallbackObserver(
      function ($value) use ($observer) {
        $decoded = json_decode($value, true);
        if (json_last_error() == JSON_ERROR_NONE) {
          $observer->onNext($decoded);
        } else {
          $msg = json_last_error_msg();
          $e = new InvalidArgumentException($msg);
          $observer->onError($e);
        }
      },
      function ($error) use ($observer) {
        $observer->onError($error);
      },
      function () use ($observer) {
        $observer->onCompleted();
      }
    );

    return $observable->subscribe($obs, $scheduler);
  }
}
```

There're a few interesting things to notice:

- When `onError` or `onComplete` notifications occur, we just pass them along without any further logic.
- The operator can send any signal any time it wants. Inside `CallbackObserver` class's `onNext` closure, we check whether any error occurred while decoding the input JSON string coming from the source Observable using `json_last_error()`.
- The operator has full access to the source Observable.
- The operator can emit values independently on values from the source Observable.

In order to use our operator, we have to use the `Observable::lift()`, method which takes a Closure as an argument that needs to return an instance of an operator (this function is a so-called operator factory):

```
// rxphp_07.php
Rx\Observable::just('{"value":42}')
    ->lift(function() {
        return new JSONDecodeOperator();
    })
    ->subscribe(new DebugSubject());
```

Using custom operators was significantly simplified in RxPHP 2, but using the `lift()` method is universal and works in both versions of RxPHP.

Valid JSON string is decoded as expected:

```
$ php rxphp_07.php
17:58:49 [] onNext: {"value": 42} (array)
17:58:49 [] onCompleted
```

On the other hand, the same invalid JSON string that we used above doesn't call `onNext`, but `onError` instead. It sends this notification with an instance of `InvalidArgumentException` class and the error message from `json_last_error_msg()`, as shown in the following output:

```
17:59:25 onError (InvalidArgumentException): Syntax error
```

As usual, we're going to reuse this class throughout this book. The next chapter is going to work with remote APIs a lot, so this operator is going to be very handy.

Simplifying propagation of notifications

In the `JSONDecodeOperator` class, we didn't want to modify either `onError` nor `onComplete` notifications and we just passed them along. However, there's an easier way to do this thanks to how PHP works with callables. A valid callable is also an array with two items: an object and a method name.

This means we can rewrite the above `CallbackObserver` instantiation as follows:

```
$callbackObserver = new CallbackObserver(
    function ($value) use ($observer) {
        // ...
    },
    [$observer, 'onError'],
    [$observer, 'onCompleted']
);
```

The functionality is exactly the same. Instead of creating an anonymous function for each notification, we can just pass the callable directly.

Using custom operators in RxPHP 2

In Chapter 1, *Introduction to Reactive Programming,* we mentioned a magic `__call()` method. RxPHP 2 uses this method to allow the use of custom operators by auto-discovering them in two namespace formats.

The first option is defining our operator class in the `Rx\Operator` namespace:

```
// JSONDecodeOperator.php
namespace Rx\Operator;

use Rx\ObservableInterface as ObservableI;
use Rx\ObserverInterface as ObserverI;
use Rx\Operator\OperatorInterface as OperatorI;
use Rx\DisposableInterface as DisposableI;

class JSONDecodeOperator implements OperatorI {
  public function __invoke(ObservableI $observable,
      ObserverI $observer): DisposableI {

    return $observable->subscribe(
      function ($value) use ($observer) {
        $decoded = json_decode($value, true);
        if (json_last_error() == JSON_ERROR_NONE) {
          $observer->onNext($decoded);
```

```
        } else {
          $msg = json_last_error_msg();
          $e = new InvalidArgumentException($msg);
          $observer->onError($e);
        }
      },
      [$observer, 'onError'],
      [$observer, 'onCompleted']
    );
  }
}
```

It's the same `JSONDecodeOperator` class, just updated for RxPHP 2. Using this operator is, then, very simple:

```
Observable::just('{"value":42}')
    ->JSONDecode()
    ->subscribe(new DebugSubject());
```

Since our operator resides under the `Rx\Operator` namespace, it's expanded by the `__call()` method to `Rx\Operator\JSONDecodeOperator`. This means we don't need to use the `lift()` method at all.

Another way is to prefix the operator name and namespace with underscores _ which are then merged into a full class name. This means we can put all application specific operators under a custom namespace:

```
// JSONDecodeOperator.php
namespace MyApp\Rx\Operator;
...
class JSONDecodeOperator implements OperatorI { ... }
```

Now we can use the operator as follows:

```
Observable::just('{"value":42}')
    ->_MyApp_JSONDecode()
    ->subscribe(new DebugSubject());
```

Writing CURLObservable

As we said, we're going to work with API calls and, for this reason, we need a comfortable way of creating HTTP requests. It's probably no surprise that we'll write a custom Observable that downloads a URL and passes it's response to its observers, where we'll decode it from JSON using the operator we created just a couple of lines above.

We're going to use PHP's cURL module, which is a wrapper around libcurl (`https://curl.haxx.se/libcurl/`) – a C library for transferring data via any protocols imaginable.

We'll start by using plain simple cURL in PHP and we'll see that it supports some sort of asynchronous approach out-of-the-box.

Imperative approach and cURL

If we just wanted to download a single URL, we wouldn't need anything special. However, we want to make this, and all future applications of `CURLObservable` class, more interactive, so we'll also keep track of the downloading progress.

A plain and simple approach could look like this:

```php
// curl_01.php
$ch = curl_init();
curl_setopt($ch, CURLOPT_URL, "http://google.com");
curl_setopt($ch, CURLOPT_RETURNTRANSFER, true);
curl_setopt($ch, CURLOPT_PROGRESSFUNCTION, 'progress');
curl_setopt($ch, CURLOPT_NOPROGRESS, false);
curl_setopt($ch, CURLOPT_HEADER, 0);
$html = curl_exec($ch);
curl_close($ch);

function progress($res, $downtotal, $down, $uptotal, $up) {
    if ($download_size > 0) {
        printf("%.2f\n", $down / $downtotal * 100);
    }
    ob_flush();
    usleep(100 * 1000);
}
```

We're using `CURLOPT_PROGRESSFUNCTION` option to set a callback function which is invoked internally by the cURL module. It takes four arguments that help us keep track of how much of the page's total size already has been downloaded.

We probably don't need to show its output because it's pretty obvious.

There's also a small subset of cURL functions that work with multiple cURL handles simultaneously. These are all prefixed with `curl_multi_` and are executed by calling `curl_multi_exec()`. Nonetheless, the `curl_multi_exec()` function is blocking and the interpreter needs to wait until it finishes.

Implementing cURL into a custom Observable

We've already seen how to write a custom observer, Subject and operator. Now is the right time to write an Observable as well. We want the Observable to emit values when downloading the URL and, at the end, return a complete response. We can distinguish between the two types of messages by checking their type. Progress will always be a double, while response will always be a string.

Let's start with our class synopsis to see how it's going to work and then implement each method separately with a short description:

```
use Rx\Observable;
use Rx\ObserverInterface as ObserverI;

class CURLObservable extends Observable {
    public function __construct($url) {}
    public function subscribe(ObserverI $obsr, $sched = null) {}
    private function startDownload() {}
    private function progress($r, $downtot, $down, $uptot, $up) {}
}
```

Every time we write an Observable, we'll extend the base `Rx\Observable` class. We could theoretically just implement `Rx\ObservableInterface`, but, most of the time, we also want to inherit all its internal logic and all existing operators.

The constructor and method `startDownload()` are going to be very simple. In `startDownload()`, we start downloading the URL while monitoring its progress.

Please note that this code goes inside the `CURLObservable` class; we're just trying to keep the code short and easy to read, so we have omitted indentation and class definition in this example:

```
public function __construct($url) {
    $this->url = $url;
}

private function startDownload() {
    $ch = curl_init();
    curl_setopt($ch, CURLOPT_URL, $this->url);
    curl_setopt($ch, CURLOPT_PROGRESSFUNCTION, [$this,'progress']);
    curl_setopt($ch, CURLOPT_RETURNTRANSFER, true);
    curl_setopt($ch, CURLOPT_NOPROGRESS, false);
    curl_setopt($ch, CURLOPT_HEADER, 0);
    curl_setopt($ch, CURLOPT_USERAGENT, 'Mozilla/5.0 ...');
    // Disable gzip compression
    curl_setopt($ch, CURLOPT_ENCODING, 'gzip;q=0,deflate,sdch');
```

```
$response = curl_exec($ch);
curl_close($ch);

return $response;
}
```

This is mostly the same as the example using an imperative approach. The only interesting difference is that we're using a callable `[$this, 'progress']` instead of just a function name, as we did earlier.

The actual emission of values happens inside the `progress()` method:

```
private function progress($res, $downtotal, $down, $uptotal, $up){
    if ($downtotal > 0) {
        $percentage = sprintf("%.2f", $down / $downtotal * 100);
        foreach ($this->observers as $observer) {
            /** @var ObserverI $observer */
            $observer->onNext(floatval($percentage));
        }
    }
}
```

Since we inherited the original Observable, we can make use of its protected property `$observers` that holds all subscribed observers, as its name suggests. To emit a value to all of them, we can simply iterate the array and call `onNext` on each observer.

The only method we haven't seen so far is `subscribe()`:

```
public function subscribe(ObserverI $obsr, $sched = null) {
    $disp1 = parent::subscribe($obsr, $sched);

    if (null === $sched) {
        $sched = new ImmediateScheduler();
    }

    $disp2 = $sched->schedule(function() use ($obsr, $started) {
        $response = $this->startDownload();
        if ($response) {
            $obsr->onNext($response);
            $obsr->onCompleted();
        } else {
            $msg = 'Unable to download ' . $this->url);
            $obsr->onError(new Exception($msg));
        }
    });

    return new CompositeDisposable([$disp1, $disp2]);
```

```
        }
```

This method combines many of the things we've seen in this chapter:

- We definitely want to keep the original functionality of the Observable, so we'll call its parent implementation. This adds the observer to the array of observers, as mentioned a moment ago.
- The `parent::subscribe()` method returns a disposable. That's the object we can use to unsubscribe the observer from this Observable.
- If we don't specify what Scheduler this Observable should use, it'll fall back to `ImmediateScheduler`. We've already mentioned `ImmediateScheduler` when we were talking about Schedulers in general. In RxPHP 2, we'd use `Scheduler::getImmediate()` instead of directly using the class name.
- Right after that, we schedule the work (in terms of Schedulers, it's usually referred to as "action") to be executed by the Scheduler. Note that the action itself is a closure.
- Then, we start downloading the URL. If we subscribe another observer to the same Observable, it'll re-download the same URL again. Download progress is then emitted with frequency according to cURL's internals. We'll talk more about the subscription process in the next chapter.
- When downloading finishes, we emit the response or an error.
- At the end of this method, it returns another disposable. This time, it's `CompositeDisposable` that is used to wrap other disposables. When calling its `dispose()` method, these wrapped ones are properly disposed as well.

So, that's it. Now we can test our Observable and see what its output is. We can try to grab a list of the most recent questions on www.stackoverflow.com tagged with *functional-programming*":

```php
$url = 'https://api.stack...&tagged=functional-programming';
$observable = new CurlObservable($url);
$observable->subscribe(new DebugSubject());
```

This prints a couple of numbers and then the response JSON string:

```
16:17:52 onNext: 21.39 (double)
16:17:52 onNext: 49.19 (double)
16:17:52 onNext: 49.19 (double)
16:17:52 onNext: 76.99 (double)
16:17:52 onNext: 100 (double)
16:17:52 onNext: {"items":[{"tags":["javascript","... (string)
16:17:52 onCompleted
```

You can see that one value was emitted twice. This is because of the timing and network latency when cURL evaluates the callback, which is nothing unusual. If we didn't want to see repeated values, we could use the `distinct()` operator that we saw when talking about "marble diagrams".

Now let's combine it with our `JSONDecodeOperator`. Since we're now interested only in the string response and want to ignore all progress emissions, we'll also use the `filter()` operator:

```
// rxphp_curl.php
$observable
    ->filter(function($value) {
        return is_string($value);
    })
    ->lift(function() {
        return new JSONDecodeOperator();
    })
    ->subscribe(new DebugSubject(null, 128));
```

This returns part of the response array (for demonstration purposes, we added indentation and made the output a little longer):

```
$ php rxphp_curl.php
16:23:55 [] onNext: {
    "items": [
        {
            "tags": [
                "javascript",
                "functional-programming",
        ... (array)
16:23:55 [] onCompleted
```

When we used the `filter()` operator, you might notice that we called it `Observable::filter()` without necessarily using the `lift()` method. This is because almost all operators are, in fact, just `lift()` calls with predefined Closures that return an appropriate operator class. A good question is whether we can write our own shorthand for `JSONDecodeOperator` when we're already extending the base Observable class. Maybe something like `Observable::jsonDecode()`?

The answer is yes, we can. However, in RxPHP 1.x, it wouldn't help us a lot. When we chain operators, they return other instances of Observables that aren't under our control. We could theoretically use `Observable::jsonDecode()` right after creating `CurlObservable` because we'd know that it's going to be an instance of this class, but chaining it with `filter()` brings us back to the original Observable that doesn't know any `jsonDecode()` methods. In particular, the `filter()` operator returns an instance of `Rx\Observable\AnonymousObservable`.

Running multiple requests asynchronously

An interesting use case could be to start multiple requests asynchronously. All calls to `curl_exec()` are blocking, which means that they block the execution context until they're finished.

Unfortunately, this is a very tricky problem that's hard to solve without using any extra PHP modules, such as **pthreads**, as we'll see much later in `Chapter 9`, *Multithreaded and Distributed Computing with pthreads and Gearman*.

We can, however, make use of PHP's standard `proc_open()` to spawn non-blocking subprocesses that can run in parallel and then just ask for their output.

The proc_open() and non-blocking fread()

Our goal is to have the means to start various subprocesses asynchronously. In this example, we'll use a simple PHP script that'll just sleep for a couple of seconds and represent our asynchronous task:

```
// sleep.php
$name = $argv[1];
$time = intval($argv[2]);
$elapsed = 0;

while ($elapsed < $time) {
    sleep(1);
    $elapsed++;
    printf("$name: $elapsed\n");
}
```

This script takes two arguments. The first one is an identifier of our choice that we'll use to distinguish between multiple processes. The second one is the number of seconds this script will run while printing its name and the elapsed time every second. For example, we can run:

```
$ sleep.php proc1 3
proc1: 1
proc1: 2
proc1: 3
```

Now, we'll write another PHP script that uses `proc_open()` to spawn a subprocess. Also, as we said, we need the script to be non-blocking. This means that we need to be able to read output from the subprocess as it is printed using `printf()` above, while being able to spawn more subprocess, if needed:

```
// proc_01.php
$proc = proc_open('php sleep.php proc1 3', [
    0 => ['pipe', 'r'], // stdin
    1 => ['pipe', 'w'], // stdout
    2 => ['file', '/dev/null', 'a'] // stderr
], $pipes);

stream_set_blocking($pipes[1], 0);

while (proc_get_status($proc)['running']) {
    usleep(100 * 1000);
    $str = fread($pipes[1], 1024);
    if ($str) {
        printf($str);
    } else {
        printf("tickn");
    }
}
fclose($pipes[1]);
proc_close($proc);
```

We spawn a subprocess `php sleep.php proc1 3` and then go into a loop. With a 100ms delay, we check whether there's any new output from the subprocess using `fread()`. If there is, we print it; otherwise, just write the word "tick". The loop will end when the subprocess terminates (that's the condition with the `proc_get_status()` function).

The most important thing in this example is calling the `stream_set_blocking()` function, which makes operations with this stream non-blocking.

Event loop and RxPHP

Applying event loop to Observables would work in a similar way. We'd create Observables, start an event loop and periodically check their progress. Luckily for us, RxPHP is prepared for this. In combination with the ReactPHP library (https://github.com/reactphp/react), we can use a Scheduler that's designed exactly for what we need.

As an example, we can have a look at `IntervalObservable` that periodically emits values:

```
// rxphp_eventloop.php
$loop = new ReactEventLoopStreamSelectLoop();
$scheduler = new RxSchedulerEventLoopScheduler($loop);

RxObservable::interval(1000, $scheduler)
    ->take(3)
    ->subscribe(new DebugSubject());

$loop->run();
```

This prints three values with 1s delays:

```
$ php rxphp_eventloop.php
23:12:44 [] onNext: 0 (integer)
23:12:45 [] onNext: 1 (integer)
23:12:46 [] onNext: 2 (integer)
23:12:46 [] onCompleted
```

In RxPHP 2, using event loops has been simplified and, most of the time, we don't even need to worry about starting the loop ourselves. We'll talk about differences between RxPHP 1.x and RxPHP 2 regarding event loops in Chapter 6, *PHP Streams API and Higher-Order Observables*.

Summary

In this chapter, we had a closer look at all the components of RxPHP.

In particular, we've seen all three types of notifications used in Rx, Observables, observers, Subjects, Singles and operators. On practical examples, we have designed our custom observer, Subject, Observable and an operator. We'll use all these in the upcoming chapters.

We saw that documentation regarding Rx operators is very often described in the form of "marble diagrams".

The next chapter is going to utilize all we did in this chapter. We're going to create a CLI Reddit reader using RxPHP and Symfony Console component. We'll also talk in more depth about the subscription process in Observable chains.

3
Writing a Reddit Reader with RxPHP

In previous chapters, we talked a lot about asynchronous programming in PHP and how this relates to reactive programming, in particular, how to start using RxPHP, and how to use common PHP functions such as `proc_open()` and cURL asynchronously.

This chapter will cover writing a CLI Reddit reader app using RxPHP, Symfony Console, and Symfony Process components. We're also going to use most of what we've learned in the previous chapter:

- We'll look in more depth into what happens internally when creating Observable chains and subscribing to Observables.
- We'll see how Disposables are used in the default classes that come with RxPHP, and how these are going to be useful for unsubscribing from Observables in our app.
- Subjects can sometimes simplify our lives when working with operator chains.
- How to use `Observable::create()` and `Observable::defer()` static methods to create new Observables with custom logic on subscription.
- Symfony Console library is going to be our tool of choice for most CLI interactions throughout this book. Before we start using it, we'll have a quick look at what its practical benefits are.
- The event loop from the previous chapter is going to be the center of our app. We're going to use it to make the app responsive (we could also say, reactive) at any given time.

- To easily work with subprocesses, we'll use Symfony Process component, which handles all the heavy work related to managing subprocesses for us.
- We'll use non-blocking stream handling we've seen already in practice, in combination with input from terminal and output from a subprocesses.
- We'll list disposable classes provided by RxPHP.

Before we dive in, now is a good time to have a closer look at the internal functionality of RxPHP, which hasn't been very important thus far. Nonetheless, this knowledge is going to be crucial in this and most of the upcoming chapters.

Examining RxPHP's internals

In the previous chapter, we briefly mentioned disposables as a means for releasing resources used by observers, Observables, Subjects, and so on. In practice, a disposable is returned, for example, when subscribing to an Observable. Consider the following code from the default `Rx\Observable::subscribe()` method:

```
function subscribe(ObserverI $observer, $scheduler = null) {
    $this->observers[] = $observer;
    $this->started = true;

    return new CallbackDisposable(function () use ($observer) {
        $this->removeObserver($observer);
    });
}
```

This method first adds the observer to the array of all subscribed observers. It then marks this Observable as started (remember the difference between "cold" and "hot" Observables from `Chapter 2`, *Reactive Programming with RxPHP*) and, at the end, it returns a new instance of the `CallbackDisposable` class. This class takes a Closure as an argument and invokes it when it's disposed. This is probably the most common use case for disposables.

This disposable just removes the observer from the array, and therefore, it receives no more values emitted from this Observable.

A closer look at subscribing to Observables

It should be obvious that Observables need to work in such a way that all their subscribed observers can be iterated. Then, unsubscribing via a disposable will need to remove one particular observer from the array of all subscribed observers.

However, if we have a look at how most of the default Observables work, we find out that they always override the `Observable::subscribe()` method and usually completely omit the part where it should hold an array of subscribers. Instead, they just emit all available values to the subscribed observer and finish with the `onComplete()` signal immediately after that. For example, we can have a look at the actual source code of the `subscribe()` method of the `Rx\ReturnObservable` class in RxPP 1:

```
function subscribe(ObserverI $obs, SchedulerI $sched = null) {
    $value = $this->value;
    $scheduler = $scheduler ?: new ImmediateScheduler();
    $disp = new CompositeDisposable();

    $disp->add($scheduler->schedule(function() use ($obs, $val) {
        $obs->onNext($val);
    }));
    $disp->add($scheduler->schedule(function() use ($obs) {
        $obs->onCompleted();
    }));

    return $disp;
}
```

The `ReturnObservable` class takes a single value in its constructor and emits this value to every observer as they subscribe.

The following is a nice example of how the lifecycle of an Observable might look:

- When an observer subscribes, it checks whether a Scheduler was also passed as an argument. Usually, it's not, so it creates an instance of `ImmediateScheduler`. Note that in RxPHP 2 the Scheduler can be set only in the class constructor.
- Then, an instance of `CompositeDisposable` is created, which is going to keep an array of all disposables used by this method. When calling `CompositeDisposable::dispose()`, it iterates all disposables it contains and calls their respective `dispose()` methods.
- Right after that, we start populating our `CompositeDisposable` with the following:

    ```
    $disposable->add($scheduler->schedule(function() { ... }));
    ```

- This is something we'll see very often. The
  `SchedulerInterface::schedule()` method returns a
  `DisposableInterface`, which is responsible for canceling the action and
  releasing resources. In this case, when we're using `ImmediateScheduler`, which
  has no other logic, it just evaluates the Closure immediately:

```
function () use ($obs, $val) {
    $observer->onNext($val);
}
```

- Since `ImmediateScheduler::schedule()` doesn't need to release any
  resources (it didn't use any), it just returns an instance
  of `Rx\Disposable\EmptyDisposable` that does literally nothing.
- Then the disposable is returned, and could be used to unsubscribe from this
  Observable. However, as we saw in the preceding source code, this Observable
  doesn't let you unsubscribe, and if we think about it, it doesn't even make sense
  because `ReturnObservable` class's value is emitted immediately on
  subscription.

The same applies to other similar `Observables`, such
as `IteratorObservable`, `RangeObservable` or `ArrayObservable`. These just contain
recursive calls with Schedulers, but the principle is the same.

A good question is, why on Earth is this so complicated? All the preceding code does could
be stripped into the following three lines (assuming we're not interested in using
Schedulers):

```
function subscribe(ObserverI $observer) {
    $observer->onNext($this->value);
    $observer->onCompleted();
}
```

Well, for `ReturnObservable` this might be true, but in real applications, we very rarely use
any of these primitive Observables. Another very important use case for Schedulers is
testing. We can provide a test Scheduler that simulates delayed execution, to make sure our
Observables and operators emit values in the correct order. We'll go into this topic in depth
in Chapter 5, *Testing RxPHP Code.*

The ability to unsubscribe from Observables or clean up any resources when unsubscribing
is very important, and we'll use it in a few moments.

Emitting multiple values with Schedulers

We've seen how to use RangeObservable already. Now, when we know why using Scheduler->schedule() is important, we can for tutorial purposes think about how we could implement RangeObservable Observable's functionality ourselves.

For example, it could look like the following:

```
// custom_range_01.php
use Rx\Observable;
use Rx\ObserverInterface;

class CustomRangeObservable extends Observable {
  private $min;
  private $max;

  public function __construct($min, $max) {
    $this->min = $min;
    $this->max = $max;
  }

  public function subscribe($observer, $sched = null) {
    if (null === $sched) {
      $sched = new \Rx\Scheduler\ImmediateScheduler();
    }

    return $sched->schedule(function() use ($observer) {
      for ($i = $this->min; $i <= $this->max; $i++) {
        $observer->onNext($i);
      }
      $observer->onCompleted();
    });
  }
}

(new CustomRangeObservable(1, 5))
    ->subscribe(new DebugSubject());
```

When we run this example, we'll see that it produces the correct results:

```
$ php custom_range_01.php
1
2
3
4
5
```

However, the original `RangeObservable` has one interesting feature. It's able to unsubscribe inside the loop, which means that we can stop generating values any time we want.

Consider the following example, where we unsubscribe inside the observer's callable:

```
// range_01.php
use Rx\Observable;
use Rx\Scheduler\EventLoopScheduler;
use React\EventLoop\StreamSelectLoop;

$loop = new StreamSelectLoop();
$scheduler = new EventLoopScheduler($loop);

$disposable = Observable::range(1, 5)
    ->subscribeCallback(function($val) use (&$disposable) {
        echo "$val\n";
        if ($val == 3) {
            $disposable->dispose();
        }
    }, null, null, $scheduler);

$scheduler->start();
```

This example emits only the first three values and then unsubscribes using `$disposable->dispose()`.

We had to use an asynchronous `EventLoopScheduler`, because we want to start executing scheduled actions after we subscribe. With `EventLoopScheduler`, the execution starts by calling `$scheduler->start()`. If we use the default `ImmediateScheduler`, then the `$disposable` variable will always be null (unassigned), because all the scheduled actions would be executed inside `subscribeCallback()` method and the `$disposable` variable will never be assigned.

When we run this demo we'll see just the first three numbers:

```
$ php range_01.php
1
2
3
```

If we try the same with our `CustomRangeObservable` we've just created, we'll see that it doesn't unsubscribe and we always receive all values. To deal with such use cases, Scheduler has a `scheduleRecursive()` method that behaves just like `schedule()` but its callable takes one argument, which is a callable itself to reschedule another emission.

In practice, we can rewrite `CustomRangeObservable::subscribe()` method to use `scheduleRecursive()` instead of `schedule()`:

```
public function subscribe($observer, $sched = null) {
    if (null === $sched) {
        $sched = new \Rx\Scheduler\ImmediateScheduler();
    }
    $i = $this->min;

    return $sched->scheduleRecursive(
        function($reschedule) use ($observer, &$i) {
        if ($i <= $this->max) {
            $observer->onNext($i);
            $i++;
            $reschedule();
        } else {
            $observer->onCompleted();
        }
    });
}
```

Notice that we're not creating any loops ourselves and we let `$reschedule()` recursively call itself. Now we can properly call `dispose()` on the disposable object returned from `$sched->scheduleRecursive()` to stop scheduling more actions. We can test this with the same scenario as we used with `RangeObservable`:

```
// php custom_range_02.php
$loop = new StreamSelectLoop();
$scheduler = new EventLoopScheduler($loop);

$disposable = (new CustomRangeObservable(1, 5))
    ->subscribeCallback(function($val) use (&$disposable) {
        echo "$val\n";
        if ($val == 3) {
            $disposable->dispose();
        }
    }, null, null, $scheduler);

$scheduler->start();
```

Now it prints only the first three numbers:

```
$ php custom_range_02.php
1
2
3
```

A closer look at operator chains

We already used operator chains in the previous chapter. Before we start writing our Reddit reader, we should talk briefly about an interesting situation that might occur, so that it doesn't catch us unprepared later.

We're also going to introduce a new type of Observable, called `ConnectableObservable`. Consider this simple operator chain with two subscribers:

```
// rxphp_filter_observables_01.php
use Rx\Observable\RangeObservable;
use Rx\Observable\ConnectableObservable;

$connObs = new ConnectableObservable(new RangeObservable(0, 6));
$filteredObs = $connObs
    ->map(function($val) {
        return $val ** 2;
    })
    ->filter(function($val) {
        return $val % 2;
    });

$disposable1 = $filteredObs->subscribeCallback(function($val) {
    echo "S1: ${val}\n";
});
$disposable2 = $filteredObs->subscribeCallback(function($val) {
    echo "S2: ${val}\n";
});

$connObs->connect();
```

The `ConnectableObservable` class is a special type of Observable that behaves similarly to the Subject (in fact, internally, it really uses an instance of the `Subject` class). Any other Observable emits all available values right after you subscribe to it. However, `ConnectableObservable` takes another Observable (the source Observable) as an argument and lets you subscribe observers to it without emitting anything. When you call `ConnectableObservable::connect()`, it subscribes to the source Observables, and all values go one by one to all subscribers.

Internally, it contains an instance of the `Subject` class, and when we called the `subscribe()` method, it just subscribed each observer to its internal Subject. Then when we called the `connect()` method, it subscribed the internal Subject to the source Observable.

In the `$filteredObs` variable we keep a reference to the Observable returned from `filter()` operator, which is an instance of `AnnonymousObservable` where, on the next few lines, we subscribe both observers.

Now, let's see what this operator chain prints:

```
$ php rxphp_filter_observables_01.php
S1: 1
S2: 1
S1: 9
S2: 9
S1: 25
S2: 25
```

As we can see, all values went through both observers in the order they were emitted. Just out of curiosity, we can also have a look at what would happen if we didn't use `ConnectableObservable`, and used just the `RangeObservable` instead:

```
$ php rxphp_filter_observables_02.php
S1: 1
S1: 9
S1: 25
S2: 1
S2: 9
S2: 25
```

This time, `RangeObservable` emitted all values to the first observer and then, again, all values to the second observer. We can see that the source Observable had to generate all the values twice, which is inefficient, and with a large dataset, this might cause a performance bottleneck.

Subscribing to ConnectableObservable

Let's go back to the first example with `ConnectableObservable`, and modify the `filter()` call so it prints all the values that go through:

```
$filteredObservable = $connObservable
    ->map(function($val) {
        return $val ** 2;
    })
```

```
        ->filter(function($val) {
            echo "Filter: $val\n";
            return $val % 2;
        });
```

Now we run the code again and see what happens:

```
$ php rxphp_filter_observables_03.php
Filter: 0
Filter: 0
Filter: 1
S1: 1
Filter: 1
S2: 1
Filter: 4
Filter: 4
Filter: 9
S1: 9
Filter: 9
S2: 9
Filter: 16
Filter: 16
Filter: 25
S1: 25
Filter: 25
S2: 25
```

Well, this is unexpected! Each value is printed twice, even though we're using `ConnectableObservable`. This doesn't always mean that the Observable has to generate all the values twice, however (as we'll see in Chapter 8, *Multicasting in RxPHP and PHP7 pthreads Extension*). It's not obvious at first sight what happened, but the problem is that we subscribed to the Observable at the end of the operator chain.

As stated previously, `$filteredObservable` is an instance of `AnnonymousObservable` that holds many nested Closures. By calling its `subscribe()` method, it runs a Closure that's created by its predecessor, and so on. This leads to the fact that every call to `subscribe()` has to invoke the entire chain. While this might not be an issue in many use cases, there are situations where we might want to do a special operation inside one of the filters.

The operator chain for this example looks like the following diagram, where each subscription is represented by an arrow:

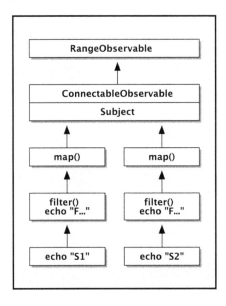

The most important consequence of all this is that neither operators nor `AnnonymousObservable` class share values that go through them. In fact, none of them keep track of subscribed observers either.

Also, note that calls to the `subscribe()` method might be out of our control, performed by another developer who wanted to use an Observable we created for them.

It's good to know that such a situation might occur and could lead to unwanted behavior.

 It's sometimes hard to see what's going on inside Observables. It's very easy to get lost, especially when we have to deal with multiple nested Closures in PHP. Schedulers are prime examples. Feel free to experiment with the examples shown here and use debugger to examine step-by-step what code gets executed and in what order.

So, let's figure out how to fix this. One way could be restructuring our code where we'll turn `$filteredObservable` into `ConnectableObservable` and not `RangeObservable` directly. Consider the following code:

```
// rxphp_filter_observables_04.php
$source = new RangeObservable(0, 6);
$filteredObservable = $source
    ->map(function($val) {
        return $val ** 2;
    })
    ->filter(function($val) {
        echo "Filter: $val\n";
        return $val % 2;
    });

$connObs = new ConnectableObservable($filteredObservable);

$disposable1 = $connObs->subscribeCallback(function($val) {
    echo "S1: ${val}\n";
});
$disposable2 = $connObs->subscribeCallback(function($val) {
    echo "S2: ${val}\n";
});
$connObs->connect();
```

When we run this code, we can see the `filter()` operator is called just once for each value:

```
$ php rxphp_filter_observables_04.php
Filter: 0
Filter: 1
S1: 1
S2: 1
Filter: 4
Filter: 9
S1: 9
S2: 9
Filter: 16
Filter: 25
S1: 25
S2: 25
```

To better understand what is different to the previous example, we can have a look at a diagram representing this operator chain:

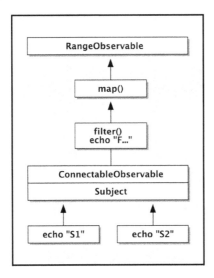

We can see that the `ConnectableObservable` was moved down the chain and it subscribes to the `filter()` operator instead of `RangeObservable`.

Using Subject instead of ConnectableObservable

We said we don't want to subscribe at the end of the chain multiple times, so we can create an instance of `Subject` class, where we'll subscribe both observers, and the `Subject` class itself will subscribe to the `$filteredObservable`, as discussed a moment ago:

```
// rxphp_filter_observables_05.php
use Rx\Subject\Subject;

$subject = new Subject();
$source = new RangeObservable(0, 6);
$filteredObservable = $source
    ->map(function($val) {
        return $val ** 2;
    })
    ->filter(function($val) {
        echo "Filter: $val\n";
        return $val % 2;
    })
    ->subscribe($subject);
```

```php
$disposable1 = $subject->subscribeCallback(function($val) {
    echo "S1: ${val}\n";
});
$disposable2 = $subject->subscribeCallback(function($val) {
    echo "S2: ${val}\n";
});
$filteredObservable->subscribe($subject);
```

We can run the script and see that it returns exactly the same output as the previous example:

```
$ php rxphp_filter_observables_05.php
Filter: 0
Filter: 1
S1: 1
S2: 1
Filter: 4
Filter: 9
S1: 9
S2: 9
Filter: 16
Filter: 25
S1: 25
S2: 25
```

This might look like an edge case, but soon we'll see that this issue, left unhandled, could lead to some very unpredictable behavior. We'll bring out both these issues (proper usage of disposables and operator chains) when we start writing our Reddit reader.

Observable::create() and Observable::defer()

We know how to create Observables using `ReturnObservable` or `RangeObservable`. We've also written a custom `CURLObservable` as well. However, in some situations we might want to create an Observable with some custom logic that isn't easily reproducible with already existing Observable classes. Of course, we could write another Observable inheriting the base Observable class, but if we need to deal with a very specific, single use-case scenario, there's an easier way with static methods `Observable::create()` and `Observable::defer()`.

Creating Observables with Observable::create()

With `Observable::create()`, we can create an Observable that automatically pushes values into each of its observers on subscription. Consider the following example:

```php
// observable_create_01.php
use Rx\Observable;
use Rx\ObserverInterface;

$source = Observable::create(function(ObserverInterface $obs) {
    echo "Observable::create\n";
    $obs->onNext(1);
    $obs->onNext('Hello, World!');
    $obs->onNext(2);
    $obs->onCompleted();
});

$source->subscribe(new DebugSubject());
$source->subscribe(new DebugSubject());
```

The callable passed to `Observable::create()` takes as a parameter an observer where it can immediately start emitting values. It's important to remember that this callable is going to be called for each observer. This example prints the following output:

```
$ php observable_create_01.php
Observable::create
21:00:52 [] onNext: 1 (integer)
21:00:52 [] onNext: Hello, World! (string)
21:00:52 [] onNext: 2 (integer)
21:00:52 [] onCompleted
Observable::create
21:00:52 [] onNext: 1 (integer)
21:00:52 [] onNext: Hello, World! (string)
21:00:52 [] onNext: 2 (integer)
21:00:52 [] onCompleted
```

Notice that string `Observable::create` is printed twice. Also, notice we called `onCompleted` ourselves to properly complete the Observable.

The callable can optionally return an instance of `Rx\DisposableInterface` that'll be disposed when unsubscribing/completing the Observable. We can modify the same example to return an instance of `CallbackDisposable`:

```php
$source = Observable::create(function(ObserverInterface $obs) {
    ...
    return new CallbackDisposable(function() {
        echo "disposed\n";
```

```
    });
  });
```

Now each `CallbackDisposable` will be called to properly cleanup resources for each observer.

Creating Observables with Observable::defer()

Imagine a use case where we want to generate a random range of numbers for each observer that subscribes to our Observable. This means we want each observer to have a different range of numbers.

Lets see what would happen if we used just `RangeObservable`:

```
// observable_defer_01.php
use Rx\Observable;
$source = Observable::range(0, rand(1, 10));

$source->subscribe(new DebugSubject('#1'));
$source->subscribe(new DebugSubject('#2'));
```

Since we created a single source Observable, both observers will always receive the same range of numbers. Range dimensions are set once when calling `Observable::range()`. So, for example, the output from this script could look like the following:

```
$ php observable_defer_01.php
21:38:29 [#1] onNext: 0 (integer)
21:38:29 [#1] onNext: 1 (integer)
21:38:29 [#1] onNext: 2 (integer)
21:38:29 [#1] onCompleted
21:38:29 [#2] onNext: 0 (integer)
21:38:29 [#2] onNext: 1 (integer)
21:38:29 [#2] onNext: 2 (integer)
21:38:29 [#2] onCompleted
```

We could of course create two source Observables, but there's a more elegant way using `Observable::defer()` static method:

```
// observable_defer_02.php
use Rx\Observable;
$source = Observable::defer(function() {
    return Observable::range(0, rand(1, 10));
});

$source->subscribe(new DebugSubject('#1'));
$source->subscribe(new DebugSubject('#2'));
```

Static method `Observable::defer()` takes as argument a callable that is called every time an observer subscribes similarly to `Observable::create()`. However, this callable needs to return another Observable where the observer will subscribe. Instead of creating a `RangeObservable` just once, we're creating a new one for each observer.

The output for this example could look like the following:

```
$ php observable_defer_02.php
21:40:58 [#1] onNext: 0 (integer)
21:40:58 [#1] onNext: 1 (integer)
21:40:58 [#1] onNext: 2 (integer)
21:40:58 [#1] onNext: 3 (integer)
21:40:58 [#1] onCompleted
21:40:58 [#2] onNext: 0 (integer)
21:40:58 [#2] onCompleted
```

Notice that each observer received a different range of numbers.

Writing a Reddit reader using RxPHP

This and many upcoming apps we're going to build will be pure CLI apps. That said, it'll be helpful to have some unified library that'll help us with things common in the CLI environment:

```
Terminal — php console_reddit.php reddit — 127×30
0 bchs is just the beginning... poshpotdllr ftw.
1 How to simulate ENOSPC errors on OS X?
2 Need some help – UNIX Batch Script
3 11 Myths about FreeBSD
4 Will switching to FreeBSD give me an advantage over Linux when it comes to gaming?
5 dual unix/OSX install on macbook 2010
6 [Question] What exactly I'm doing wrong compiling this...?
7 A set of custom unix-like utilities that any developer could benefit from
8 Tutorials | EuroBSDcon 2016
9 HELP: Messed up renaming user and accidentally hid it?
10 I just finished and published my first eBook! What do you think?
11 Are any of you gov admins who have gone through a DISA or Army CCRI inspection? What should i expect?
12 How does homebrew compare to other package managers?
13 Linux vs. *BSD – what where why now?
14 Yes, Linux is Unix too.
15 Script wont return when called via SSH.
16 A ZFS developer's analysis of the good and bad in Apple's new APFS file system
17 Tool analogous to Emacs' Quail for typing non-ASCII and non-Latin on X
18 Balmer: I suggest a new function for the Unix standard C library: BREXIT(3): perform normal programme termination and remove
   the binary from the disc. (Just if it wasn't clear: brexit(3) stands for "binary remove exit". Should we vote on it?)
19 Do i need to know a programing language to learn UNIX?
20 The file just loaded does not appear to be executable
21 Using Grep To Find Argument?
22 For those who are interested in the tool curl and how it came about..
23 rsync on OS X says its complete but it's really not?
24 Dennis Ritchie's cousin
[q] Quit, [0-25]: Read article
```

The tool of choice for us is going to be Symfony Console component (http://symfony.com/doc/current/components/console.html). It's an open-source library developed along with the Symfony framework, but it's designed to be used independently in any project, which is ideal for us.

It handles everything from inputs to outputs, and on top of that, it comes with a few very nifty helpers as well. In particular, we're going to use the following:

- Coloring and formatting the console output
- Splitting a CLI app into multiple independent commands
- Automatically generating help from an input parameter definition
- Handling input parameters, including validation and default values
- Creating a unified set of functions to handle user input

In this example, we're going to use just the first two bullet points, but in later chapters, we'll use all the features listed here.

Using the Symfony Console component

Start by installing the Symfony Console component via composer:

```
$ composer require symfony/console
```

Each CLI app is divided into multiple commands that can be run on their own. We'll set one default command because our app is very simple and we can put all its logic into a single command.

The entrance point of our app is just going to register the command and then let the Console library handle everything for us:

```
// console_reddit.php
require_once __DIR__ . '/../vendor/autoload.php';
require_once 'RedditCommand.php';

$application = new Symfony\Component\Console\Application();
$application->setDefaultCommand('reddit');
$application->add(new RedditCommand());
$application->run();
```

Running the `$application::run()` method checks CLI parameters from PHP globals and chooses the right command based on that. Since our app has only one command, we don't need to pass any parameters from terminal; the app will use the default one, `RedditCommand`, which we'll start writing right now.

Each command inherits the `Symfony\Component\Console\Command` class and should at least define its name:

```
// RedditCommand.php
use Symfony\Component\Console\Command\Command;
use Symfony\Component\Console\Input\InputInterface as InputI;
use Symfony\Component\Console\Output\OutputInterface as OutputI;

class RedditCommand extends Command {
    protected function configure() {
        $this->setName('reddit');
        $this->setDescription(
            'CLI Reddit reader created using RxPHP library.');
    }

    protected function execute(InputI $input, OutputI $output) {
        $output->writeln('<info>Hello, World!</info>');
    }
}
```

This command's name is `reddit`, which needs to match the name we set using `setDefaultCommand()`.

Notice that we can use tags similar to HTML for some basic styling, which is very limited, but it's enough for the purposes of typical CLI apps. There are four predefined colors that we'll use, but if you want to go into more detail feel free to check the documentation on coloring outputs at `http://symfony.com/doc/current/console/coloring.html`:

- `<info>` = green
- `<comment>` = yellow
- `<question>` = black on cyan background
- `<error>` = white text on red background

When Symfony Console library recognizes a command, it calls its `execute()` method while passing two objects used to handle inputs and outputs. We don't usually want to handle input or output by ourselves because there are inconsistencies across different platforms and Console library can do everything for us.

One suitable exception is when we want to use non-blocking user input instead of the built-in question helper. As it happens, this is exactly what we're going to do in a moment, but let's first see how to run this command from terminal:

```
$ php console_reddit.php
Hello, World!
```

Since `RedditCommand` is also the default command, we didn't have to set any CLI parameters to execute it. This is actually identical to running the following:

```
$ php console_reddit.php reddit
```

One CLI app can hold multiple commands, as stated previously. We can list all commands supported by this app with the following:

```
$ php console_reddit.php list
```

This prints a nicely colored overview of all commands, and some common options allowed by all apps by default:

```
martin:Chapter 03 martin$ php console_reddit.php list
Console Tool

Usage:
  command [options] [arguments]

Options:
  -h, --help            Display this help message
  -q, --quiet           Do not output any message
  -V, --version         Display this application version
      --ansi            Force ANSI output
      --no-ansi         Disable ANSI output
  -n, --no-interaction  Do not ask any interactive question
  -v|vv|vvv, --verbose  Increase the verbosity of messages: 1 for normal output, 2 for more verbose out
put and 3 for debug

Available commands:
  help    Displays help for a command
  list    Lists commands
  reddit  CLI Reddit reader created using RxPHP library.
martin:Chapter 03 martin$
```

Among them, there's also our `reddit` command with the description we set above. We could also use the `help` command to get detailed information about a particular command, but since our `reddit` command has no input parameters, we won't see anything interesting, so we'll keep it for later.

Notice that `help` and `list` are just commands like any other.

Non-blocking user input and an event loop

At the end of the previous chapter, we talked about blocking and non-blocking streams in PHP using `proc_open()` and `stream_set_blocking()`. We also mentioned that we need some kind of event loop that, while periodically checking for user input, doesn't block the execution thread, in order to make the app responsive at any time.

The basic principles that we're going to use for our command are as follows: We'll create an Observable that emits a value for every line of input it receives (that's a string followed by *Enter* key). This Observable will have multiple observers that will subscribe and unsubscribe based on the current app's internal state. We'll always have at least one observer active, which is going to look for the q (quit) string that terminates the event loop and ends the app.

Let's extend the `execute()` method to read a user's input from terminal and the event loop itself:

```
use Rx\Observable\IntervalObservable;

class RedditCommand extends Command {
  /** @var \Rx\Subject\Subject */
  private $subject;
  private $interval;

  protected function execute(InputI $input, OutputI $output) {
    $this->subject = new \Rx\Subject\Subject();
    $stdin = fopen('php://stdin', 'r');
    stream_set_blocking($stdin, false);

    $loop = new React\EventLoop\StreamSelectLoop();
    $scheduler = new Rx\Scheduler\EventLoopScheduler($loop);
    $this->interval = new IntervalObservable(100, $scheduler);

    $disposable = $this->interval
      ->map(function($count) use ($stdin) {
        return trim(fread($stdin, 1024));
      })
      ->filter(function($str) {
        return strlen($str) > 0;
```

```
        })
        ->subscribe($this->subject);
    $loop->run();
  }
}
```

There are already a few concepts used worth noting, so let's take a look at each of them separately:

- We opened an input stream with `fopen('php://stdin', 'r')` and made it non-blocking using the `stream_set_blocking()` function. This is exactly the same principle as we used in the previous chapter, with `proc_open()`.
- The event loop works exactly the same way as we saw in the previous chapter. We use it here to create a stable timer that fires (or "ticks," as it's referred in `EventLoopScheduler`) every 100 ms.
- All user input is buffered, which means that `fread()` will always return an empty string until we hit the *Enter* key.
- With the `filter()` operator, we filter out all empty strings.
- Values that successfully go through this operator chain are then observed by a `Subject` class. This is the class where we'll subscribe our observers later, and it emits only valid user inputs.

Using `EventLoopScheduler` is in fact very simple. It makes sure it emits values at precise intervals, even though there's always some code executed down the operator chain. It internally measures the time it fired the last time and the time it spent in propagating the value and then sleeps only for the interval necessary.

Note that we've already addressed the issue regarding operator chains we explained at the beginning of this chapter. The Observable where we'll subscribe/unsubscribe is always `$this->subject`, and never the `IntervalObservable` directly.

Also, note that we're creating a `$disposable` variable that holds a `Disposable` object created by calling `subscribe($this->subject)`. This is basically the subscription to the `IntervalObservable`. If we unsubscribe (this means invoking `$disposable->dispose()`) the event loop will end automatically, and so will the entire app.

Subscribing to user inputs

We've already mentioned that when a user enters q, the app should gracefully end. We can implement this functionality right now. Once we have our instance of Subject prepared, we can start subscribing to it:

```
protected function execute(InputI $input, OutputI $output) {
  // The rest of the method is the same as above

  $this->subject
    ->filter(function($value) {
      return strval($value) == 'q';
    })
    ->take(1)
    ->subscribeCallback(null, null,
        function() use ($disposable, $output, $stdin) {
      fclose($stdin);
      $output->writeln('<comment>Good bye!</comment>');
      $disposable->dispose();
    }
  );

  $loop->run();
}
```

> To save space and keep code examples short, we're omitting class name, indentation, and already defined methods that remain unchanged.

This works exactly the same as subscribing to any other Observable. What's interesting here is that we pass the $disposable variable to the Closure, where we call its dispose() method, which unsubscribes the Subject from the IntervalObservable and in turn terminates the event loop. This time, we don't need to keep any reference to a Disposable object return from subscribeCallback(), because we know we'll never want to unsubscribe this observer.

Notice that we're using take(1) to accept always at most one quit signal. Then the following subscribe() call defines only one callable for complete signal and completely ignores the remaining two.

We addressed this at the beginning of this chapter when we talked about disposables and how these are, in fact, necessary.

We obviously want to let users choose their favorite subreddit. This is going to be just another subscriber to $this->subject, but this time we'll keep its disposable, because later, we need to be able to subscribe other observers and unsubscribe this one, which needs to be subscribed only to enter subreddit name and nothing more:

```
/** @var string */
private $subreddit;
/** @var \Rx\DisposableInterface */
private $subredditDisposable;

protected function execute(InputI $input, OutputI $output) {
  // The rest of the method is the same as above
  $this->askSubreddit();

  $loop->run();
}

protected function askSubreddit() {
  $this->output->write('Enter subreddit name: ');
  $this->subredditDisposable =
    $this->subject->subscribeCallback(function($value) {
      $this->subreddit = $value;
      $this->subredditDisposable->dispose();
      $this->refreshList();
    });
}
```

Right before we start the event loop, we schedule an action that asks the user for the name of the subreddit they want to download and then subscribe a new observer. When it receives a valid value, we store it in the $this->subreddit variable and then it unsubscribes itself using $this->subredditDisposable->dispose().

We can already see that there's a call to another method, called refreshList(). This method will download posts for this subreddit via Reddit API in JSON and print a list with their titles, where the user can choose which one of them they want to read by entering the post's index number.

To download the list, we're going to use the cURL PHP module. We've already used it in
Chapter 2, *Reactive Programming with RxPHP*, where we created CURLObservable for this
purpose, which comes in handy here as well. Also, we've already
written JSONDecodeOperator for decoding JSON strings, which we'll also use:

```
const API_URL = 'https://www.reddit.com/r/%s/new.json';

protected function refreshList() {
    $curlObservable = new CurlObservable(
        sprintf(self::API_URL, $this->subreddit));

    $curlObservable
      ->filter(function($value) {
        return is_string($value);
      })
      ->lift(function() {
        return new JSONDecodeOperator();
      })
      ->subscribeCallback(function(array $response) {
        $articles = $response['data']['children'];
        foreach ($articles as $i => $entry) {
          $this->output->writeln("<info>${i}</info> " .
              $entry['data']['title']);
        }

        $this->printHelp();
        $template = ', <info>[%d-%d]</info>: Read article';
        $this->output->writeln(
            sprintf($template, 0, count($articles)));

        $this->chooseArticleDetail($articles);
      }), function($e) {
        $this->output->writeln(
            '<error>Unable to download data</error>');
      });
}
```

This is what we've already seen and it should be very easy to follow. We use
CURLObservable to download the URL, and then JSONDecodeOperator to decode it from
a JSON to a PHP array. We then iterate the list of all articles it contains and print their
indices and titles.

We introduced one more small method, called `printHelp()`, which only prints a hint that typing `q` and hitting *Enter* will quit the app. We then append some more hints relative only to the current state, such as **[b] Back to the list**, as we can see in the following screenshot:

```
● ◎ ●                        Terminal — php console_reddit.php — 127×30
Script wont return when called via SSH.

I am calling a script via ssh client like this:

    ssh root@host "su - oracle -c '~/bin/weblogic start'"

The `~/bin/weblogic` is a bash script that actually starts the web server in the background and reads and displays its log unti
l certain pattern is found ('Server state changed to RUNNING') at which point it exits. When I call it from the remote location
 it hangs after the last bash command is executed. I am sure it has something to do with what is explained at SO (http://stacko
verflow.com/questions/8122780/exiting-shell-script-with-background-processes), however I can't start `weblogic` bash script in
the background - I must wait for it to finish and get its exit code along with regular stdout up to the specific pattern.

The bash code is like this:

        function start_server {
            ~/bin/weblogic.py
            echo 'Python script finished'
            exit 1
        }


        ....
        start_server

The output is

    ... server output ...
    ...
    ... Server state
[q] Quit, [b] Back to the list
```

Then, similarly, it calls `chooseArticleDetail()`, which lets the user enter the index number of the article they want to see.

This could go on and on but the principle is always the same. We subscribe an observer to the main `Subject` class stored in `$this->subject`, check only values relevant to the current application state, perform some action, and then unsubscribe. It's probably not necessary to include the complete source code here because it would be very repetitive.

 If you want to see all methods for this app implemented, then check out the full source codes for this chapter.

Instead, let's focus on another thing related to `CURLObservable` and subprocesses, with Symfony Process component.

Non-blocking CURLObservable

In our Reddit reader app, we download data from a remote API using PHP's cURL. Even when using its asynchronous callbacks, such as CURLOPT_PROGRESSFUNCTION, it's important to keep in mind that curl_exec() is still a blocking call, no matter what options we choose.

This is due to the fact that PHP runs in a single execution thread and when it starts executing curl_exec(), everything else needs to wait until it finishes. It's true that this method might call some callback functions, but if any of them got stuck, for example, in an infinite loop, the curl_exec() function would never end.

This has serious implications for the actual responsiveness of our Reddit reader. While CURLObservable is downloading data, it doesn't respond to any user input, which is probably not what we want.

When we talked about IntervalObservable and how it's able to keep the desired interval very precisely, we didn't mention that this is, in fact, a type of situation it can't handle.

Let's make a small script that demonstrates such behavior. We'll use IntervalObservable to fire every second:

```php
use Rx\Observable\IntervalObservable;

function getTime() {
    $t = microtime(true);
    $micro = sprintf("%06d", ($t - floor($t)) * 1000000);
    return date('H:i:s') . '.' . $micro;
}

$loop = new React\EventLoop\StreamSelectLoop();
$scheduler = new Rx\Scheduler\EventLoopScheduler($loop);
$observable = new IntervalObservable(1000, $scheduler);

$observable->map(function($tick) {
    printf("%s Map: %d\n", getTime(), $tick);
    return $tick;
})->subscribeCallback(function($tick) {
    printf("%s Observer: %d\n", getTime(), $tick);
});
$loop->run();
```

This example prints the current time very precisely, including microseconds. If we keep it running for a while, we'll still see that it holds to microseconds pretty well while incrementing by one second:

```
$ php blocked_intervalobservable.php
00:27:14.306441 Map: 0
00:27:14.306509 Observer: 0
00:27:15.305033 Map: 1
00:27:15.305116 Observer: 1
. . .
00:28:22.306071 Map: 68
00:28:22.306124 Observer: 68
```

We can already observe that the map() operator is called shortly before the observer. Now, let's add a usleep(1250 * 1000); call into the map() operator. We can see that the gap is even larger than the 1-second interval of IntervalObservable, which makes it completely out of sync:

```
$ php blocked_intervalobservable.php
00:41:25.606327 Map: 0
00:41:26.859891 Observer: 0
00:41:26.860455 Map: 1
00:41:28.113972 Observer: 1
```

This implies that, even when we rely on IntervalObservable to do all the timing necessary, it can't do anything when there's code anywhere in the operator chain blocking the execution. This is what happened to us with CURLObservable, and the app not responding when curl_exec() is running.

Unfortunately, PHP itself, without any extra modules, doesn't give us many options to write non-blocking code.

But in the previous chapter, we used proc_open() and stream_set_blocking() to run a non-blocking subprocess, so we can use the same technique and wrap CURLObservable into a standalone app that we can run as a subprocess.

Since we already know how to write CLI apps using Symfony Console component, we're going to use it here as well:

```php
// wrap_curl.php
use Symfony\Component\Console\Command\Command;
use Symfony\Component\Console\Input\InputInterface as InputI;
use Symfony\Component\Console\Output\OutputInterface as OutputI;
use Symfony\Component\Console\Input\InputArgument;

class CURLCommand extends Command {
```

```
    protected function configure() {
      $this->setName('curl');
      $this->setDescription(
          'Wrapped CURLObservable as a standalone app');
      $this->addArgument('url',
          InputArgument::REQUIRED, 'URL to download');
    }

    protected function execute(InputI $input, OutputI $output) {
      $returnCode = 0;
      (new CURLObservable($input->getArgument('url')))
        ->subscribeCallback(function($res) use ($output) {
          if (!is_float($response)) {
            $output->write($res);
          }
        }, function() use (&$returnCode) {
          $returnCode = 1;
        });
      return $returnCode;
    }
}

$application = new Symfony\Component\Console\Application();
$application->add(new CURLCommand());
$application->run();
```

This command has one required argument, which is the URL it's supposed to download. It uses CURLObservable internally to download the URL, and then just prints the response to its standard output. It also sets proper UNIX return code when an error occurs.

If we try to run the command without any arguments, it prints an error telling us that this command has to have exactly one argument:

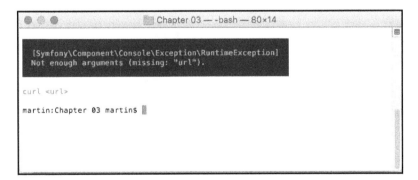

We can test the command manually; for example with the following:

```
$ php wrapped_curl.php curl https://www.reddit.com/r/php/new.json
{"kind": "Listing", "data": {"modhash": "", "children": ...
```

Now, we could use `proc_open()` like in the previous chapter, but apart from just spawning the process, there are a lot of things to handle by ourselves, so it's easier to leave all the heavy work to another library.

Using Symfony Process component

As usual, we'll install this library using composer:

```
$ php composer require symfony/process
```

This library lets us create new processes, read their outputs in a non-blocking way, send inputs, send signals, use timeouts, terminate processes, and so on.

To test things out, we'll make a small script that uses `IntervalObservable` to print a number every second while waiting for the subprocess to finish:

```php
// php curl_subprocess.php
use Symfony\Component\Process\Process;
use Rx\Observable\IntervalObservable;

$c='php wrap_curl.php curl https://www.reddit.com/r/php/new.json';
$process = new Process($c);
$process->start();

$loop = new React\EventLoop\StreamSelectLoop();
$scheduler = new Rx\Scheduler\EventLoopScheduler($loop);

(new IntervalObservable(1000, $scheduler))
    ->takeWhile(function($ticks) use ($process) {
        return $process->isRunning();
    })
    ->subscribeCallback(function($ticks) {
        printf("${ticks}\n");
    }, function() {}, function() use ($process) {
        echo $process->getOutput();
    });
$loop->run();
```

The `Process` class takes in its constructor a full command it's supposed to execute. Then, calling `Process::start()` will start the subprocess in an asynchronous non-blocking way, just like we did before. We can check for available output anytime with the `getOutput()` method. Then, the `isSuccessful()` and `isRunning()` methods return `true` when the process has successfully terminated (return code equals 0), and whether the process is still running, respectively.

The takeWhile() operator

We have also used one new operator, called `takeWhile()`. This operator takes a predicate Closure as an argument, which is executed for every value it receives. If the predicate returns `true`, it passes the value down the chain (by calling `onNext()` on its observer), but if the predicate returns `false`, it signals `onComplete()`, and therefore, the loop ends because there are no other observers subscribed to it. It's exactly the same situation we saw earlier in this chapter, when we used disposable to unsubscribe from `IntervalObservable` and end the app. The following Marble diagram represents `takeWhile()` operator in RxJS (`http://reactivex.io/rxjs/class/es6/Observable.js`):

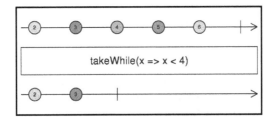

If we run this example, it'll print a few ticks, then dump the entire response and end. This is exactly what we need. So, we can remove the temporary `printf()` statement and use this subprocess in our Reddit reader app.

Implementing subprocesses into the Reddit reader app

This final improvement will require some modifications to the existing code. First, the method `refreshList()` doesn't need to use either `CURLObservable` or `JSONDecodeOperator`, because we'll read the response from the instance of the `Process` class directly.

Also, both the main `Subject` class checking for user input and the observer checking whether the subprocess has terminated need to use the same instance of Scheduler. It's easier to share the same instance of `IntervalObservable` than create a new one every time we want to refresh the list of posts, so we'll keep its reference as a `property` class in `$this->intervalObservable`:

```php
protected function refreshList() {
    $url = sprintf(self::API_URL, $this->subreddit);
    $this->process = new Process(
        'php wrap_curl.php curl '.$url);
    $this->process->start();

    $this->intervalObservable
        ->takeWhile(function() {
          return $this->process->isRunning();
        })
        ->subscribeCallback(null, null, function() {
          $jsonString = $this->process->getOutput();
          if (!$jsonString) {
            return;
          }

          $response = json_decode($jsonString, true);
          $articles = $response['data']['children'];
          // ... the rest is unchanged
```

Then, when we want to quit the app, we have to make sure the subprocess has already terminated, or eventually terminate by ourselves. If we don't terminate it, the PHP interpreter will have to wait until it finishes.

This is what the updated observer checking for the quit entry will look like:

```php
$this->subject->filter(function($value) {
  return strval($value) == 'q';
})
->take(1)
->subscribeCallback(null, null,
  function() use ($disposable, $output, $stdin) {
    fclose($stdin);
    $output->writeln('<comment>Good bye!</comment>');
    if ($this->process && $this->process->isRunning()) {
      $this->process->stop();
    }
    $disposable->dispose();
  }
);
```

So, at the end, this all allows us to quit (or perform any other action) any time we want, even when cURL is downloading data at that very moment, because we run the download as a separate non-blocking process that we check periodically for a response in the same event loop as all user input.

> In `Chapter 6`, *PHP Streams API and Higher-Order Observables*, we'll see how to use `StreamSelectLoop` to directly read from file handles created with `fopen()`.

Types of disposable classes

Throughout this chapter, we've been subscribing and unsubscribing to Observables a lot. Although we know what disposables are, we haven't talked about what different types of disposable classes are available out of the box in RxPHP.

We're not going to write examples for each one of them, because these are very simple classes and if you're not sure about their implementation details, feel free to check their source code.

- `BinaryDisposable`: A class internally containing two more disposable objects. Then by calling its `dispose()` it automatically calls `dispose()` on the two internal disposables as well.
- `CallbackDisposable`: This class wraps a callable that is executed later when calling `dispose()`.
- `CompositeDisposable`: A collection of disposables that'll be disposed all together.
- `EmptyDisposable`: A dummy disposable that does nothing. Sometimes it's required to pass or return an instance of `DisposableInterface` even when we have nothing to dispose.
- `RefCountDisposable`: A disposable containing another disposable and a counter that'll be disposed when the counter reaches 0 (basically the same principle as automatic reference counting in programming languages).
- `ScheduledDisposable`: This class wraps another disposable that won't be disposed directly but scheduled with `Scheduler::schedule()` instead.

- `SerialDisposable`: A collection of disposables where, when adding a new disposable, the previous one is automatically disposed (the `Scheduler::scheduleRecursive()` method returns this type of disposable).
- `SingleAssignmentDisposable`: A wrapper around another disposable that can be assigned only once. If we try to assign this disposable twice, it'll result in exception.

 Since RxPHP is based mostly on RxJS 4, it uses its style of disposables. If you're coming from RxJS 5, you're used to always using only `Subscription` class, which is very similar to `CompositeDisposable`.

Summary

In this chapter, we looked in more depth at how to use disposables and operators, how these work internally, and what it means for us. We also saw how to use `Observable::create()` and `Observable::defer()` to create new Observables with custom logic.

The app that we have built was meant to be a simple Reddit reader that combines all the aspects of RxPHP we've learned so far. We also saw how we can achieve a truly responsive app by making all long running tasks non-blocking. We used Symfony Console component to handle user input and output from terminal. Also, we used Symfony Process component to easily spawn and have control over subprocesses.

We also looked at a couple of new classes from RxPHP, such as `ConnectableObservable`, `CompositeDisposable`, or `takeWhile()` operator.

In the following chapter, we'll work with some event-based systems used in popular PHP frameworks, such as Symfony, Silex, and Zend Framework, and see how we can combine them with the principles of reactive programming.

4
Reactive versus a Typical Event-Driven Approach

So far, we've been focused mainly on CLI applications. In this chapter, we'll apply what we've already learned to a typical component of all web frameworks, and add a little on top of that. We're going to use the Symfony `EventDispatcher` component, which is an independent library that can be used in any framework.

Its main purpose is dispatching events during an application's lifetime, and easy extendability. Most notably, it's a core building block of the Symfony3 framework and the Silex micro-framework.

In this chapter, we're going to do the following:

- Have a look at error handling in RxPHP and explain the `retry()`, `retryWhen()`, and `catchError()` operators. We'll see how these three relate to what we've talked about in the previous chapter.
- We'll see how to combine two Observables using `concat()` and `merge()` operators. Then we'll also have a look at `concatMap()` and its very common use-case with ordered HTTP requests.
- Have a quick introduction to `EventDispatcher` component using examples.
- Write a drop-in replacement for the default `EventDispatcher` class called `ReactiveEventDispatcher` that's built on the top of the default `EventDispatcher`, with a reactive approach using RxPHP.
- See how we can use Subjects to construct Observable chains on the fly.

- Enhance our event dispatcher implementation using Observables instead of closures as event listeners.
- Test our event-dispatcher implementation on the same examples we used when introducing the default `EventDispatcher`.

Before we jump into the `EventDispatcher` component, we should also talk about how to handle error states in operator chains.

We've worked with `onError` handlers already in Chapter 2, *Reactive Programming with RxPHP*, with `CURLObservable`, for example. However, we haven't seen how to gracefully recover from errors and what unexpected implications these might have.

Handling error states in operator chains

If we go back to Chapter 2, *Reactive Programming with RxPHP*, and `CURLObservable`, we know that it emits `onError` when it wasn't able to download any data. The question is, what if we want to try downloading the URL again? And even more interestingly, repeat the failed attempt every few seconds.

Subscribing only to `onError` signals is simple with the second parameter to the `subscribeCallback()` method:

```
(new CURLObservable('https://example.com'))
    ->subscribeCallback(null, function ($e) { ... });
```

It's obvious that nesting another `CURLObservable` into `onError` handler is probably not an option. This is exactly what the `retry()` operator is designed for.

The retry() operator

When the `retry()` operator receives an `onError` signal, it captures it and tries to resubscribe to its source Observable. It takes as an argument the number of times it tries to resubscribe until it passes the error signal down the operator chain.

Let's rewrite the preceding example with the `retry()` operator:

```
(new CURLObservable('https://example.com'))
    ->retry(3)
    ->subscribe(new DebugSubject());
```

This tries to resubscribe to the CURLObservable three times, until DebugSubject receives the onError signal. By default, the retry() operator takes no parameters and tries to resubscribe infinitely.

Well, testing error states on third-party web services isn't very convenient, because we can't force it to return error states. For this reason, we're better off using the map() operator to trigger onError signals from now on.

To our advantage, the map() operator calls its callable wrapped inside a try...catch block, so any exception thrown will be turned into an onError signal:

```
// snippet from Rx\Operator\MapOperator class
try {
    $value = call_user_func_array($this->selector, [$nextValue]);
} catch (\Exception $e) {
    $observer->onError($e);
}
```

Consider the following code, which is supposed to print numbers from 1 to 6, but fails every time on number 3:

```
// retry_01.php
Observable::range(1, 6)
    ->map(function($val) {
        if ($val == 3) {
            throw new \Exception('error');
        }
        return $val;
    })
    ->retry(3)
    ->subscribe(new DebugSubject());
```

Now, try to guess what happens before looking at the actual output, and keep in mind what we talked about in Chapter 03, *Writing a Reddit Reader with RxPHP*, in the section called *A closer look at Operator chains* and *A closer look on subscribing to Observables*:

```
$ php retry_01.php
09:18:32 [] onNext: 1 (integer)
09:18:32 [] onNext: 2 (integer)
09:18:32 [] onNext: 1 (integer)
09:18:32 [] onNext: 2 (integer)
09:18:32 [] onNext: 1 (integer)
09:18:32 [] onNext: 2 (integer)
09:18:32 [] onError (Exception): error
```

It prints only the numbers 1 and 2 three times and then ends with onError.

What might be confusing at first is that common sense tells us to expect this code to print the numbers 1, 2, 4, 5, and 6. Number 3 throws an exception, but thanks to the retry() operator it continues with the next value.

However, this is not what happens, due to the fact that retry() resubscribes to its source Observable, and emitting an onError signal always makes the chain stop propagating further values. In Chapter 03, *Writing a Reddit Reader with RxPHP*, we saw that subscribing to an Observable triggers generation of the entire chain of Observables that subscribe to each other in the order they were defined. At the end, it subscribes to the source Observable that starts emitting values.

We've encountered the exact same situation here. When the map() operator signals onError, it's immediately resubscribed thanks to the retry() operator, which in turn resubscribes to RangeObservable and starts emitting values from the beginning.

This is nicely demonstrated by the following marble diagram for this operator (note the red and yellow marbles):

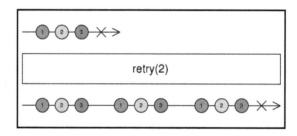

Marble diagram representing the retry() operator, from http://reactivex.io/documentation/operators/retry.html

If we wanted to simulate a situation where we get numbers from 1 to 6 except number 3, we could make an external variable, $count, and increment it, instead of relying on values coming from RangeObservable. To stop emitting values, we can use takeWhile(), which calls onCompleted when its callable returns false:

```
// retry_05.php
$count = 0;
Rx\Observable::range(1, 6)
    ->map(function($val) use (&$count) {
        if (++$count == 3) {
            throw new \Exception('error');
        }
        return $count;
    })
```

```
    ->retry(3)
    ->takeWhile(function($val) {
        return $val <= 6;
    })
    ->subscribe(new DebugSubject());
```

The output is then as we expected:

```
$ php retry_05.php
14:18:01 [] onNext: 1 (integer)
14:18:01 [] onNext: 2 (integer)
14:18:01 [] onNext: 4 (integer)
14:18:01 [] onNext: 5 (integer)
14:18:01 [] onNext: 6 (integer)
14:18:01 [] onCompleted
```

CURLObservable and the retry() operator

We can make a simple test scenario that is closer to a real world application. We'll take our CURLObservable and try to repeat an HTTP request three times. We'll choose any non-existing URL to be sure it fails every time to see how the error is propagated through the operator chain when using retry():

```
// retry_04.php
Rx\Observable::defer(function() {
        echo "Observable::defer\n";
        return new CurlObservable('https://example.com123');
    })
    ->retry(3)
    ->subscribe(new DebugSubject());
```

We've already seen the Observable::defer() static method in Chapter 3, *Writing a Reddit Reader with RxPHP*. We're using it here to show that the retry() operator causes resubscription to the source Observable.

This example prints to the console the following output:

```
$ php retry_04.php
Observable::defer()
Observable::defer()
Observable::defer()
13:14:20 [] onError (Exception): Unable to download https://ex...
```

We can see that it took three iterations before the error (in fact an exception) reached DebugSubject.

The retryWhen() operator

Similar to `retry()`, there's also an operator called `retryWhen()`, which in contrast to `retry()`, doesn't re-subscribe immediately. Operator `retryWhen()` takes as an argument a callable that returns another Observable. This Observable is then used when the `onError` signal occurs, to schedule resubscription.

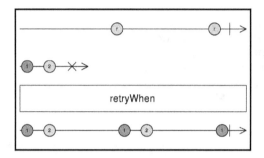

Marble diagram representing the retryWhen() operator, from http://reactivex.io/rxjs/class/es6/Observable.js~Observable.html#instance-method-retryWhen

CURLObservable and the retryWhen() operator

For example, we can consider our `CURLObservable` once more and imagine we want to repeat the failed request after a one-second delay. Since the functionality of `retryWhen()` is a little more complicated, we'll start with an example:

```php
// retry_when_01.php
$loop = new \React\EventLoop\StreamSelectLoop();
$scheduler = new \Rx\Scheduler\EventLoopScheduler($loop);

(new CURLObservable('https://example.com123'))
    ->retryWhen(function($errObs) use ($scheduler) {
        $notificationObs = $errObs
            ->delay(1000, $scheduler)
            ->map(function() {
                echo "\$notificationObs\n";
                return true;
            });
        return $notificationObs;
    })
    ->subscribe(new DebugSubject(), $scheduler);

$scheduler->start();
```

We need to use an event loop to schedule the `delay()` operator.

The callable to `retryWhen()` takes an Observable as an argument and has to return an Observable. Then, when an error signal occurs, it's pushed to `$errObs` as `onNext` so we can decide based on the type of error what we want to do. Depending on the emissions from the returned `$notificationObs` we can control what happens next:

- `onNext`: When `$notificationObs` emits the `onNext` signal, the `retryWhen()` operator resubscribes to its source Observable. Note that the value emitted is not important.
- `onError`: The error is propagated further down the operator chain.
- `onComplete`: The `onComplete` signal is propagated further down the operator chain.

What the preceding example does should be obvious. When `CURLObservable` fails (emits `onError`), the `retryWhen()` operator waits one second, thanks to the `delay()` operator, and then resubscribes, which will make CURLObservable try to download the URL again indefinitely. The output from this example looks like the following:

```
$ php retry_when_01.php
onNext
onNext
onNext
. . .
```

Since the `retryWhen()` operator is slightly more complicated, we can have a look into its internals to understand why it works the way it works:

- It creates an instance of `Subject` and stores its reference in a variable called `$errors`. Subjects work as both Observables and observers. It needs to use Subject, because it's important to be able to manually trigger signals such as `onNext`, which is not possible with just an Observable.
- When the operator calls its callable, it passes along the `$errors->asObservable()` and expects to receive an Observable, which is stored in another variable, called `$when`. The method `asObservable()` wraps Subject with an `AnonymousObservable`, and thus hides that it is, in fact, an instance of `Subject`.
- Then, `CallbackObserver` is subscribed to `$when`, which can later resubscribe to the source Observable of this operator.

- This means that we have the "head" and "tail" of the chain of Observables in variables $errors and $when, respectively.
- Later on, when an onError signal is received, the operator calls $errors->onNext(), which sends the value through the chain of Observables. In our case, it goes through the delay() operator.

If we rewrote the preceding points into an actual heavily simplified code it would look like the following:

```
$errors = new Subject();
$when = call_user_func($callable, $errors->asObservable());

$subscribe = function() use ($observable, $observer, $errors) {
    $observable->subscribe(new CallbackObserver(
        [$observer, 'onNext'],
        function() use ($errors) {
            $errors->onNext($errors);
        }),
        [$observer, 'onCompleted']
    );
};
$when->subscribe(new CallbackObserver(function() use ($subscribe){
    $subscribe();
}));

$subscribe();
```

This operator doesn't care about onNext or onComplete, and passes them right into $observer. The only signal it needs to handle is onError, which calls $errors->onNext(), and therefore triggers the chain of Observables, eventually resulting in resubscribing to the source Observable inside the $when->subscribe() callable.

This technique of using an instance of Subject to be able to manually trigger signals and at the same time subscribe observers to it is very useful. We're going to use it in a moment, when we implement our event dispatcher.

CURLObservable and controlled number of retries

When talking about the retry() operator, we made a demo where we tried to download a URL three times and then failed. The number of retries was fixed to 3.

We can create the same example with the `retryWhen()` operator while having more control if and when we want to retry the HTTP request. Consider the following example where we make three attempts to download a URL and then propagate the error further:

```php
// retry_when_02.php
use Rx\Observable;
$loop = new \React\EventLoop\StreamSelectLoop();
$scheduler = new \Rx\Scheduler\EventLoopScheduler($loop);

(new CURLObservable('https://example.com123'))
    ->retryWhen(function($errObs) use ($scheduler) {
        echo "retryWhen\n";
        $i = 1;
        $notificationObs = $errObs
            ->delay(1000, $scheduler)
            ->map(function(Exception $val) use (&$i) {
                echo "attempt: $i\n";
                if ($i == 3) {
                    throw $val;
                }
                $i++;
                return $val;
            });

        return $notificationObs;
    })
    ->subscribe(new DebugSubject(), $scheduler);

$loop->run();
```

In this example, we make three attempts where each is delayed by one second and then re-throw the exception, which is caught by the `map()` operator and passed as an `onError` signal. Since `$notificationObs` sends the `onError` signal, the `retryWhen()` operator passes this error further as explained previously. We also print the string `retryWhen` to prove that the callable is called just once even when there're multiple retries.

The output from this example is the following:

```
$ php retry_when_02.php
retryWhen
attempt: 1
attempt: 2
attempt: 3
14:36:13 [] onError (Exception): Unable to download https://ex...
```

What's interesting about this demo is that it doesn't need to end with the error at all. We could use $notificationObs to signal onComplete instead.

The inner callable could look, for example, like the following code:

```
// retry_when_03.php
...
$notificationObs = $errObs
    ->delay(1000, $scheduler)
    ->map(function(Exception $val) use (&$i) {
        echo "attempt: $i\n";
        $i++;
        return $val;
    })
    ->take(3);
...
```

In contrast to the previous example we're not re-throwing the exception, and just emitting onComplete instead:

```
$ php retry_when_03.php
retryWhen
attempt: 1
attempt: 2
attempt: 3
15:30:01 [] onCompleted
```

This might be useful in situations where even multiple failed retries don't necessarily mean an error state.

The catchError() operator

The operator catchError() also handles only error signals. When it receives an onError, it calls a callable that returns an Observable, which is then used to continue the Observable sequence instead of the source Observable.

Consider the following example:

```
use Rx\Observable;
Observable::range(1,6)
    ->map(function($val) {
        if ($val == 3) {
            throw new Exception();
        }
        return $val;
    })
```

```
->catchError(function(Exception $e, Observable $sourceOb) {
    return Observable::just(42);
})
->subscribe(new DebugSubject());
```

In this example, the `onError` signal is captured by `catchError()` and, instead of ending the entire Observable sequence, it continues with a single value, thanks to `Observable::just()`, and then ends with `onComplete`:

```
$ php catch_01.php
06:43:04 [] onNext: 1 (integer)
06:43:04 [] onNext: 2 (integer)
06:43:04 [] onNext: 42 (integer)
06:43:04 [] onCompleted
```

The concat() and merge() operators

With `retry()` and `retryWhen()` we've stumbled upon operators that take as parameters other Observables and work with their emissions. Combining multiple Observables into a single chain is a common practice mostly in RxJS due to the asynchronous nature of JavaScript by design. In RxPHP we don't use them as often, but it's worth having a quick look at them.

The merge() operator

In order to merge two Observables into a single one that emits all values from both of them (including `onError` signals) we can use the `merge()` operator.

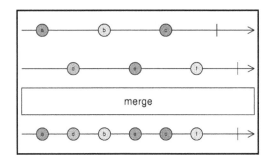

Marble diagram representing the merge() operator, from http://reactivex.io/rxjs/class/es6/Observable.js~Observable.html#static-method-merge

As we can see from the marble diagram, this operator reemits values from source and the merged Observables. This means it subscribes to both of them and emits values as they arrive.

To better understand how it works, we can make a simple example with two interval Observables where each emits three values with different delays:

```php
// merge_01.php
use Rx\Observable;
$loop = new \React\EventLoop\StreamSelectLoop();
$scheduler = new \Rx\Scheduler\EventLoopScheduler($loop);

$merge = Observable::interval(100)
    ->map(function($value) {
        return 'M' . $value;
    })
    ->take(3);

$source = Observable::interval(300)
    ->map(function($value) {
        return 'S' . $value;
    })
    ->take(3)
    ->merge($merge)
    ->subscribe(new DebugSubject(), $scheduler);

$loop->run();
```

The `$merge` Observable emits its values faster than `$source`. We also prefix each value to mark where it came from so the output from this example is the following:

```
$ php merge_01.php
22:00:28 [] onNext: M0 (string)
22:00:28 [] onNext: M1 (string)
22:00:28 [] onNext: S0 (string)
22:00:28 [] onNext: M2 (string)
22:00:29 [] onNext: S1 (string)
22:00:29 [] onNext: S2 (string)
22:00:29 [] onCompleted
```

We can see that the values are mixed together. However, there's only one `onComplete` signal when both Observables complete, so overall it behaves like a single Observable.

The concat() operator

In contrast to `merge()` sometimes we might want to combine two Observables but first emit all values from the first Observable and, when it completes, subscribe to the second one and emit all values from that as well. For this reason, there's also the `concat()` operator:

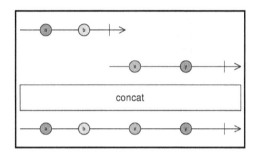

Marble diagram representing the concat() operator, from http://reactivex.io/rxjs/class/es6/Observable.js~Observable.html#instance-method-concat

We can take the same example as we made for `merge()` and just switch the `merge()` operator to `concat()`:

```
// concat_01.php
use Rx\Observable;
$loop = new \React\EventLoop\StreamSelectLoop();
$scheduler = new \Rx\Scheduler\EventLoopScheduler($loop);

$concat = Observable::interval(100)
    ->map(function($value) {
        return 'C' . $value;
    })
    ->take(3);

$source = Observable::interval(300)
    ->map(function($value) {
        return 'S' . $value;
    })
    ->take(3)
    ->concat($concat)
    ->subscribe(new DebugSubject(), $scheduler);

$loop->run();
```

Since `concat()` should subscribe to the source and concatenated Observables one after another we should expect to receive first all values from the source Observable and, when it completes, all values from `$concat` Observable.

```
$ php concat_01.php
22:25:45 [] onNext: S0 (string)
22:25:45 [] onNext: S1 (string)
22:25:46 [] onNext: S2 (string)
22:25:46 [] onNext: C0 (string)
22:25:46 [] onNext: C1 (string)
22:25:46 [] onNext: C2 (string)
22:25:46 [] onCompleted
```

Even though the concatenated Observable emits values faster than the source Observable, its values follow after all the values from source.

The concatMap() and flatMap() operators

Both the `merge()` and `concat()` operators have their `*map()` variants. In particular these are `flatMap()` and `concatMap()`. These operators combine the functionality of `merge()`/`concat()` with the `map()` operator. If we look at both examples we made a moment ago, we'll see that we need to know the inner Observable beforehand. This means the inner Observable is passed to `concat()`/`merge()` once when creating the Observable chain.

We'll pick one of the two operators and explain its benefits in an example.

Let's imagine we want to make three HTTP requests one after another. This looks like an ideal use case for the `concat()` operator. However, each request is going to be dependent on the result from the previous one, so we need to use `concatMap()` instead because its callable takes the current value from the source Observable as a parameter and returns an Observable that'll be concatenated to the chain:

```php
// concat_map_01.php
use Rx\Observable;

function createCURLObservable($num) {
    $url = 'http://httpbin.org/get?num=' . $num;
    echo "$url\n";
    return (new CURLObservable($url))
        ->filter(function($response) {
            return is_string($response);
        });
}
```

```
$source = Observable::emptyObservable()
    ->concat(createCURLObservable(rand(1, 100)))
    ->concatMap(function($response) {
        $json = json_decode($response, true);
        return createCURLObservable(2 * $json['args']['num']);
    })
    ->concatMap(function($response) {
        $json = json_decode($response, true);
        return createCURLObservable(2 * $json['args']['num']);
    })
    ->subscribe(new DebugSubject());
```

We're using the `http://httpbin.org/get` web service that serves as a test server and returns the request we sent as a JSON string.

We used `Observable::emptyObservable()` to create an empty Observable that completes immediately, and chain it with one `concat()` and two `concatMap()` operators. Each `concatMap()` then decodes the JSON from the previous requests, takes its `num` parameter multiplied by 2 and resends the HTTP request.

Then, from the console output, we can see the requests are called in order and the random `num` parameter created in the `concat()` operator call is multiplied by 2 with every request:

```
$ php concat_map_01.php
http://httpbin.org/get?num=51
http://httpbin.org/get?num=102
http://httpbin.org/get?num=204
22:54:37 [] onNext: {
  "args": {
    "num": "204"
  },
  "headers": {
    "Accept"... (string)
22:54:37 [] onCompleted
```

With `flatMap()` the example would be the same. However, since PHP isn't asynchronous like JavaScript, `flatMap()` operator isn't as useful in this particular use case.

We'll have a look at more operators that combine multiple Observables in Chapter 6, *PHP Streams API and Higher-Order Observables*.

Writing a reactive event dispatcher

The Symfony `EventDispatcher` component is a PHP library for exchanging messages between objects. It's based on the Mediator design pattern (`https://en.wikipedia.org/wiki/Mediator_pattern`), and its implementation is relatively simple.

A very common scenario is when we have an application that we want to make extendable via plugins. In this case, we'd create a single instance of `EventDispatcher` and let plugins listen to various events. Each event is an object that can hold references to other objects as well. This is what the Symfony3 framework does extensively.

A quick introduction to EventDispatcher

If you haven't done so already, install the Event Dispatcher component via `composer`:

```
$ composer require symfony/event-dispatcher
```

First, we're going to have a look at how the default implementation is used in practice, so we can later compare it to our reactive implementation, and check that both work the same from a developer's perspective while the internal implementation is different.

Working with event listeners

In the most basic situation, we just want to set up a couple of listeners and dispatch events:

```php
// event_dispatcher_01.php
use Symfony\Component\EventDispatcher\EventDispatcher;
use Symfony\Component\EventDispatcher\Event;

$dispatcher = new EventDispatcher();
$dispatcher->addListener('my_action', function() {
    echo "Listener #1\n";
});
$dispatcher->addListener('other_action', function() {
    echo "Other listener\n";
});
$dispatcher->addListener('my_action', function() {
    echo "Listener #2\n";
});

$dispatcher->dispatch('my_action');
```

We created three event listeners to two different events, my_action and other_action. Then, with $dispatcher->dispatch(), we tell the event dispatcher to notify all event listeners that the event called my_action occurred.

The output in the console should be obvious:

```
$ php event_dispatcher_01.php
Listener #1
Listener #2
```

The dispatch() method takes an optional second argument with an instance of Event class that can contain further information about the event. Event listeners can also modify event data if necessary. Also, all callables receive exactly one argument with the event object, which comes from the initial call to the dispatch() method. Since we didn't provide any event object, our callables don't need to accept any parameter.

Note that the event dispatcher doesn't need to know what events it supports, as they are created on the fly. This also means you can accidentally try to dispatch a non-existent event:

```
$dispatcher->dispatch('foo_my_action');
```

This won't throw an error, but no event will be dispatched.

The EventDispatcher class supports two important features:

- **Priority**: By default, listeners are executed in the order they subscribe to the event dispatcher. We can alter this behavior by supplying a third argument to the addListener() method with priority for this particular listener (it's 0 by default). Listeners with higher priority are executed first. If more listeners have the same priority, then the order they were added matters.
- **Stopping event propagation**: In some scenarios, it's important to be able to stop propagating a particular event to subsequent listeners. For this reason, the Event class has a method called stopPropagation(). The event dispatcher is then responsible for not propagating this event further.

These two features can be used in a situation such as the following:

```
// event_dispatcher_02.php
$dispatcher = new EventDispatcher();

$dispatcher->addListener('my_action', function(Event $event) {
    echo "Listener #1\n";
});
$dispatcher->addListener('my_action', function(Event $event) {
    echo "Listener #2\n";
```

```
        $event->stopPropagation();
    }, 1);

    $dispatcher->dispatch('my_action', new Event());
```

The first event listener should be called after the second one because it has higher priority, but it stops further propagation of this event using `$event->stopPropagation()`, so it's never invoked.

The console output is then very short:

```
$ php event_dispatcher_02.php
Listener #2
```

Working with event subscribers

While `addListener()` subscribes to a single event listener, there's also the `addSubscriber()` method, which accepts an instance of a class implementing `EventSubscriberInterface` and subscribes to multiple events at once. In fact, `addSubscriber()` uses `addListener()` internally to add listeners. Sometimes it's just easier to wrap all listeners into a single class than add them one by one.

Throughout this and upcoming examples in this chapter, we're also going to use a custom `Event` class in order to properly test that both the default and our reactive implementations work the same.

First, let's declare our event class:

```
// MyEvent.php
use Symfony\Component\EventDispatcher\Event;

class MyEvent extends Event {
    private $name;
    private $counter = 0;

    public function __construct($name = null, $counter = 0) {
        $this->name = $name;
        $this->counter = $counter;
    }
    public function getCounter() {
        return $this->counter;
    }
    public function inc() {
        $this->counter++;
    }
```

```
    public function __toString() {
        return sprintf('%s (%d)', $this->name, $this->counter);
    }
}
```

It's a pretty simple class. We'll use the `inc()` method to see that all the listeners work with the same instance of `MyEvent`. We also use the `__toString()` magic method so we can convert this class to string just by typecasting it.

Now, for demonstration purposes, we'll declare a `MyEventSubscriber` class with three event listeners:

```
// MyEventSubscriber.php
use Symfony\Component\EventDispatcher\EventDispatcher;
use Symfony\Component\EventDispatcher\Event;
use Symfony\Component\EventDispatcher\EventSubscriberInterface;

class MyEventSubscriber implements EventSubscriberInterface {
    public static function getSubscribedEvents() {
        return [
            'my_action' => [
                ['onMyActionA'],
                ['onMyActionAgain', 1],
            ],
            'other_action' => 'onOtherAction',
        ];
    }

    public function onMyActionA(MyEvent $event) {
        $event->inc();
        echo sprintf('Listener [onMyAction]: %s\n', $event);
    }

    public function onMyActionAgain(MyEvent $event) {
        $event->inc();
        echo sprintf('Listener [onMyActionAgain]: %s\n', $event);
    }

    public function onOtherAction(Event $event) { }
}
```

The interface `EventSubscriberInterface` requires only the static method `getSubscribedEvents()`, which returns an associative array of event names and their appropriate callables.

This example class declares two listeners for the my_action event (where the second one has higher priority than the first) and one listener for the other_action event.

Subscribing to this class works the same way as subscribing to listeners:

```
$dispatcher = new EventDispatcher();
$dispatcher->addSubscriber(new MyEventSubscriber());
$dispatcher->dispatch('my_action', new MyEvent('my-event'));
```

This time, the example also prints a string representation of the event:

```
$ php event_dispatcher_03.php
Listener [onMyActionAgain]: my-event (1)
Listener [onMyAction]: my-event (2)
```

This is yet another thing we need to handle, because we want to allow defining event Observables in an event subscriber class.

Now we know how the default EventDispatcher class can be used and what use cases it's supposed to fulfill. Our goal will be to write our own implementation based on RxPHP and reactive programming.

Writing ReactiveEventDispatcher with RxPHP

Event dispatchers need to implement an EventDispatcherInterface interface that defines all the methods we've seen previously, and we'll also add a few more. Luckily for us, we can reuse a large part of the default EventDispatcher class. For example, the removeListener() or removeSubscriber() methods will work without any modification.

Internal representation of event listeners as observers

The original EventDispatcher had a very easy task. On the dispatch() call, it just sorted the array of listeners for that particular event by their priority and evaluated them one by one, in a loop:

```
// snippet from Symfony\Component\EventDispatcher\EventDispatcher
foreach ($listeners as $listener) {
    if ($event->isPropagationStopped()) {
        break;
    }
    call_user_func($listener, $event, $eventName, $this);
}
```

In our case, we're going to represent all event listeners as observers. In fact, when we add a new event listener, we'll transform its callable into an observer. Then, when calling `dispatch()`, we'll create a chain of Observables where all observers are already subscribed at specific points. Of course, we also need to handle the `isPropagationStopped()` condition by ourselves.

For example, let's consider the simplest usage of the event dispatcher, as shown previously:

```
$dispatcher->addListener('my_action', function() {
    echo "Listener #1\n";
});
$dispatcher->addListener('my_action', function() {
    echo "Listener #2\n";
});
```

We have to turn these two event listeners into a chain of Observables while making sure that, before each event listener is executed, we check that the event object hasn't got the stop propagation flag set:

```
// reactive_dispatcher_03.php
$subject = new Subject();

$tail = $subject->filter(function(Event $event) {
    return !$event->isPropagationStopped();
});
$tail->subscribe(new CallbackObserver(function(Event $event) {
    echo "Listener #1\n";
    $event->stopPropagation();
}));

$tail = $tail->filter(function(Event $event) {
    return !$event->isPropagationStopped();
});
$tail->subscribe(new CallbackObserver(function(Event $event) {
    echo "Listener #2\n";
}));

$subject->onNext(new Event());
```

We're using Subject here for the same reason as we explained earlier in the chapter when we talked about the `retryWhen()` operator. Still, let's explain this code in more detail:

- The `$subject` variable holds a reference to the "head" of the chain of Observables

- The $tail variable always holds a reference to the last Observable in the chain. This is where we further chain more Observables, and where we append the filter() operator that checks for stopped events.
- When we want to dispatch an event, we just need to call $subject->onNext().

To be extra clear what the current chain of Observables looks like, we can represent it as a tree structure:

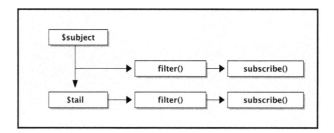

Now we just need to turn all this into a real PHP class.

Writing a ReactiveEventDispatcher class

The good thing is that we can actually reuse a lot of the logic already written in EventDispatcher and just overload certain methods that need to work differently.

First, we'll just write a class stub to see what's waiting ahead of us, and talk a little about each method:

```php
// ReactiveEventDispatcher.php
class ReactiveEventDispatcher extends EventDispatcher {
  /**
   * @var Subject[];
   */
  private $subjects = [];

  public function dispatch($eventName, Event $event = null) {}

  public function addListener($eventName, $listener, $prio=0) {}

  public function addObservable($eventName, $create, $prio=0) {}

  public function addSubscriber($subscriber) {}

  private function observerFromListener($listener) {}
```

```
    private function getSubject($eventName) {}
}
```

Only the methods `dispatch()`, `addListener()`, and `addSubscriber()` from `EventDispatcher` need to be overwritten; the rest can remain as they are. We also added three more methods to help us deal with Observables.

Let's see what the purpose of each component is:

- `$subjects`: An associative array that holds references to all heads of Observable chains (their Subjects).
- `addListener()`: We already know this method from previous examples. However, now the method also accepts observers as event listeners.
- `addObservable()`: This is a method that lets us append an Observable to a specific point in the chain of Observables generated by `getSubject()`.
- `addSubscriber()`: This subscribes to multiple events with the subscription class. It uses the `addObserver()` method.
- `dispatch()`: This method takes the instance of `Subject` for this particular event and calls `onNext()`, with the event object as a parameter.
- `observerFromListener()`: A helper method that transforms any listener into an observer. Basically, this just wraps every callable with a `CallbackObserver` object.
- `getSubject()`: Our event dispatcher is going to work with Subjects. This method internally sorts an array of listeners by their priority and constructs a chain of Observables from them. It'll also keep Subjects in the `$subjects` associative array, to be easily reused without necessarily creating the Observable chain all over again on every `dispatch()` call.

So, we have a pretty good picture of how this event dispatcher is going to work, and we can start implementing each method.

Adding event listeners

The first two methods are going to be `addListener()` and `observerFromListener()`. The first one is dependent on the second one, so we'll write both of them at the same time:

```
// ReactiveEventDispatcher.php
class ReactiveEventDispatcher extends EventDispatcher {
    /**
     * @param string $eventName
```

```
 * @param callable|ObserverInterface $listener
 * @param int $prio
 * @throws Exception
 */
public function addListener($eventName, $listener, $prio = 0) {
  $observer = $this->observerFromListener($listener);
  parent::addListener($eventName, $observer, $prio);
  unset($this->subjects[$eventName]);
}

/**
 * @param callable|ObserverInterface $listener
 * @return ObserverInterface
 */
private function observerFromListener($listener) {
  if (is_callable($listener)) {
    return new CallbackObserver($listener);
  } elseif ($listener instanceof ObserverInterface) {
    return $listener;
  } else {
    throw new \Exception();
  }
}

/* rest of the class */
}
```

 In the rest of the examples in this chapter, we're also going to include doc blocks and type hints for each method to clarify what arguments it accepts.

The `observerFromListener()` method checks the runtime type of `$listener` and always turns it into an instance of observer.

The method `addListener()` uses `observerFromListener()` internally, and then calls its parent's `addListener()` with the observer as an argument, even though it originally accepted only callables. The parent method stores the listener in a nested associative array by event name and priority. Since the parent's code is pretty universal, we don't need to make any changes to it and will leave it as is.

Note that, after we call the parent `addListener()`, we remove a Subject from the `$subjects` array for this particular event. This is because we modified the Observable chain for this event and it needs to be created from scratch. This happens later, when calling the `dispatch()` method.

Adding Observables

Speaking of listeners, we can now also implement `addObservable()`, which is a slightly modified version of `addListener()`. This method is going to be used differently than `addListener()`, so it deserves special attention:

```
class ReactiveEventDispatcher extends EventDispatcher {
  /**
   * @param string $evtName
   * @param callable $create
   * @param int $prio
   */
  public function addObservable($evtName, $create, $prio=0) {
    $subject = new Subject();
    $create($subject->asObservable());
    $this->addListener($evtName, $subject, $prio);
  }

  /* rest of the class */
}
```

We create an instance of `Subject` and call `asObservable()` to let the user-defined callable append its operators to it. Then we call `addListener()` with the `$subject` variable that we explained a moment ago. Again, this is the same technique we described with the `retryWhen()` operator.

This method is interesting, because it lets us add a "sub-chain" of Observables as a listener. Consider the following code:

```
$dispatcher->addObservable('my_action', function($observable) {
  $observable
    ->map(function($value) { return $value; })
    ->filter(function($value) { return true; })
    ->subscribe(new DebugSubject());
});
```

If we represent this code as a tree structure as we did before, inside the $dispatcher, it will look like the following (this structure is generated later inside the getSubject() method):

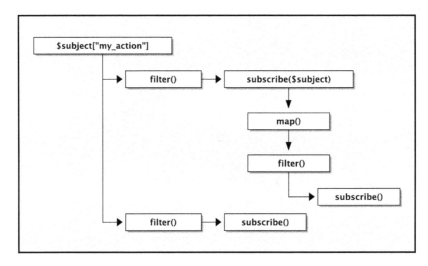

Event "my_action" with two event listeners

So, this event listener appends a series of operators in its callable and then subscribes to it. In the addObservable() method, we pass only the $subject itself to the addListener(), which is later appended to the filter() operator, when calling dispatch(). This works thanks to the fact that Subjects work as observers as well and can subscribe to Observables.

This is the major benefit of writing our custom ReactiveEventDispatcher. We're using reactive programming to easily manipulate events that interest us in a very straightforward way. If we used the default event dispatcher, we'd have to put all the listener-specific conditions inside the callable.

Adding event subscribers

Similar to the original EventDispatcher, we want to be able to subscribe multiple listeners to multiple events at once, using a subscriber class. However, we're also going to support adding listeners as Observables, just like we did with addObservable(). This is not going to work without overloading the parent's addSubscriber() method and handling Observables in a special way.

Basically, we need to call `addObservable()` instead of the `addListener()` method:

First, let's define an interface that we can use to recognize an event subscriber class that also defines Observables as listeners:

```
// EventObservableSubscriberInterface.php
use Symfony\Component\EventDispatcher\EventSubscriberInterface;

interface EventObservableSubscriberInterface extends
    EventSubscriberInterface {
  public static function getSubscribedEventsObservables();
}
```

Now, `addSubscriber()` can check whether the class is an instance of this interface and, if it is, process all its listeners as if they were Observables:

```
use EventObservableSubscriberInterface as RxEventSubscriber;
class ReactiveEventDispatcher extends EventDispatcher {
  /**
   * @param EventSubscriberInterface $subscriber The subscriber
   */
  public function addSubscriber(EventSubscriberInterface $sub) {
    parent::addSubscriber($sub);

    if ($sub instanceof RxEventSubscriber) {
      $events = $sub->getSubscribedEventsObservables();
      foreach ($events as $evt => $params) {
        if (is_callable($params)) {
          $this->addObservable($evt, $params);
        } else {
          foreach ($params as $listener) {
            $prio = isset($listener[1]) ? $listener[1] : 0;
            $this->addObservable($evt, $listener[0], $prio);
          }
        }
      }
    }
  }

  /* rest of the class */
}
```

The array of event listeners can be defined as an array, with a key as the event name and its value as a callable. However, our implementation also supports using array values as another array defining the callable and priority (that's the second nested `foreach` loop).

At the beginning of this method, we also call its parent because we want to allow the default functionality as well.

For demonstration purposes, we're going to extend the MyEventSubscriber class we defined earlier and implement the getSubscribedEventsObservables() method, which is going to return two event listeners:

```php
// MyObservableEventSubscriber.php
use Symfony\Component\EventDispatcher\EventSubscriberInterface;
use Rx\Observable;
require_once __DIR__ . '/MyEventSubscriber.php';

class MyObservableEventSubscriber extends MyEventSubscriber
    implements EventObservableSubscriberInterface {
  public static function getSubscribedEventsObservables() {
    return [
      'my_action' => [
        [
          function(Observable $observable) {
            $observable->subscribe(new DebugSubject());
          }, 10
        ], [
          function(Observable $observable) {
            $observable
              ->subscribe(new DebugSubject());
          }
        ]
      ],
      'other_action' => function(Observable $observable) {
        $observable->subscribe(new DebugSubject());
      }
    ]
  }
}
```

We defined three event listeners for two different events, where the first one for my_action event has priority 10 and the second the default, 0.

Creating the Observable chain for an event

The method `getSubject()` is the place where Observable chains are being generated. This method is then called only when dispatching an event:

```
class ReactiveEventDispatcher extends EventDispatcher {
  /**
   * @param string $eventName
   * @return Subject
   */
  private function getSubject($eventName) {
    if (isset($this->subjects[$eventName])) {
      return $this->subjects[$eventName];
    }

    $subject = new Subject();
    $this->subjects[$eventName] = $subject;
    $tail = $subject->asObservable();

    foreach ($this->getListeners($eventName) as $listener) {
      $newTail = $tail->filter(function (Event $event) {
        return !$event->isPropagationStopped();
      });
      $newTail->subscribe($listener);
      $tail = $newTail;
    }
    return $subject;
  }

  /* rest of the class */
}
```

If the Subject for this event doesn't exist, we create a new one and then call `getListeners()`. This method is defined in the parent `EventDispatcher` class and returns a sorted array of listeners (or observers, in our case). Then we iterate the array and add a `filter()` operator followed by subscribing the observer or Subject, depending on whether we used `addListener()` or `addObservable()`.

 Note that operators (such as `filter()`, in this example) always return a new Observable, while calling `subscribe()` returns a disposable object.

We don't need to create the `$subject` every time we call this method, because it doesn't change until we add new listeners, so we can keep a reference to it in the `$subjects` array.

Comparing filter() to takeWhile()

In the previous Chapter 3, *Writing a Reddit Reader with RxPHP*, we mentioned an operator that might work well instead of `filter()`. We used `takeWhile()`, which also takes a predicate callable as a parameter and can stop propagating values down the Observable chain.

The important distinction is that the `filter()` operator decides whether or not it internally calls `onNext()` on its associated observer. On the other hand, `takeWhile()` decides whether or not it calls `onComplete()`. Calling `onComplete()` would lead to invoking disposables, which would unsubscribe the observers, and this is definitely not what we want. If we did unsubscribe, we'd have to create the Subject for each event on every `dispatch()` call.

> In Chapter 8, *Multicasting in RxPHP and PHP7 pthreads Extension*, we'll talk more about what unexpected consequences calling `onComplete` on a `Subject` might have.

Dispatching events

Finally, dispatching events is very simple:

```
class ReactiveEventDispatcher extends EventDispatcher {
  public function dispatch($eventName, Event $event = null) {
    if (null === $event) {
      $event = new Event();
    }
    $subject = $this->getSubject($eventName);
    $subject->onNext($event);
    return $event;
  }

  /* rest of the class */
}
```

Dispatching an event in our reactive dispatcher means taking the Subject for this particular event and calling its `onNext()` method, with the event as an argument. The event then gets propagated unless its `stopPropagation()` method is called, because we check its state before calling every observer with the `filter()` operator.

We also return the event from the method, to stay compatible with the default `EventDispatcher` implementation.

And that's it. Our `ReactiveEventDispatcher` is complete and we can run a few test scenarios.

Practical example of ReactiveEventDispatcher

We dedicated the first part of this chapter to explaining how the default `EventDispatcher` that comes out of the box with the Symfony `EventDispatcher` component works, and what use cases we expect it to deal with.

Now we need to make sure the same applies to `ReactiveEventDispatcher` as well.

Working with event listeners

We know that our overridden `addListener()` method now accepts both callables and observers, so we can test both use cases in one example:

```
// reactive_dispatcher_02.php
$disp = new ReactiveEventDispatcher();
$disp->addListener(' my.action ', function(Event $event) {
  echo "Listener #1\n";
});
$disp->addListener(' my.action ', new CallbackObserver(function($e) {
  echo "Listener #2\n";
}), 1);
$disp->dispatch(' my.action ', new Event());
```

This example calls the second listener and then the first listener, because the second one has a higher priority:

```
$ php reactive_dispatcher_02.php
Listener #2
Listener #1
```

Now, let's test event subscribers with the same `MyEventSubscriber` class we used in the preceding example. The usage and the output are exactly the same, so we don't need to print the output here again:

```
// reactive_dispatcher_04.php
$dispatcher = new ReactiveEventDispatcher();
$dispatcher->addSubscriber(new MyEventSubscriber());
$dispatcher->dispatch('my_action', new MyEvent());
```

An important feature of ReactiveEventDispatcher is the addObservable() method. We've seen a short snippet of how it can be used when explaining the method itself, but it's worth showing this in context with addListener() as well.

A slightly modified example, which dispatches multiple events, uses Observables and fiddles with conditional stopping event propagation, could look like the following:

```
// reactive_dispatcher_05.php
$dispatcher = new ReactiveEventDispatcher();
$dispatcher->addListener('my_action', function(MyEvent $event) {
  echo "Listener #1\n";
});
$dispatcher->addObservable('my_action', function($observable) {
  $observable
    ->map(function(MyEvent $event) {
      $event->inc();
      return $event;
    })
    ->doOnNext(function(MyEvent $event) {
      if ($event->getCounter() % 2 === 0) {
        $event->stopPropagation();
      }
    })
    ->subscribe(new DebugSubject());
}, 1);

foreach (range(0, 5) as $i) {
  $dispatcher->dispatch('my_action', new MyEvent('my-event', $i));
}
```

Its output is obvious. When the event's getCounter() method returns a number divisible by 2, the event is stopped and never reaches the first event listener added using addListener():

```
$ php reactive_dispatcher_05.php
23:27:08 [] onNext: my-event (1) (MyEvent)
Listener #1
23:27:08 [] onNext: my-event (2) (MyEvent)
23:27:08 [] onNext: my-event (3) (MyEvent)
Listener #1
23:27:08 [] onNext: my-event (4) (MyEvent)
23:27:08 [] onNext: my-event (5) (MyEvent)
Listener #1
23:27:08 [] onNext: my-event (6) (MyEvent)
```

Working with event subscribers

Let's also test that the event subscriber `MyObservableEventSubscriber` we defined earlier works as expected:

```
// reactive_dispatcher_06.php
$dispatcher = new ReactiveEventDispatcher();
$dispatcher->addSubscriber(new MyObservableEventSubscriber());
$dispatcher->dispatch('my_action', new MyEvent('my-event'));
```

Remember that we extended the original `MyEventSubscriber` and added two more listeners, so the event dispatcher first adds listeners returned from `getSubscribedEvents()`, and then adds those from `getSubscribedEventsObservables()`:

```
$ php reactive_dispatcher_06.php
11:14:01 [] onNext: my-event (0) (MyEvent)
Listener [onMyActionAgain]: my-event (1)
Listener [onMyAction]: my-event (2)
11:14:01 [] onNext: my-event (2) (MyEvent)
```

The listener with the highest priority is called first. In our case, it's the first Observable listener with priority 10, then `onMyActionAgain()` is called, with priority 1, and then the two remaining listeners are called in the order they were added.

Summary

This chapter has focused mainly on the practical usage of RxPHP in combination with typical non-reactive code, and presented a different approach to existing event-based solutions.

Specifically, we stumbled across Error handling in Observable chains with `retry()`, `RetryWhen()`, and `catch()` operators. We combined Observables with the `concat()`, `merge()`, and `concatMap()` operator. We used Subjects to dynamically create Observable chains and manually emit values. You were also given an introduction to the Symfony `EventDispatcher` component, with a series of examples presenting how the default `EventDispatcher` class that comes out of the box can be used. We extended and partially rewrote the `EventDispatcher` class and created `ReactiveEventDispatcher`, which adds support for Observables. And lastly, we reused examples for `EventDispatcher` with `ReactiveEventDispatcher` to demonstrate that our implementation can work as a drop-in replacement.

The Symfony `EventDispatcher` component serves as an easily implementable solution to a common problem in larger applications, which is communication between object and extendability. We wrote `ReactiveEventDispatcher` to add capabilities to also use observers as event listeners.

In the next chapter, we'll learn how to write unit tests to test Observables, operators, and observers. We'll also have a better look at Schedulers and see how important are they in testing RxPHP code.

5
Testing RxPHP Code

In this chapter, we're going to start testing code based on RxPHP. So far, we've been testing code by just running it and watching for the expected output in console. Of course, this isn't a very systematic approach, so it's time to start testing our code in an automatic way.

More precisely, in this chapter we will do the following:

- Introduce the `doOn*()` operators
- Start using the PHPUnit library for unit testing code
- Talk about testing asynchronous code in general and try some common pitfalls ourselves
- Explore classes that come with RxPHP intended for testing and see how to use them separately, and how they fit into the great scheme of things
- For demonstration purposes, create a `SumObservable` class that calculates the sum of all integers going through, and test it using RxPHP testing tools
- Write a simplified `ForkJoinObservable` class and test it
- Stress how important it is to be aware of timing when testing Observables and operators

This chapter is going to be very code-intensive, although most of these examples are simple and aim to put things from previous chapters to the perspective of unit testing. Previous experience with unit testing with PHPUnit is helpful, but not required.

Apart from writing unit tests, there's a very common way of debugging Observable chains with `doOn*()` operators.

The doOn*() operators

In the previous chapter, we've used the `map()` operator a couple of times to just print to the console what's happening inside our Observable chains. However, this isn't very convenient. The `map()` operator always needs to return a value that is passed further down the chain, and it can catch only `onNext` signals.

That's why RxPHP has a couple of operators with the common prefix `doOn*`:

- `doOnNext()`, `doOnError()`, `doOnCompleted()`: Each of these operators takes a callable as a parameter that is executed when they receive their respective signal
- `doOnEach()`: This operator takes an instance of `ObserverInterface` as a parameter and executes its handlers for each signal

So these operators are very similar to the methods `subscribeCallback()` and `subscribe()`. The biggest advantage is in the way `doOn*` operators work internally. They never modify the value going through and just execute our callables, which is ideal for quickly debugging Observable chains or to perform side-effects without creating subscriptions (this includes everything related to subscribing to Observables as we talked about in Chapter 3, *Writing a Reddit Reader with RxPHP*).

We can see this with a very simple example:

```php
// do_01.php
use Rx\Observable;
use Rx\ObserverInterface;

Observable::create(function(ObserverInterface $obs) {
        $obs->onNext(1);
        $obs->onNext(2);
        $obs->onError(new \Exception("it's broken"));
    })
    ->doOnError(function(\Exception $value) {
        echo $value->getMessage() . "\n";
    })
    ->subscribeCallback(function($value) {
        echo "$value\n";
    }, function() {});
```

We have a single subscriber that handles `onNext` and `onError` signals. Note that the `onError` handler is empty and it's the `doOnError()` operator that prints the exception messages. Console output for this example is as follows:

```
$ php do_01.php
1
2
doOnError: it's broken
```

Using the remaining `doOn*()` operators is exactly the same. We're obviously not going to use these operators to test RxPHP code, but these are often the easiest way to see what's emitted by our Observables.

These operators have been simplified in RxPHP v2 and have the same signature as the `subscribe()` method in RxPHP v2, which is just `do()` instead of all its variants. Its functionality remains unchanged.

Installing the PHPUnit package

Since we're installing all dependencies throughout this book from the composer, we will do the same for PHPUnit:

```
composer require phpunit/phpunit
```

This also creates a symlink into `vendor/bin/phpunit`, which we'll use to run our unit tests from the console.

PHPUnit supports multiple ways to install, including **PHAR** (**PHP archive**) format and installing it globally using the following:

```
composer global require phpunit/phpunit
```

If you run into trouble installing PHPUnit, head over to the installation instructions at `https://phpunit.de/manual/5.6/en/installation.html`.

However, unless you have a good reason to use one global instance of PHPUnit, it's better to install it per project. This way we can avoid dealing with issues involving unit testing code written for different PHPUnit versions.

Basics of writing tests using PHPUnit

We're not going to go into very much detail about how to use PHPUnit, and instead leave it to its in-depth documentation (https://phpunit.de/manual/5.6/en/index.html). For the purpose of this chapter, we should, however, have a quick look at some of the basics we're going to use for the purposes of testing RxPHP code.

There are some basic rules we should follow:

- All tests for a single class, `MyClass`, go into a class called `MyClassTest`, which should inherit from `PHPUnit\Framework\TestCase`.
- Each test scenario is represented by a function prefixed with `test` or annotated with `@test` annotation. This way it can be auto-discovered by PHPUnit.
- Each test function consists of one or more assertions using `assert*` methods (more on them later). If any one of them fails, the whole test scenario (one test function) is marked as failed. All assertions are inherited from `PHPUnit\Framework\TestCase`.
- We can specify dependencies between test scenarios using `@depends testname` annotation to change the order in which tests are executed.

So, let's write a minimalistic test class that demonstrates the preceding points. We can call this test class `DemoTest`, and it can make just a few assertions:

```php
// phpunit_01.php
use PHPUnit\Framework\TestCase;

class DemoTest extends TestCase {
    public function testFirstTest() {
        $expectedVar = 5;
        $this->assertTrue(5 == $expectedVar);
        $this->assertEquals(5, $expectedVar);

        $expectedArray = [1, 2, 3];
        $this->assertEquals([1, 2, 3], $expectedArray);
        $this->assertContains(2, $expectedArray);
    }
}
```

We used three different types of assertion. In general, all assertions compare an expected value and an actual value returned from a tested function. The following three assertions work in this way too:

- `assertTrue($condition)`: The tested condition needs to be true.

- `assertEquals($expected, $actual)`: Checks that `$expected` and `$actual` values are equal. This single assertion handles multiple types of data separately, even those that aren't comparable with the `==` operator. Apart from comparing basic types, such as strings, arrays, Booleans, and numbers, it can also compare `DOMDocument` instances, or any objects to match their attributes.

- `assertContains($needle, $haystack)`: Typically, checks that an array (haystack) contains a value, but can also check that a string contains another string.

PHPUnit contains dozens of different assertion methods, and all of them work on the same principle. A full list is available in the documentation (`https://phpunit.de/manual/current/en/appendixes.assertions.html`), and we can, of course, write our own. We're going to use a very limited number of assertions that are relevant for us, so we're good to go with these basic ones.

Then, we can execute all test scenarios in the class from the console, using the PHPUnit command-line executable. It's located in `vendor/bin`, and since we're going to use it a lot we'll make a symlink to the project root. We'll do the same for the `autoload.php` script located in the vendor directory that we need as well:

```
$ ln -s vendor/bin/phpunit ./phpunit
$ ln -s vendor/autoload.php ./autoload.php
```

Now we can run our test class with the following command:

```
$ ./phpunit --bootstrap autoload.php phpunit_01.php
PHPUnit 5.6.2 by Sebastian Bergmann and contributors.
.                                                   1 / 1 (100%)
Time: 72 ms, Memory: 4.00MB
OK (1 test, 4 assertions)
```

 Some empty lines from the CLI output are purposely removed to keep them reasonably short.

We used two CLI parameters here:

- `--bootstrap`: Since we expect tests to work with various classes and functions from our project, we need to tell PHPUnit where it can find them. This parameter lets you specify a custom class loader (basically a PHP SPL autoloader). Fortunately, Composer already does everything for us, and generates `autoload.php` from our `composer.json` file. If we don't use the `--bootstrap` parameter, PHPUnit will throw an error because it will be unable to find `PHPUnit\Framework\TestCase`.

- `phpunit_01.php`: This is the file containing the test we want to run. Note that we could also use a directory path to test all the files in that directory, or just a dot (`.`), to test all the files in the current directory.

> PHPUnit allows the creation of a custom XML file with its configuration, so we don't have to include the `--bootstrap` parameter every time. To keep things simple, we're not using it. For more information, see the documentation at `https://phpunit.de/manual/current/en/appendixes.configuration.html`.

The console output summarizes everything we need to know about the tests processed. We can see it ran one test case with four assertions. The line with a single dot (`.`) followed by `1 / 1 (100%)` means we executed a single test case and it succeeded. This isn't very descriptive, so we can use another argument, `--testdox`, to make it more human-readable:

```
$ ./phpunit --testdox --bootstrap autoload.php phpunit_01.php
PHPUnit 5.6.2 by Sebastian Bergmann and contributors.
Demo
 [x] First test
```

Now, instead of the dot (`.`), PHPUnit converted the class and function names into strings, and marked those that passed. This is definitely more understandable; however, it doesn't show error messages on the failed test, so we don't know why it failed.

We'll use both formats in this chapter depending on the situation. Usually, when we expect a test to pass, we'll use the second, more readable, format. When we expect the test to fail, we'll use the first format to see where it failed and why (if it failed).

For demonstration purposes, we'll also add a test that fails and another test that depends on the first test:

```
class DemoTest extends TestCase {
    // ...
    public function testFails() {
        $this->assertEquals(5, 6);
        $this->assertContains(2, [1, 3, 4]);
    }

    /**
     * @depends testFails
     */
    public function testDepends() {
        $this->assertTrue(true);
    }
}
```

The first test case fails because it asserts that 5 == 6. The second test case is skipped because the test it depends on failed. The failed test is then properly marked as failed, while the skipped test is omitted:

```
$ ./phpunit --testdox --bootstrap autoload.php phpunit_01.php
PHPUnit 5.6.2 by Sebastian Bergmann and contributors.
Demo
  [x] First test
  [ ] Fails
```

This is all we need to know for now. Before jumping into testing RxPHP code, we should quickly talk about testing asynchronous code in general and one common pitfall we need to be aware of.

Testing asynchronous code

There's one important caveat we need to know about when testing asynchronous code, and since everything we do with RxPHP is asynchronous it's very relevant to us. Let's consider the following function `asyncPowIterator()`, which we're about to test:

```
// phpunit_async_01.php
use PHPUnit\Framework\TestCase;

function asyncPowIterator($num, callable $callback) {
    foreach (range(1, $num - 1) as $i) { // intentional
        $callback($i, pow($i, 2));
    }
```

```
    }

    class AsyncDemoTest extends TestCase {
        public function testBrokenAsync() {
            $callback = function($i, $pow) use (&$count) {
                $this->assertEquals(pow($i, 2), $pow);
            };
        }
    }
```

We have a function, `asyncPowIterator()`, that calls a callable on each number in the range 1 to 5. Notice that we made an intentional bug and instead of iterating the range 1 to 5, we'll just iterate 1 to 4.

In order to test that this method produces correct values, we placed the assertion right into the callable. So, let's run the test and see what happens:

```
$ ./phpunit --testdox --bootstrap autoload.php phpunit_async_01.php
PHPUnit 5.6.2 by Sebastian Bergmann and contributors.
AsyncDemo
 [x] Broken async
```

Well, the test passed, even though there's a bug that we know about.

The function in fact generates correct results, it's just not called as many times as we expect. This means that to test this function properly, we need to count the calls of the callable as well, and then compare it to the expected value:

```
    class AsyncDemoTest extends TestCase {
        public function testBrokenAsync() {
            $count = 0;
            $callback = function($i, $pow) use (&$count) {
                $this->assertEquals(pow($i, 2), $pow);
                $count++;
            };
            asyncPowIterator(5, $callback);
            $this->assertEquals(5, $count);
        }
    }
```

Now, we're incrementing the `$count` variable every time we go through the callable and, if we run the test again, we'll see it fails as it's supposed to:

```
$ ./phpunit --bootstrap autoload.php phpunit_async_01.php
PHPUnit 5.6.2 by Sebastian Bergmann and contributors.
F                                                      1 / 1 (100%)
Time: 57 ms, Memory: 4.00MB
```

```
There was 1 failure:
1) AsyncDemoTest::testBrokenAsync
Failed asserting that 4 matches expected 5.
/path/Chapter 05/phpunit_async_01.php:22
FAILURES!
Tests: 1, Assertions: 5, Failures: 1.
```

Now it fails as we want and we know that something's wrong.

This is an important paradigm. When testing asynchronous code, we can't just test that it returns correct results; we also need to be sure it gets called at all.

What we already know about unit testing could be enough to start testing our Observables and operators. RxPHP comes with a couple of classes intended for testing RxPHP code that can make our lives easier. All of these are used internally by RxPHP to test itself, so it's worth spending a little time learning about them, and start using them as well when testing our own code.

Testing RxPHP code

Since `Chapter 2`, *Reactive Programming with RxPHP*, where we introduced Schedulers, we've been using them via `ImmediateScheduler` and `EventLoopScheduler`.
Internally, `EventLoopScheduler` extends another Scheduler, called `VirtualTimeScheduler`, which is also used internally by `TestScheduler`, which we'll use for testing in a moment. But before we do that, let's see what's so interesting about `VirtualTimeScheduler`.

Introducing VirtualTimeScheduler

With `ImmediateScheduler`, everything is executed immediately.
The `VirtualTimeScheduler` keeps a priority queue of actions to be executed and gives us control over the order they're called.

In this example, we'll make an instance of `VirtualTimeScheduler` and stack a couple of actions that will be executed with different delays using the `schedule($actionCallable, $delay)` method:

```
// virtual_time_scheduler_01.php
use Rx\Scheduler\VirtualTimeScheduler;

$scheduler = new VirtualTimeScheduler(0, function($a, $b) {
```

```
        return $a - $b;
});

$scheduler->schedule(function() {
    print("1\n");
}, 300);
$scheduler->schedule(function() {
    print("2\n");
}, 0);
$scheduler->schedule(function() {
    print("3\n");
}, 150);
$scheduler->start();
```

When we instantiate the VirtualTimeScheduler class, we also need to pass a starting time and a typical comparer function that decides which action is called first. Then, to actually start executing all the actions in the correct order, we need to call the start() method manually.

The schedule() method also takes as its last argument a delay from the starting time when it'll be executed. This means we can define actions in a different order than they're supposed to be executed.

This example will print numbers in the following order:

```
$ php virtual_time_scheduler_01.php
2
3
1
```

This is actually what EventLoopScheduler does when we use it with an Observable that allows delayed execution, such as IntervalObservable. Let's look again at the very basic example with the interval() operator in RxPHP 1.x:

```
$loop = new React\EventLoop\StreamSelectLoop();
$scheduler = new Rx\Scheduler\EventLoopScheduler($loop);

Rx\Observable::interval(1000, $scheduler)
    ->subscribe(...);
$loop->run();
```

The EventLoopScheduler class is based on the same principle as VirtualTimeScheduler (it also inherits VirtualTimeScheduler). The primary difference is that EventLoopScheduler uses a loop to reschedule action calls over and over again in the specified interval. In this example, by "action" we mean an onNext() call from IntervalObservable.

The default delay for `schedule()` is 0, so we can also use `VirtualTimeScheduler` instead of `ImmediateScheduler`. Consider the following example:

```php
// virtual_time_scheduler_02.php
use Rx\Scheduler\VirtualTimeScheduler;
use Rx\Observable;
use Rx\Observer\CallbackObserver;
$scheduler = new VirtualTimeScheduler(0, function($a, $b) {
    return $a - $b;
});
$observer = new CallbackObserver(function($val) {
    print("$val\n");
});

$observable = Observable::fromArray([1,2,3,4]);
$observable->subscribe($observer, $scheduler);
$scheduler->start();
```

As expected, this prints all items in the array in the order they're specified:

```
$ php virtual_time_scheduler_02.php
1
2
3
4
```

Now it should be obvious why we always check in all our methods whether there's a Scheduler passed, and if there isn't, we use the simplest `ImmediateScheduler`. This allows us to easily switch to any other Scheduler if we have a reason to. Well, one good reason is unit testing, of course.

The `VirtualTimeScheduler` itself isn't used when testing RxPHP code, but it's wrapped with another Scheduler called `TestScheduler` that uses its principles under the hood and lets us schedule even more than just actions. Since `TestScheduler` uses a few other classes related to testing internally, we'll first have a look at them and then go back to `TestScheduler`.

 As its name suggests the `VirtualTimeScheduler` doesn't work with real time. The delays we set when calling the `schedule()` method are only used to execute actions in the correct order.

HotObservable and ColdObservable

We know what hot and cold Observables are from Chapter 02, *Reactive Programming with RxPHP*. These have their universal variants as HotObservable and ColdObservable classes. Note that these are intended only for testing and not for production usage.

We'll first have a look at how HotObservable can be used, and then talk about each class used in this example separately:

```
// hot_observable_01.php
use Rx\Scheduler\VirtualTimeScheduler;
use Rx\Testing\HotObservable;
use Rx\Testing\Recorded;
use Rx\Notification\OnNextNotification;

$scheduler = new VirtualTimeScheduler(0, function($a, $b) {
    return $a - $b;
});
$observable = new HotObservable($scheduler, [
    new Recorded(100, new OnNextNotification(3)),
    new Recorded(150, new OnNextNotification(1)),
    new Recorded(80, new OnNextNotification(2)),
]);
$observable->subscribeCallback(function($val) {
    print("$val\n");
});
$scheduler->start();
```

We used two new classes, Recorded and OnNextNotification, which we haven't met yet, so let's talk about them:

- HotObservable/ColdObservable: This class creates a hot or cold Observable, respectively. It takes as its argument a Scheduler and an array of actions that need to be scheduled for execution on the Scheduler we provide.
- Recorded: This class represents a single message (instead of a callable we used in the previous examples) scheduled for delayed execution. This class has a very important method, equal(), to compare two instances for equal value, time of invocation, and message type.
- OnNextNotification: The action itself is represented by an instance of this class. It takes only one parameter representing its value, and its only purpose is to call onNext() on an observer when invoked. There are also OnErrorNotification and OnCompletedNotification classes, calling onError and OnComplete methods, respectively.

When we run this example, we get the following result:

```
$ php hot_observable_01.php
2
3
1
```

The difference between `HotObservable` and `ColdObservable` is when they schedule their actions. The `HotObservable` class schedules everything right in its constructor, while `ColdObservable` does everything on subscription.

MockObserver

Just like when we talked about testing asynchronous code and that we need to be able to tell when callables weren't called at all, we need the same thing in RxPHP when testing Observables. RxPHP comes with class `MockObserver`, which records all the messages it receives (including the exact time for each record from the Scheduler), so we can later compare them with expected messages in the correct order.

Consider the following code printing all messages from `MockObserver`:

```php
// mock_observer_01.php
use Rx\Testing\MockObserver;
use Rx\Scheduler\VirtualTimeScheduler;
use Rx\Testing\HotObservable;
use Rx\Testing\Recorded;
use Rx\Notification\OnNextNotification;
use Rx\Notification\OnCompletedNotification;

$scheduler = new VirtualTimeScheduler(0, function($a, $b) {
    return $a - $b;
});
$observer = new MockObserver($scheduler);

(new HotObservable($scheduler, [
    new Recorded(100, new OnNextNotification(3)),
    new Recorded(150, new OnNextNotification(1)),
    new Recorded(80, new OnNextNotification(2)),
    new Recorded(140, new OnCompletedNotification()),
]))->subscribe($observer);
$scheduler->start();

foreach ($observer->getMessages() as $message) {
    printf("%s: %s\n", $message->getTime(), $message->getValue());
}
```

Notice that we've also included OnCompletedNotification, which is called before the last value:

```
$ php mock_observer_01.php
80: OnNext(2)
100: OnNext(3)
140: OnCompleted()
150: OnNext(1)
```

We can see that the value in each message is wrapped with the type of notification we used. Also, the last onNext call is recorded as well, even though it was emitted after onComplete. This is the correct behavior of MockObserver, because its only goal is to record messages and not to perform any logic.

TestScheduler

Now let's come back to the TestScheduler class we mentioned when talking about VirtualTimeScheduler. This class inherits VirtualTimeScheduler and provides a couple of methods related to scheduling events.

We'll start with an example again and see what TestScheduler does for us:

```
$scheduler = new TestScheduler();
$observer = $scheduler
    ->startWithCreate(function() use ($scheduler) {
        return new HotObservable($scheduler, [
            new Recorded(200, new OnNextNotification(3)),
            new Recorded(250, new OnNextNotification(1)),
            new Recorded(180, new OnNextNotification(2)),
            new Recorded(240, new OnCompletedNotification()),
            new Recorded(1200, new OnNextNotification(4)),
        ]);
});

$expected = [
    new Recorded(200, new OnNextNotification(3)),
    new Recorded(240, new OnCompletedNotification()),
    new Recorded(250, new OnNextNotification(1)),
];

$actual = $observer->getMessages();
printf("Count match: %d\n", count($actual) == count($expected));
foreach ($actual as $i => $message) {
    printf("%s: %d\n", $message->getTime(),
        $message->equals($expected[$i]));
```

```
}
```

We created five messages and we're expecting to receive only three. Also, this time, we're using the method `equals()` on instances of `Recorded` to compare them to each other. This will make sure we're receiving the correct number of messages in the correct order.

Let's run this example and check that we receive messages as we expect in the `$expected` array, and then talk about what happens inside and why:

```
$ php mock_observer_02.php
Count match: 1
200: 1
240: 1
250: 1
```

So, where did the other two messages disappear to? The `TestScheduler` class has two very important methods for scheduling actions, which we're going to use when testing RxPHP code:

- `startWithTiming($create, $createTime, $subscribeTime, $disposeTime)`: This method schedules three actions. These actions are: creating an instance of the source Observable, subscribing to the Observable and finally disposing a disposable returned from the `subscribe()` call. Each action is scheduled for a specific time by one of the arguments. Since creating an instance of Observable is one of the scheduled actions, it needs to be passed as a callable that returns the Observable, and not directly as an argument.
- `startWithCreate($create)`: This method calls the `startWithTiming()` method with default values. It's equal to calling `startWithTiming($create, 100, 200, 1000)`. The only argument is a callable that returns the source Observable.

Both these methods return an instance of `MockObserver`, which is also used to subscribe to the source Observable, so we don't need to create it ourselves.

Now it should be obvious why we received just three messages when we actually scheduled five. The message delayed by 180 happens before we subscribe to the source Observable, and the last message, with a delay of 1200, happens after we've already called `dispose()`, which unsubscribed `TestObserver` from the source Observable.

Comparing actual and expected messages with a `foreach` loop is, of course, possible, but it would be very tedious to do this in every single test we write. That's why RxPHP comes with `Rx\Functional\FunctionalTestCase` class, which we can use instead of `PHPUnit\Framework\TestCase` and which adds assertion methods specific to RxPHP code, most notably the `assertMessages()` method, which compares arrays of messages, just as we did in this example.

Testing SumOperator

All these classes are used by RxPHP to test its own code. Now we'll use them to test our own Observables and operators as well.

For testing purposes, we're going to write a simple operator that calculates the sum of all the integers it receives. When an `onComplete` arrives, it emits a single `onNext` with the sum of all numbers. It also emits `onError` when a non-integer value arrives:

```php
// SumOperator.php
class SumOperator implements OperatorInterface  {
  private $sum = 0;

  function __invoke($observable, $observer, $scheduler=null) {
    $observable->subscribe(new CallbackObserver(
      function($value) use ($observer) {
        if (is_int($value)) {
          $this->sum += $value;
        } else {
          $observer->onError(new Exception());
        }
      },
      [$observer, 'onError'],
      function() use ($observer) {
        $observer->onNext($this->sum);
        $observer->onCompleted();
      }
    ));
  }
}
```

This operator is very straightforward, and since we already know all the utilities we need to properly test it, we can jump right into unit testing with PHPUnit.

In fact, RxPHP already has a sum() operator, which is internally implemented as a reduce() operator that just adds values.

Instead of PHPUnit\Framework\TestCase, we'll use Rx\Functional\FunctionalTestCase, which creates TestScheduler internally and automatically passes it to new hot/cold Observables, so we don't need to worry about Schedulers at all.

RxPHP also contains a few helper functions to simplify creating Recorded objects. Instead of calling new Recorded(200, new OnNextNotification(3)), we can use onNext(200, 3) function defined in the rxphp/test/helper-functions.php file.

In order to use these functions, and also the FunctionalTestCase class, we need to tell the autoloader where to find them by updating our composer.json:

```
{
    "name": "rxphp_unittesting_demo",
    ...
    "require": {
        "reactivex/rxphp": "^1.5",
        "phpunit/phpunit": "^5.6",
        ...
    },
    "autoload": {
        "psr-4": {
            "Rx": "vendor/reactivex/rxphp/test/Rx"
        },
        "files": [
            "vendor/reactivex/rxphp/test/helper-functions.php"
        ]
    }
}
```

After updating composer.json, we need to regenerate the autoload.php script as well:

```
$ composer update
```

Now we can use onNext(), onComplete(), onError(), and also the FunctionalTestCase class (don't interchange the onNext() function from helper-functions.php with the onNext() method in observers; these are two separate things). Thanks to all this, the test class will then be pretty short:

```
// SumOperatorTest.php
use Rx\Functional\FunctionalTestCase;
```

```
class SumOperatorTest extends FunctionalTestCase {
  public function testSumSuccess() {
    $observer = $this->scheduler->startWithCreate(function () {
      return $this->createHotObservable([
        onNext(150, 3),
        onNext(210, 2),
        onNext(450, 7),
        onCompleted(460),
        onNext(500, 4),
      ])->lift(function () {
        return new SumOperator();
      });
    });

    $this->assertMessages([
      onNext(460, 9),
      onCompleted(460)
    ], $observer->getMessages());
  }
}
```

This test schedules a couple of messages and completes the Observable at time 460, which causes the SumOperator to emit its accumulated value, and also to complete right after that.

The callable for the startWithCreate() method creates a HotObservable class and connects it with our SumOperator using the lift() method we talked about extensively and used in Chapter 03, *Writing a Reddit Reader with RxPHP*. At the end, we used assertMessages() to compare messages received by MockObserver with expected messages, just as we did in the previous example. Using assertMessages() from FunctionalTestCase is just more comfortable.

We can run the test to see that it really passes successfully:

```
$ ./phpunit --bootstrap ./vendor/autoload.php SumOperatorTest.php
PHPUnit 5.6.2 by Sebastian Bergmann and contributors.
.                                                          1 / 1 (100%)
Time: 84 ms, Memory: 4.00MB
OK (1 test, 1 assertion)
```

Note that even when assertMessages() has to compare two messages and make sure both arrays are the same size, it counts as a single assertion.

Now let's also test a situation where we pass an invalid value (a string in this case) that causes an onError message:

```
class SumOperatorTest extends FunctionalTestCase {
  // ...
  public function testSumFails() {
    $observer = $this->scheduler->startWithCreate(function () {
      return $this->createHotObservable([
        onNext(150, 3),
        onNext(250, 'abc'),
        onNext(300, 2),
        onCompleted(460)
      ])->lift(function() {
        return new SumOperator();
      });
    });

    $this->assertMessages([
      onError(250, new Exception()),
    ], $observer->getMessages());
  }
}
```

We expect to receive an onError message at 250 and that's all. Even though there are two more messages scheduled, they won't arrive at TestObservable.

Of course, these two tests pass as expected:

```
$ ./phpunit --testdox --bootstrap autoload.php SumOperatorTest
PHPUnit 5.6.2 by Sebastian Bergmann and contributors.
SumOperator
 [x] Sum success
 [x] Sum fails
```

Testing ForkJoinObservable

Now we can have a look at a slightly more complicated example. In RxPHP, there's an interesting operator called forkJoin(). This operator takes as its parameter an array of Observables, collects the last value emitted for each of them, and when they all complete, emits a single array with the last values for each Observable.

This will make better sense when we look at the following marble diagram for `forkJoin()` operator in RxJS:

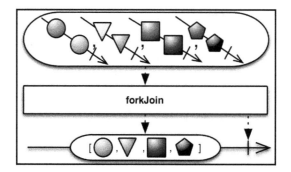

Marble diagram representing the forkJoin() operator in RxJS (http://reactivex.io/documentation/operators/zip.html)

We're going to implement a simplified version of the `forkJoin()` operator as an Observable. To make it extra clear what it does, we'll start with an example:

```php
// fork_join_test_01.php
use Rx\Observable;

(new ForkJoinObservable([
    Observable::fromArray([1, 2, 3, 4]),
    Observable::fromArray([7, 6, 5]),
    Observable::fromArray(['a', 'b', 'c']),
]))->subscribeCallback(function($values) {
    print_r($values);
});
```

This will print the last value from each source Observable:

```
$ php fork_join_test_01.php
Array
(
    [0] => 4
    [1] => 5
    [2] => c
)
```

Our implementation will subscribe to each source Observable and keep the latest value emitted for each of them. Then, when all of them complete, it emits one `onNext()` and one `onComplete`:

```php
// ForkJoinObservable.php
class ForkJoinObservable extends Observable {
    private $observables;
    private $lastValues = [];
    private $completed = [];

    public function __construct($observables) {
        $this->sources = $observables;
    }

    public function subscribe($observer, $sched = null) {
        $disp = new CompositeDisposable();

        if (null == $sched) {
            $sched = new ImmediateScheduler();
        }

        foreach ($this->observables as $i => $obs) {
            $inDisp = $obs->subscribeCallback(function($v) use ($i) {
                $this->lastValues[$i] = $v;
            }, function($e) use ($observer) {
                $observer->onError($e);
            }, function() use ($i, $observer) {
                $this->completed[$i] = true;
                $completed = count($this->completed);
                if ($completed == count($this->observables)) {
                    $observer->onNext($this->lastValues);
                    $observer->onCompleted();
                }
            }
            );
            $disp->add($inDisp);
        }
        return $disp;
    }
}
```

There are just a couple of nested anonymous functions. Note that we also need to store all disposables in `CompositeDisposable` to be able to properly dispose all of them.

Testing this class is very similar to what we did before. Pay special attention to the delays we use for each of the message calls:

```php
// ForkJoinObservableTest.php
class ForkJoinObservableTest extends FunctionalTestCase {

    public function testJoinObservables() {
        $observer = $this->scheduler->startWithCreate(function () {
            return new ForkJoinObservable([
                $this->createHotObservable([
                    onNext(200, 1),
                    onNext(300, 2),
                    onNext(400, 3),
                    onCompleted(500),
                    onNext(600, 4),
                ]),
                $this->createHotObservable([
                    onNext(200, 8),
                    onNext(300, 7),
                    onNext(400, 6),
                    onCompleted(800),
                ])
            ]);
        });

        $this->assertMessages([
            onNext(800, [3, 6]),
            onCompleted(800)
        ], $observer->getMessages());
    }
}
```

We expect to receive onNext() with the last values for each source Observable at 800, because this is the time when the second Observable completes. Also, even though the first Observable emitted one more value after its onComplete call, this will be ignored because it has already completed.

Then, if we run the test case, it will pass as expected:

```
$ ./phpunit --testdox --bootstrap autoload.php
ForkJoinObservableTest
PHPUnit 5.6.2 by Sebastian Bergmann and contributors.
ForkJoinObservable
  [x] Join observables
```

The most important thing we should keep in mind when testing RxPHP code is that time of invocation matters.

We could, of course, just test that our Observables and operators produce the correct values, but this could leave some bugs unnoticed and hard to find. To take a specific example, a bug could cause an Observable to pass along values even after it was supposed to complete, or to fail on an error.

Another interesting scenario we can test is when one of the Observables never completes. In this case `ForkJoinObservable` won't emit any value and not even the `onComplete` signal:

```
public function testJoinObservablesNeverCompletes() {
    $observer = $this->scheduler->startWithCreate(function () {
        return new ForkJoinObservable([
            $this->createHotObservable([
                onNext(200, 1),
                onNext(300, 2),
                onCompleted(500),
            ]),
            $this->createHotObservable([
                onNext(200, 8),
                onNext(300, 7),
            ])
        ]);
    });

    $this->assertMessages([], $observer->getMessages());
}
```

If we reran the `ForkJoinObservableTest` class, we'd see that this test passes as well.

> The real implementation of `ForkJoinObservable` is in RxPHP available since version 1.5 and is slightly more complicated. We'll come back to it in `Chapter 10`, *Using Advanced Operators and Techniques in RxPHP*. In `Appendix`, *Reusing RxPHP Techniques in RxJS*, we'll learn about the new way of testing Rx code called "marble tests" implemented in RxPHP 2 and RxJS 5.

Summary

This chapter covered unit testing code written using PHPUnit with utilities provided by the RxPHP package.

Most importantly, we went through the doOn*() operators and the basics of unit testing with PHPUnit, and the problems we need to be aware of when unit testing asynchronous code. Next, we went in-depth into which classes aimed at unit testing are provided by RxPHP, how to use each of them, and which problems they solve. In particular, these were the VirtualTimeScheduler, HotObservable, ColdObservable, TestScheduler, and FunctionalTestCase classes. In addition to this, we wrote example SumOperator and ForkJoinObservable classes to demonstrate how important it is to test that messages are emitted and received at the correct times.

In the following chapter, we'll have a deeper look at event loops in PHP and we'll introduce a more advanced concept of higher-order Observables in RxPHP.

6
PHP Streams API and Higher-Order Observables

In this chapter, we'll introduce a lot of new features that we need for the next chapter. Almost everything covered in this chapter is related to **PHP Streams API**, Promises and event loops (`reactphp/event-loop` project in our case). This also includes a couple of more advanced RxPHP operators working with so-called higher-order Observables.

In particular, in this chapter, we'll do the following:

- Quickly look at using Promises in PHP with the `reactphp/promise` library
- Introduce PHP Streams API and, with examples, see what benefits it brings with minimal or no effort
- Examine the internals of `StreamSelectLoop` class, this time in the context of PHP Streams API
- See what caveats we need to be aware of when working with non-blocking code in event loops
- Talk about higher-order Observables
- Introduce four new and more advanced operators, `concatAll()`, `mergeAll()`, `combineLatest()` and `switchMap()`, which are intended to work with higher-order Observables

This chapter is going to introduce a lot of new things we haven't encountered yet. However, all of them have their benefits in practice, as we'll see in the next chapter, where we'll write an application that spawns multiple subprocesses on the go. Each subprocess will be a self-sufficient WebSocket server itself, and we'll use knowledge gained in this chapter to communicate with them and to collect information from them.

Using Promises in PHP

While using Reactive Extensions, we think of data as continuous streams that emit data over time. A similar, and probably more familiar, concept is Promises, which represent a single value in the future.

You've probably met Promises in libraries such as jQuery, where it's commonly used to handle responses from an AJAX request. There are multiple implementations in PHP, but the principle is always the same. We're going to use a library called `reactphp/promise` (`https://github.com/reactphp/promise`), which follows Promises/A proposal (`http://wiki.commonjs.org/wiki/Promises/A`) and adds some extra functionality as well. Since we're going to use this library for this and the next chapter, we will have a look at how to use it.

Install `react/promise` package via composer:

```
$ composer require react/promiseWe
```

We will use two basic classes:

- `Promise`: This class represents a result of a deferred computation that will be available in the future.
- `Deferred`: This class represents an action that's pending. It returns a single instance of Promise, which is resolved or rejected. Usually, by resolving a Promise, we understand that the action ended successfully, while rejection means it failed.

Each Promise is going to be resolved or rejected, and we can handle its results via multiple methods (we can call them operators as well, since they serve a similar purpose, like in Rx). Each of these methods returns a new Promise, so we'll be able to chain them in a very similar way to how we do it in Rx:

- `then()`: This method takes two callbacks as arguments. The first one is called only when the Promise is resolved, while the second one is called only when it's rejected. Each callback can return a modified value, which is passed to the next operator.
- `done()`: Similarly to `then()`, it takes two callbacks as arguments. However, this method returns null, so it doesn't allow chaining. It's intended only to consume the result and prevents you from modifying it any further.

- otherwise(): This is a handler when the Promise is rejected or when the preceding then() method throws an exception.
- always(): This is the cleanup method called when the Promise is either resolved or rejected.

Using the then() and done() methods

We can demonstrate how to use a Promise and Deferred classes with the then() and done() methods in the following example:

```php
// deferred_01.php
use React\Promise\Deferred;
$deferred = new Deferred();

$deferred->promise()
    ->then(function($val) {
        echo "Then #1: $val\n";
        return $val + 1;
    })
    ->then(function($val) {
        echo "Then #2: $val\n";
        return $val + 1;
    })
    ->done(function($val) {
        echo "Done: $val\n";
    });

$deferred->resolve(42);
```

The promise() method returns an instance of the Promise class, which is then chained with two then() and one done() calls. We've mentioned that a Promise class represents a single value in the future. For this reason, calling promise() method multiple times always returns the same Promise object.

In the first then() call, we'll print the value and return $val + 1. This modified value will be passed to the consecutive then() call, which again updates the value and passes it to done(). The done() method returns null, so it can't be chained with any more operators.

The output is then as follows:

```
$ php deferred_01.php
Then #1: 42
Then #2: 43
Done: 44
```

Notice that it's the instance of the `Deferred` class that is responsible for resolving or rejecting the `Promise` class because it represents the asynchronous action. The `Promise` class, on the other hand, represents just the result of the `Deferred` class.

Using the otherwise() and always() methods

Similarly to using `then()` and `done()`, we'll handle exceptions with `otherwise()`, and we'll also append `always()`, which will be called regardless of the `Promise` class being resolved or rejected:

```
// deferred_02.php
$deferred = new Deferred();
$deferred->promise()
    ->then(function($val) {
        echo "Then: $val\n";
        throw new \Exception('This is an exception');
    })
    ->otherwise(function($reason) {
        echo 'Error: '. $reason->getMessage() . "\n";
    })
    ->always(function() {
        echo "Do cleanup\n";
    });

$deferred->resolve(42);
```

Now, the callable for `then()` throws an exception, which is caught by the following `otherwise()` method. This chain of Promises is always finished by an `always()` call, even when we threw an exception in `then()`.

If we run this example, we'll receive the following output:

```
$ php deferred_02.php
Then: 42
Error: This is an exception
Do cleanup
```

The `otherwise()` method is, in fact, just a shortcut for `then(null, $onRejected)`, so we could write it as a single call. However, this notation is split into two separate method calls, making it easier to understand. We can also test a scenario where we reject the `Promise` class instead of resolving it:

```
$deferred->reject(new \Exception('This is an exception'));
```

This skips the `then()` call and triggers only the `otherwise()` callable:

```
$ php deferred_02.php
Error: This is an exception
Do cleanup
```

Notice that the `always()` method was called in both situations. Also, note that the `otherwise()` method allows creating multiple handlers for different exception classes. If we don't specify the class type in the callable definition, it'll be triggered on any exception.

PHP Streams API

If we want to work with sockets in PHP, we're offered two sets of methods, starting with one of these two prefixes:

- `socket_*`: Low-level API to the socket communication available since PHP 4.1. This extension needs to be enabled when compiling PHP with the `--enable-sockets` option. You can check whether your PHP supports this API by running `php -i` in the console and watching for `--enable-sockets` under the `Configure Command` option.
- `stream_*`: API introduced in PHP 4.3 that generalizes usage of file, network, and other operations under a unified set of functions. Streams in the sense of this API are resource objects that share some common behavior. This extension is part of PHP and doesn't require any extra steps to be enabled. More stream functions were added in PHP 5, such as `stream_socket_server()`, which we'll use in a moment.

In general, we'll always want to use the newer `stream_*` API because it's a built-in part of PHP and offers better functionality.

The core feature is that it's built around using resources. A resource in PHP is a special variable holding a reference to some external resource (this can be a socket connection, file handler, and so on). These have some limitations. For instance, they can't be serialized, for obvious reasons, and certain methods are not applicable with particular types of resources, such as `fseek()`.

Working with resources and streams is unified, so we can use `stream_*` functions when, for example, writing data to files instead of the typical `fwrite()` function. Consider the following example, where we copy the content of a file to another file and instead of using `fwrite()`, or `file_get_content()` and `file_put_content()`, we'll use `stream_copy_to_stream()`:

```
// streams_00.php
$source = fopen('textfile.txt', 'r');
$dest = fopen('destfile.txt', 'w');
stream_copy_to_stream($source, $dest);
```

Both `$source` and `$dest` are resources. The `stream_copy_to_stream()` function just copies the content of one stream to another. How one resource reads the data and how the second resource writes the data is up to the inner implementation of this resource. We could also use `fseek()` to move the read cursor to some position instead of reading data from the beginning of the file:

```
$source = fopen('textfile.txt', 'r');
fseek($source, 5);
...
```

Now we have skipped the first five bytes of the file.

There are many types of resources. We can see what types we're supporting with the `get_resource_type()` function.

In the following example, we create three different types of resources:

```
// streams_01.php
$source = fopen('textfile.txt', 'r');
echo get_resource_type($source) . "\n";

$xml = xml_parser_create();
echo get_resource_type($xml) . "\n";

$curl = curl_init();
echo get_resource_type($curl) . "\n";
```

We can see that each resource type is identified by a different string:

```
$ php streams_01.php
stream
xml
curl
```

In Chapter 3, *Writing a Reddit Reader with RxPHP*, we read inputs from the console by opening a stream to php://stdin and using fread() to periodically (with IntervalObservable) get content of the current read buffer. We also used the stream_set_blocking() function to make the read stream nonblocking, which makes fread() return an empty string if there was no data available.

Using an event loop is, of course, a viable option, but there's also a function made exactly for this purpose, called stream_select().

Using the stream_select() function

Instead of looping over all streams and checking manually whether they have any data available, we can use the stream_select() function (http://php.net/manual/en/function.stream-select.php). This function takes arrays of streams as parameters and waits until there's some activity on at least one of them.

Since any resource created with fopen() is a stream, we can use this function to wait for user input instead of using a loop:

```
// streams_02.php
$stdin = fopen('php://stdin', 'r');
stream_set_blocking($stdin, false);

$readStreams = [$stdin];
$writeStreams = [];
$exceptStreams = [];

stream_select($readStreams, $writeStreams, $exceptStreams, 5);
echo "stdin: " . strrev(fgets($stdin));
```

The `stream_select()` function returns the number of active streams, or zero if the timeout elapsed. It takes five arguments in total, where the first four of them are required:

- `array &$read`: This is the array of read streams (streams are checked for any available data to be read).
- `array &$write`: This is the array of write streams. Streams listed here need to indicate they're ready to write data.
- `array &$except`: This is the array of streams with higher priority.
- `int $tv_sec`: This is the maximum time in seconds spent waiting for at least one of the streams to be active.
- `int $tv_usec` (optional): This is the time in microseconds added to the timeout in seconds.

Each array is passed by reference, so we can't leave it with just `[]`; we need to pass it as a variable (`null` is also acceptable). The last integer parameter 5 is the timeout after which this function returns, even though it didn't catch any activity on any of its streams.

So in this example, we create a resource `$stdin` using `fopen()`, then wait for five seconds for any user input (the data is sent to the buffer by terminal after we press the *Enter* key) and then use `fgets()` to get the data from buffer and print it in reversed order.

Notice that we had to make the `$stdin` stream nonblocking anyway. If we didn't, the `stream_select()` would never end, regardless the timeout.

StreamSelectLoop and stream_select() function

We've been using the `StreamSelectLoop` class in Chapter 3, *Writing a Reddit Reader with RxPHP*, to periodically emit values with `IntervalObservable`, or in Chapter 2, *Reactive Programming with RxPHP*, to check for user input. Let's combine what we've learned about PHP streams, `stream_select()` function, and `StreamSelectLoop` together and update the previous example to use `StreamSelectLoop`.

The `StreamSelectLoop` class has an `addReadStream()` method to add streams (resources) and callables, which are executed when the stream is active. Then it calls `stream_select()` internally and waits for activity on any of the streams in a loop:

```
// stdin_loop_01.php
use React\EventLoop\StreamSelectLoop;
$stdin = fopen('php://stdin', 'r');

$loop = new StreamSelectLoop();
```

```
$loop->addReadStream($stdin, function($stream) {
    $str = trim(fgets($stream));
    echo strrev($str) . "\n";
});

$loop->run();
```

Finally, it should be obvious why the event loop class is called StreamSelectLoop and not EventLoop or just Loop: it uses stream_select() internally.

Now we know how StreamSelectLoop is able to work with PHP streams. However, a very good question is, how do Observables such as IntervalObservable, which periodically emit values, work when they don't use any streams?

Scheduling events with StreamSelectLoop

Apart from using StreamSelectLoop to handle streams, we can also schedule one-time or periodical events by just specifying an interval and a callable.

Consider the following example, which creates two timers:

```
// loop_01.php
use React\EventLoop\StreamSelectLoop;

$loop = new StreamSelectLoop();
$loop->addTimer(1.5, function() {
    echo "timer 1\n";
});

$counter = 0;
$loop->addPeriodicTimer(1, function () use (&$counter, $loop) {
    printf("periodic timer %d\n", ++$counter);
    if ($counter == 5) {
        $loop->stop();
    }
});
$loop->run();
```

The periodic timer fires every second, while the one-time timer is fired just once after 1500ms. Output in the console will print values for the increasing $counter variable:

```
$ php loop_01.php
periodic timer 1
timer 1
periodic timer 2
```

```
periodic timer 3
periodic timer 4
. . .
```

So how is `StreamSelectLoop` able to schedule events when we're not using streams at all?

The answer is the `stream_select()` function and its fourth and fifth arguments. Even when we're not waiting for any stream activity, we can still make use of the timeouts provided to `stream_select()`. We could, in fact, achieve the same result if we used just the `usleep()` function to hold the script execution for a period of time. However, if we did use `usleep()`, we wouldn't be able to combine timers with streams.

When we start the event loop with `$loop->run()`, it iterates all its times and checks which timer is supposed to fire first. In our case it's the periodic timer that'll fire after one second, so `StreamSelectLoop` calls `stream_select()` and sets its fourth parameter (timeout) to one second. Since we didn't add any streams to the loop, the `stream_select()` call will always end with a timeout, which is intentional in this case.

If we did add a stream to the loop that would signal activity any time before the timer is supposed to fire, then `stream_select()` might be interrupted and the stream would be handled before the timer.

We can go back to our example where the `StreamSelectLoop` class works as follows:

- We scheduled a one-second timeout that makes `stream_select()` return even when there's no stream activity.
- The `StreamSelectLoop` class checks what timers are due and calls their callables. Then, if the timer was periodical, it reschedules the timer to fire again in the future.
- This was the first iteration of the internal loop where `stream_select()` caused the pause.
- At the second iteration, it checks for the nearest timers again. This time it's the one-time timer that'll fire in 500ms (1000ms already elapsed), so the timeout for `stream_select()` is going to be just 500ms.

This goes on until we call `$loop->stop()` from one of the callables.

We can rewrite this example with a periodic timer to use `IntervalObservable`, while also reading any input from `php://stdin`:

```php
// loop_02.php
use React\EventLoop\StreamSelectLoop;
use Rx\Observable;
```

```
use Rx\Scheduler\EventLoopScheduler;

$loop = new StreamSelectLoop();
$scheduler = new EventLoopScheduler($loop);

Observable::interval(2000, $scheduler)
    ->subscribeCallback(function($counter) {
        printf("periodic timer %d\n", $counter);
    });

$stdin = fopen('php://stdin', 'r');
$loop->addReadStream($stdin, function($stream) {
    $str = trim(fgets($stream));
    echo strrev($str) . "\n";
});

$loop->run();
```

Observables don't work directly with StreamSelectLoop, so we need to wrap it with a Scheduler. The EventLoopScheduler class inherits the VirtualTimeScheduler class that we explained in detail in the previous chapter, when we talked about testing and how it's used with the TestScheduler class. The principle with EventLoopScheduler is the same.

The EventLoopScheduler class schedules timers on the StreamSelectLoop instance, which doesn't forbid us from using the same loop for streams also.

Minimalistic HTTP Server with StreamSelectLoop

A nice example of using just StreamSelectLoop to create a simple HTTP web server is available on the GitHub page for the react/event-loop package:

```
// streams_03.php
$loop = new React\EventLoop\StreamSelectLoop();
$server = stream_socket_server('tcp://127.0.0.1:8080');
stream_set_blocking($server, 0);

$loop->addReadStream($server, function ($server) use ($loop) {
  $c = stream_socket_accept($server);
  $data = "HTTP/1.1 200 OK\r\nContent-Length: 3\r\n\r\nHi\n";

  $loop->addWriteStream($c, function($c) use (&$data, $loop) {
    $written = fwrite($c, $data);
    if ($written === strlen($data)) {
      fclose($conn);
      $loop->removeStream($c);
    } else {
```

```
            $data = substr($data, 0, $written);
        }
    });
});

$loop->addPeriodicTimer(5, function () {
    $memory = memory_get_usage() / 1024;
    $formatted = number_format($memory, 3).'K';
    echo "Current memory usage: {$formatted}\n";
});

$loop->run();
```

This demo uses `stream_socket_server()` to create a listening TCP socket server accepting connections only from localhost on port `8080`. The `$server` stream is then added to the event loop, and every time a new connection is established, it's captured by `stream_select()`. Then, to actually accept the connection, we need to call the `stream_socket_accept()` function, which returns another stream representing the stream to this client. Then, with `addWriteStream()` we'll know when the client is ready to start receiving data.

There are four important things to notice:

- With `stream_socket_server()`, we can use multiple different protocols. The most common are `tcp`, `udp`, and `unix`. We can get a full list of all the available protocols with `stream_get_transports()`.
- If we have *N* clients there are always *N+1* streams in the loop. This is because the server stream that accepts connections is inside the event loop as well.
- When we write data to the client stream, we need to be aware that it might not be able to write the entire response at once and we'll need to send it in chunks. That's why we always check how many bytes were written to the stream with `fwrite()`.
- After we're done writing data to the write stream, we close it with `fclose()` and remove it from the loop because we don't need it anymore. When a new client connection is accepted it'll have its own write stream.

A note on nonblocking event loops

The implementation details of `StreamSelectLoop` suggest that it can't guarantee that all timers will fire exactly at the time they should. For example, if we created two timers that both need to fire after 500ms, then we can predict pretty accurately that the first callable will be executed after exactly 500ms. However, the callable for the second timer is dependent on the execution time of the first callable. This means that if the first callable took 100ms to execute; the second callable will be trigger after 600ms instead of 500ms.

An implication of this is that the event loop is nonblocking – as long as our code is nonblocking.

There's no parallelism in PHP, thus all code is strictly sequential. If we write code that takes long to execute or needs to be blocking from its nature, it's going to cause the entire event loop to also be blocking.

Using multiple StreamSelectLoop instances

In real-world PHP applications, where we need to work asynchronously with PHP streams, Observables, HTTP servers/clients, or WebSocket servers/clients (and basically any asynchronous code), we might need to use multiple event loops. This means a situation where each nonblocking part of the application requires its own event loop.

For example, we need to use an event loop to use `IntervalObservable`, but we also need an event loop for a WebSocket server that needs to read data from a PHP stream.

Consider the following example, where we simulate a similar scenario:

```
// loop_03.php
use React\EventLoop\StreamSelectLoop;

$loop1 = new StreamSelectLoop();
$loop1->addPeriodicTimer(1, function() {
    echo "timer 1\n";
});

$loop2 = new StreamSelectLoop();
$loop2->addTimer(2, function() {
    echo "timer 2\n";
});

$loop1->run();
$loop2->run();
```

In this example, the second `$loop2` will never start. The PHP interpreter will only stay in the first `$loop1`, which never ends because of the periodic timer. If we did it in reverse order (calling `$loop2` first and then `$loop1`) it would actually work. The second loop would just be delayed by two seconds because the first loop runs just one action and then ends (there are no other timers active, so it'll end automatically).

This is something we need to be aware of. In Chapter 7, *Implementing Socket IPC and WebSocket Server/Client*, we'll write an app that uses a WebSocket server and a Unix socket client that need to run at the same time. This means they both need to be able to read data from streams in a loop. The good thing is that the WebSocket server will use the same event loop implementation from `react/event-loop` package.

The outcome of this is that, in PHP, we need to have just a single event loop, which might be a problem with certain libraries that need to work with their own event loop implementations, but don't expose any way we can hook them.

However, this doesn't necessarily apply to RxJS or, in general, to JavaScript applications where the interpreter works differently to PHP. We'll talk about the differences when using RxJS and RxPHP in more depth in the last chapter of this book.

Event loop interoperability in PHP

To tackle this problem there's an attempt to standardize even loop implementations to follow the same API.

The `async-interop/event-loop` package defines a set of interfaces that an even loop needs to implement to be truly interchangeable. This means that we can write a library that only relies on the interfaces provided by `async-interop/event-loop` and the end user can decide which even loop implementation they want to use.

We can have a look at an example of `StreamSelectLoop` we know already and use it only via the interface provided by `async-interop/event-loop`. As of now, `StreamSelectLoop` doesn't implement this interface natively so we'll need one more package `wyrihaximus/react-async-interop-loop` that wraps the event loop implementation from `react/event-loop` with `async-interop/event-loop` interface.

Our `composer.json` file will be very simple because we'll have just a single required package:

```
{
    "require": {
        "wyrihaximus/react-async-interop-loop": "^0.1.0"
```

```
        }
    }
```

The `wyrihaximus/react-async-interop-loop` package requires as dependencies
both `async-interop/event-loop` and `react/event-loop` so we don't need to include
them ourselves.

Then we'll write a minimal example that schedules two actions using the `Loop`
interoperability interface:

```
// event_interop_01.php
use Interop\Async\Loop;
use WyriHaximus\React\AsyncInteropLoop\ReactDriverFactory;

Loop::setFactory(ReactDriverFactory::createFactory());

Loop::delay(1000, function() {
    echo "second\n";
});
Loop::delay(500, function() {
    echo "first\n";
});

Loop::get()->run();
```

Notice that all our operations are done only on the `Loop` class which comes from
the `async-interop/event-loop` package and its static methods. We already know that
we always have to have only one event loop running at a time. This is why all the methods
on the `Loop` class are static.

The `setFactory()` method tells the `Loop` class how to create an instance of our event loop.
In our case we're using `react/event-loop` that is wrapped inside `ReactDriverFactory`
to follow the `async-interop` interface.

Event loops and future versions of RxPHP

Using event loops (and thus all operators requiring asynchronous scheduling) has been
significantly simplified in RxPHP 2 and most of the time we don't even need to worry about
starting the event loop ourselves.

RxPHP 2 was supposed to be based on the async-interop/event-loop interface. However, the specification is still unstable so the RxPHP team decided to rollback to the RxPHP 1 style of event loops. The following paragraphs describe how the event loops should be used in the future versions of RxPHP (maybe RxPHP 3). At the end, RxPHP 2 is based on the `StreamSelectLoop` class from the `reactphp` library as we're used to.

RxPHP in the future will rely on the `async-interop/event-loop` interface. Since we don't want to start the loop ourselves we can autoload a bootstrap script from RxPHP to start the loop automatically at the end of the script execution using PHP's `register_shutdown_function()`. We'll update our `composer.json` again and add the `autoload` directive:

```
"autoload": {
    "files": ["vendor/reactivex/rxphp/src/bootstrap.php"]
}
```

Now we can write any asynchronous code:

```
// rxphp2_01.php
use Rx\Observable;

Observable::interval(1000)
    ->take(5)
    ->flatMap(function($i) {
        return \Rx\Observable::of($i + 1);
    })
    ->subscribe(function($value) {
        echo "$value\n";
    });
```

Notice that we're neither creating a Scheduler nor starting the loop. In RxPHP 2 all operators have their default Scheduler predefined so we don't need to pass it in the `subscribe()` method.

If we wanted to follow a similar approach as with RxPHP 1 we could hardcode the Scheduler:

```
use Rx\Scheduler;
Observable::interval(1000, Scheduler::getAsync())
    ->take(5)
    ...
```

However, in some situations, we might not want to wait until the end of the script for `register_shutdown_function()` to start the loop and we want to start it ourselves.

Let's have a look at the following example:

```
// rxphp2_02.php
use Rx\Observable;

Observable::interval(1000)
    ->take(3)
    ->subscribe(function($value) {
        echo "First: $value\n";
    });

Observable::interval(1000)
    ->take(3)
    ->subscribe(function($value) {
        echo "Second: $value\n";
    });
```

Both Observables will start emitting values at the same time when the loop is started so the output will be as follows:

```
$ php rxphp2_02.php
First: 0
Second: 0
First: 1
Second: 1
First: 2
Second: 2
```

We can also manually start the event loop after we create the first Observable:

```
// rxphp2_03.php
Observable::interval(1000)
    ->take(3)
    ->subscribe(function($value) {
        echo "First: $value\n";
    });

Loop::get()->run();

Observable::interval(1000)
    ->take(3)
    ->subscribe(function($value) {
        echo "Second: $value\n";
    });
```

The loop will end after printing three values and then we carry on with the second Observable. The event loop will be automatically started again at the end the script execution. The output is then the following:

```
$ php rxphp2_03.php
First: 0
First: 1
First: 2
Second: 0
Second: 1
Second: 2
```

 Note that at the time of writing this book (April 2017) both `async-interop/event-loop` and RxPHP 2 are in pre-release state and their APIs might change.

Higher-order Observables

When talking about the prerequisites for functional programming we mentioned higher-order functions. These are functions that return other functions. A very similar concept is applied in RxPHP as well, when using Observables.

A higher-order Observable is an Observable that emits other Observables. To illustrate how higher-order Observables differ from first-order Observables, consider the following simple example:

```
// higher_order_01.php
use Rx\Observable;
Observable::range(1, 3)
    ->subscribe(new DebugSubject());
```

This example just prints three values and completes as expected. This is what we expect from any first-order Observable:

```
$ php higher_order_01.php
22:54:05 [] onNext: 1 (integer)
22:54:05 [] onNext: 2 (integer)
22:54:05 [] onNext: 3 (integer)
22:54:05 [] onCompleted
```

Now, we can make this more complicated by adding the `map()` operator that, instead of returning an integer, returns another Observable:

```
// higher_order_02.php
use Rx\Observable;

Observable::range(1, 3)
    ->map(function ($value) {
        return Observable::range(0, $value);
    })
    ->subscribe(new DebugSubject());
```

We create an Observable using `range()` for each value from the source Observable. In our example, Observables that arrive to the `DebugSubject` instances are supposed to emit values `[0]`, `[0, 1]`, and `[0,1,2]`, respectively.

The output in console is not satisfactory. The `DebugSubject` instance prints what it receives, which is an instance of `RangeObservable`.

This is correct behavior. We're really returning Observables from the `map()` operator, and `subscribe()` method doesn't care what values it passes through:

```
$ php higher_order_02.php
23:29:46 [] onNext: RangeObservable (Rx\Observable\RangeObservable)
23:29:46 [] onNext: RangeObservable (Rx\Observable\RangeObservable)
23:29:46 [] onNext: RangeObservable (Rx\Observable\RangeObservable)
23:29:46 [] onCompleted
```

The value for each `onNext` is `RangeObservable` (`Rx\Observable\RangeObservable`) because `DebugSubject` receives an object and transforms it into a string. Then it prints the class name, including its namespace, in parentheses.

So, what if we want to flatten the inner Observables and re-emit all values from them?

RxPHP has a couple of operators intended to work with higher-order Observables. In particular the most useful are `mergeAll()`, `concatAll()`, and `switchLatest()`.

For this purpose, we can choose `mergeAll()` or `concatAll()`. The difference between these two is the same as `merge()` and `concat()`. The `mergeAll()` operator subscribes to all inner Observables right when it receives them, and re-emits all their values immediately. On the other hand, `concatAll()` will subscribe to the inner Observables one at the time, in the order it receives them.

The concatAll() and mergeAll() operators

In this example, it doesn't matter which one we choose. The `RangeObservable` is a cold Observable that uses `ImmediateScheduler`, so all values are always emitted in the correct order.

Implementation with `mergeAll()` could look like the following:

```
// higher_order_03.php
Observable::range(1, 3)
    ->map(function($value) {
        return Observable::range(0, $value);
    })
    ->mergeAll()
    ->subscribe(new DebugSubject());
```

Now `Observable::range(1, 3)` emits three instances of `RangeObservable`. The `mergeAll()` operator subscribes to each of them and re-emits all their values to its observer, which is a `DebugSubject` instance.

How `mergeAll()` works is obvious from the following marble diagram:

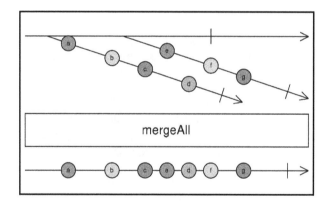

Marble diagram representing the mergeAll() operator in RxJS (http://reactivex.io/rxjs/class/es6/Observable.js)

The source Observable, represented as a horizontal line at the top, doesn't emit values directly (there are no circles on the line). Instead, it emits other Observables, represented by diagonal lines.

If we run this example, we'll get values as described above, which are 0, 0, 1, 0, 1, and 2:

```
$ php higher_order_03.php
00:02:26 [] onNext: 0 (integer)
00:02:26 [] onNext: 0 (integer)
00:02:26 [] onNext: 1 (integer)
00:02:26 [] onNext: 0 (integer)
00:02:26 [] onNext: 1 (integer)
00:02:26 [] onNext: 2 (integer)
00:02:26 [] onCompleted
```

We can also test what happens if we work with Observables that emit values asynchronously. In this case, it matters whether we use mergeAll() or concatAll(), so we'll test both scenarios.

Let's start with mergeAll() and an example similar to the previous one. We'll use IntervalObservable and take(3) to emit three Observables that asynchronously emit three values:

```php
// higher_order_04.php
$loop = new StreamSelectLoop();
$scheduler = new EventLoopScheduler($loop);

Observable::interval(1000, $scheduler)
    ->take(3)
    ->map(function($value) use ($scheduler) {
        return Observable::interval(600, $scheduler)
            ->take(3)
            ->map(function($counter) use ($value) {
                return sprintf('#%d: %d', $value, $counter);
            });
    })
    ->mergeAll()
    ->subscribe(new DebugSubject());

$loop->run();
```

Each value from the inner Observable is transformed into a string to be easily identifiable. We can describe what happens in this example by time-stamping each value:

- 1000ms: The first value is emitted from the outer IntervalObservable, which is via the map() operator turned into another IntervalObservable. At this point, mergeAll() subscribes to this first inner Observable.
- 1600ms: The inner IntervalObservable emits a first-value (integer 0), which is converted to a string and printed by the DebugSubject instance.

- 2000ms: The second inner Observable is created. The mergeAll() operator subscribes to it as well. It's subscribed to two Observables now.
- 2200ms: The first inner IntervalObservable emits its second value (1).
- 2600ms: The second inner IntervalObservable emits its first value (0).
- 2800ms: The first inner IntervalObservable emits its last value (2).
- 3000ms: The third inner IntervalObservable is created.

This continues until all inner IntervalObservable emit three values, thanks to the take(3) operator.

We can see that the values from inner Observables are really emitted asynchronously and, if we want to consume them, it's very easy to use the mergeAll() operator.

The full console output is as follows:

```
$ php higher_order_04.php
00:43:55 [] onNext: #0: 0 (string)
00:43:55 [] onNext: #0: 1 (string)
00:43:56 [] onNext: #1: 0 (string)
00:43:56 [] onNext: #0: 2 (string)
00:43:56 [] onNext: #1: 1 (string)
00:43:57 [] onNext: #2: 0 (string)
00:43:57 [] onNext: #1: 2 (string)
00:43:57 [] onNext: #2: 1 (string)
00:43:58 [] onNext: #2: 2 (string)
00:43:58 [] onCompleted
```

Implementation using concatAll() is exactly the same. The only thing that changes is how we use this operator:

```
// higher_order_05.php
...
    ->map(function($value) use ($scheduler) {
        // ...
    })
    ->concatAll()
    ->subscribe(new DebugSubject());
...
```

Just like the concat() operator, concatAll() keeps the order of Observables and subscribes to the next Observable only after the previous Observables are completed. The output in the console is in the order the inner IntervalObservables are created:

```
$ php higher_order_05.php
00:55:30 [] onNext: #0: 0 (string)
00:55:30 [] onNext: #0: 1 (string)
00:55:31 [] onNext: #0: 2 (string)
00:55:32 [] onNext: #1: 0 (string)
00:55:32 [] onNext: #1: 1 (string)
00:55:33 [] onNext: #1: 2 (string)
00:55:34 [] onNext: #2: 0 (string)
00:55:34 [] onNext: #2: 1 (string)
00:55:35 [] onNext: #2: 2 (string)
00:55:35 [] onCompleted
```

The core principle of higher-order Observables isn't easy to grasp at first sight, so feel free to experiment by yourself.

Although it's hard to see the real benefit of concat(), concatAll(), merge(), and mergeAll() in RxPHP, these all are very common in RxJS. Typically, when we need to run multiple HTTP requests in order or independently of each other, it's very convenient to use one of these operators. More on this topic is in the final chapter, which shows some interesting use-cases of RxJS.

The switchLatest Operator

With concatAll() or mergeAll(), we know we'll always receive all values emitted from all inner Observables. In some use cases, we might care only about values from the most recent Observable, while discarding all other Observables. This is something we can't do with either concatAll() or mergeAll() because these always wait until the current Observable completes or all Observables complete, respectively.

This is why there's a switchLatest() operator that's always subscribed only to the most recent Observable and automatically unsubscribes from the previous one.

The following marble diagram explains this principle very well:

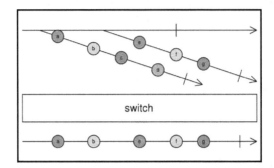

Marble diagram representing the switch() operator in RxJS (http://reactivex.io/rxjs/class/es6/Observable.js)

 This operator is called, simply, `switch()` in RxJS. There are also the `switchMap()` and `switchMapTo()` operators, currently available only in RxJS.

In this figure, we can see that the source Observable emits two Observables. The first inner Observable emits four values, but only two of them ("a" and "b") are re-emitted. Before the third value is emitted the source Observable emits another inner Observable and the current one is unsubscribed. Then it carries on by re-emitting values from the new inner Observable.

Also, note that the inner Observable is consumed even after the source Observable completes.

So, how is this operator going to change the output from the same example we used for `concatAll()` and `mergeAll()`? Take a look at the following:

```
// higher_order_06.php
...
    ->map(function($value) use ($scheduler) {
        // ...
    })
    ->switchLatest()
    ->subscribe(new DebugSubject());
...
```

We know for sure we won't receive all values from all inner Observables because each one of them is created before the previous one completes:

```
$ php higher_order_06.php
01:26:24 [] onNext: #0: 0 (string)
01:26:25 [] onNext: #1: 0 (string)
01:26:26 [] onNext: #2: 0 (string)
01:26:27 [] onNext: #2: 1 (string)
01:26:27 [] onNext: #2: 2 (string)
01:26:27 [] onCompleted
```

Each inner Observable was able to emit only its first value, and then they were unsubscribed except for the last Observable. Since there are no more emissions from the source Observable, `switchLatest()` stays subscribed to it.

The combineLatest() operator

Both `concatAll()` and `mergeAll()` re-emit all values emitted by their inner Observable (or Observables) one by one. There's one more operator with a similar functionality, called `combineLatest()`.

In contrast to the previous two, `combineLatest()` takes arguments as an array of Observables and immediately subscribes to all of them. Then, the last value emitted by each Observable is internally stored in a buffer by `combineLatest()` and when all source Observables have emitted at least one value, it emits the entire buffer as a single array. Then on any emission from any of the source Observables the updated buffer is re-emitted again.

This is demonstrated in the following marble diagram:

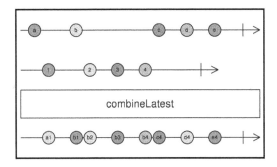

Marble diagram representing the combineLatest() operator in RxJS (http://reactivex.io/rxjs/class/es6/Observable.js)

Notice that when the first Observable emitted **a**, it wasn't immediately re-emitted. Only after the second Observable emits its first value the combineLatest() operator reemitted both of them. This means that, if we have an array of *N* Observables, the observer for combineLatest() will always receive an array of *N* values.

An important implication of this is that, if we had an Observable in the source array that, for some reason, didn't emit any value, then combineLatest() won't emit any value either because it needs to have at least one value for each source Observable. This can be easily avoided by using the startWith() or startWithArray() operators that prepend value emissions before the source Observable.

Consider the following example, where we have an Observable with just a single value, created using Observable::just(). We want to combine it using the combineLatest() operator with an array of IntervalObservable instances:

```php
// combine_latest_01.php

use React\EventLoop\StreamSelectLoop;
use Rx\Scheduler\EventLoopScheduler;
use Rx\Observable;

$loop = new StreamSelectLoop();
$scheduler = new EventLoopScheduler($loop);

$source = Observable::just(42)
  ->combineLatest([
    Observable::interval(175, $scheduler)->take(3),
    Observable::interval(250, $scheduler)->take(3),
    Observable::interval(100, $scheduler)->take(5),
  ])
  ->subscribe(new DebugSubject());

$loop->run();
```

We know for sure that the output array will always start with integer 42. This array will be emitted for every change in the array of source Observables.

Notice that the second IntervalObservable emits its first value after 250ms, while the third IntervalObservable emits its first value after just 100ms. This means that we'll never receive the first value from the third IntervalObservable. It'll never be re-emitted, because combineLatest() needs all Observables to emit at least one value, and in our case, it's going to wait for the second IntervalObservable, which is the slowest one.

The console output confirms our expected behavior:

```
$ php combine_latest_01.php
09:42:45 [] onNext: [42,0,0,1] (array)
09:42:46 [] onNext: [42,0,0,2] (array)
09:42:46 [] onNext: [42,1,0,2] (array)
09:42:46 [] onNext: [42,1,0,3] (array)
09:42:46 [] onNext: [42,1,1,3] (array)
09:42:46 [] onNext: [42,1,1,4] (array)
09:42:46 [] onNext: [42,2,1,4] (array)
09:42:46 [] onNext: [42,2,2,4] (array)
09:42:46 [] onCompleted
```

The last two emissions happened only because of the second `IntervalObservable`. Also, notice that, since every emission from the source Observables triggers `combineLatest()` to re-emit its current values, there's always only one updated value in the array.

If we want to be sure we'll catch all values emitted from all Observables, we can use `startWith()` to set default values for each of them:

```
...
->combineLatest([
  Observable::interval(175, $scheduler)->take(3)->startWith(null),
  Observable::interval(250, $scheduler)->take(3)->startWith(null),
  Observable::interval(100, $scheduler)->take(5)->startWith(null),
])
...
```

Now the output is going to start with `null` values, and we can be sure we'll receive all values from all source Observables:

```
$ php combine_latest_01.php
09:53:46 [] onNext: [42,null,null,null] (array)
09:53:46 [] onNext: [42,null,null,0] (array)
09:53:46 [] onNext: [42,0,null,0] (array)
09:53:46 [] onNext: [42,0,null,1] (array)
09:53:46 [] onNext: [42,0,0,1] (array)
09:53:46 [] onNext: [42,0,0,2] (array)
...
```

These four operators belong to a category of more advanced Rx features. Although these aren't commonly used in either RxPHP or RxJS, it's very useful to know that they exist, because it leverages the true power of Reactive Extensions. The internal logic provided by `switchMap()` or `combineLatest()` lets us avoid using any state variables to keep track of where we need to subscribe/unsubscribe and what values we need to store.

We'll encounter `combineLatest()` and `switchMap()` used in one operator chain in the next chapter. Also, in the final chapter of this book, when talking about similarities with RxJS, we'll use a slightly modified version of `combineLatest()` in JavaScript. The `concatAll()` and `mergeAll()` Operators are useful in RxJS as well, and we can do some tricks with them that aren't possible in RxPHP as of now; but more on that in the final chapter.

Summary

This chapter covered a lot of new topics. We're going to use all of what we just learned in the next chapter, where we'll use Unix sockets for inter-process communication and WebSocket server for a simple chat application. Most importantly, we're going to use spawning subprocesses with `ProcessObservable`, PHP Streams API for Unix socket communication. We are also going to look into event loops, including use cases, where we need to share the same instance of the event loop among Unix socket streams and a WebSocket server. Then we will move on to higher-order Observables to collect statuses from multiple subprocesses, and a WebSocket server and client. PHP Streams API and higher-order Observables are, in principle, a little harder to understand at first glance, so feel free to take your time and experiment by yourself.

In the next chapter, we'll also introduce the concept of backpressure in Rx, which is a common way to avoid overloading the consumer by emitting more values that the observer is able to process.

7
Implementing Socket IPC and WebSocket Server/Client

In the previous chapter, we had a sneak peek at the application we're about to build in this chapter. We already know that we'll use the PHP Streams API for interprocess communication. We'll also write WebSocket servers and, later, a simple WebSocket client. We also emphasized the importance of understanding how event loops work in an asynchronous and non-blocking application, and this will apply for both server and client applications in this chapter.

This chapter will also be very source code-intensive, so we'll split it into three smaller sections covering three different applications:

- **Server Manager application**: This is the application we'll run when testing this whole project. It'll spawn subprocesses and communicate with them via Unix socket streams (wrapped with the PHP Streams API). Each subprocess represents a single WebSocket server that listens to a specific port.
- **WebSocket Server application**: This is a single instance of the WebSocket server that allows multiple clients to be connected at the same time, enabling them to chat. This means we'll have to distribute each message to all clients in real time. We'll also keep a history of a few most recent messages that'll be populated to each new client. This application will communicate with the Server Manager via the Unix socket and provide its current status (the number of clients currently connected and the number of messages in the chat history).
- **WebSocket Client application**: This is our test client that'll connect to WebSocket servers and listen to the user input that'll be sent to the server.

Before we start working on the Server Manager application, we should talk about one more concept that arises mostly in an RxJS environment, but which is also very relevant to this chapter.

Backpressure in Reactive Extensions

We usually think of Observables as streams of data that are produced by the source Observable on one end and consumed by an observer at the other end. While this is still correct, we're not aware of situations where the Observable is emitting values so fast that the consumer (the observer) is not able to handle them.

This could lead to significant memory or CPU usage, which we definitely want to avoid.

There're two groups of operators suitable for backpressure, although most of them aren't available in RxPHP and are related mostly to RxJS:

- **Lossy**: In this group, some values are discarded and never arrive at the observers. For example, this could be the mouse position sampled over a certain timespan. We're usually interested in the current mouse position right now; we don't care about position in the past, and so this can be completely ignored.
- **Loss-less**: In this group, values are stacked in operators and are typically emitted in batches. We don't want to lose any data, so a typical inner implementation of a loss-less operator is a buffer.

As we said, backpressure is more typical for RxJS than RxPHP, but let's have a look at examples of both of these types in RxPHP.

Lossy backpressure

In the previous chapter, we used the `switchLatest()` operator to work with higher-order Observables. This automatically subscribed only to the latest Observable emitted from the source Observable and unsubscribed from the previous source. This is, in fact, a lossy operator because we know we're not guaranteed to receive all values.

In practice, we usually deal with use cases similar to the RxJS operator `throttleTime()`. This operator takes the timespan as a parameter, which defines how long after emitting a value it'll ignore all subsequent emissions from the source Observable.

We can have a look at its marble diagram to be clear as to what it does:

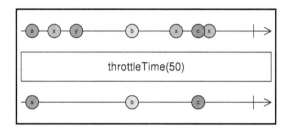

This operator is already implemented in RxPHP, but we can implement it ourselves using just `filter()`, or even better, by creating a custom operator to see how this and similar functionality can be implemented internally.

Implementing throttleTime() with the filter() operator

We can simulate a hot source Observable with the `IntervalObservable` class, which periodically emits values, and we'll filter out everything that arrives less than a second after the previous emission.

The following example simulates a similar functionality as the `throttleTime()` operator:

```
// filter_01.php
$loop = new StreamSelectLoop();
$scheduler = new EventLoopScheduler($loop);
$lastTimestamp = 0;

Observable::interval(150, $scheduler)
    ->filter(function() use (&$lastTimestamp) {
        if ($lastTimestamp + 1 <= microtime(true)) {
            $lastTimestamp = microtime(true);
            return true;
        } else {
            return false;
        }
    })
    ->subscribe(new DebugSubject());

$loop->run();
```

 From now on in this book we won't include the `use` statements for classes we've been using so far to keep the examples as short as possible.

If we run this example, we'll see that it does what we need:

```
$ php filter_01.php
14:51:01 [] onNext: 0 (integer)
14:51:02 [] onNext: 7 (integer)
14:51:03 [] onNext: 14 (integer)
14:51:04 [] onNext: 21 (integer)
...
```

As we can see, the `IntervalObservable` class emits ever-increasing counter values, where most of them are ignored. However, this is not a very systematic approach. We have to keep the last timestamp in a variable, which is what we usually want to avoid with Rx.

Note that our callable for `filter()` doesn't take any arguments (the current value) because it doesn't matter to us.

So let's reimplement this into a standalone `ThrottleTimeOperator` class:

```php
// ThrottleTimeOperator.php
class ThrottleTimeOperator implements OperatorInterface {
  private $duration;
  private $lastTimestamp = 0;

  public function __construct($duration) {
    $this->duration = $duration;
  }

  public function __invoke($observable, $observer, $sched=null) {
    $disposable = $observable->filter(function() use ($observer) {
      $now = microtime(true) * 1000;
      if ($this->lastTimestamp + $this->duration <= $now) {
        $this->lastTimestamp = $now;
        return true;
      } else {
        return false;
      }
    })->subscribe($observer);

    return $disposable;
  }
}
```

As we saw multiple times in previous chapters, when implementing custom operators we need to be aware of correctly propagating not only `onNext` signals, but also `onError` and `onComplete`. We can delegate all this responsibility by reusing already existing operators, which is in fact a recommended way of implementing new operators to Rx. This means that our operator just sets up a `filter()` operator that takes care of everything for us.

Using this operator is simple with the `lift()` method:

```php
// throttle_time_01.php
$loop = new StreamSelectLoop();
$scheduler = new EventLoopScheduler($loop);
$lastTimestamp = 0;

Observable::interval(150, $scheduler)
    ->lift(function()  {
        return new ThrottleTimeOperator(1000);
    })
    ->subscribe(new DebugSubject());

$loop->run();
```

The result printed to the console is exactly the same as we saw in the preceding code, so we don't need to list it here again.

So this is a lossy operator. All values that don't pass the predicate function to `filter()` are lost forever.

In RxJS 5, typical lossy operators are `audit()`, `auditTime()`, `throttle()`, `throttleTime()`, `debounce()`, `debounceTime()`, `sample()`, and `sampleTime()`. In RxJS 4, we also have the `pause()` operator.

Loss-less backpressure

Loss-less operators are those that don't discard any values. Values are just stacked and sent to observers in batches.

In RxPHP, we can use the `bufferWithCount()` operator that takes as an argument the number of items stored in the buffer before emitting them to the observers. Optionally, we can also specify the number of items from the beginning of the previous buffer we want to skip.

The marble diagram explains this very well (this operator is available in RxJS 5 as `bufferCount()`):

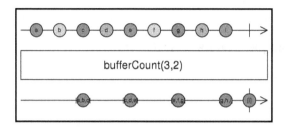

As you can see, using the `bufferWithCount()` operator is very simple. We'll use the same example as shown previously and just switch operators:

```
// buffer_with_count_01.php
$loop = new StreamSelectLoop();
$scheduler = new EventLoopScheduler($loop);
$lastTimestamp = 0;

Observable::interval(500, $scheduler)
    ->bufferWithCount(4)
    ->subscribe(new DebugSubject());

$loop->run();
```

We're always buffering four values, so when the source `IntervalObservable` class emits a value every 500 ms, the observer will receive a value every two seconds:

```
$ php buffer_with_count_01.php
15:24:24 [] onNext: [0,1,2,3] (array)
15:24:26 [] onNext: [4,5,6,7] (array)
15:24:28 [] onNext: [8,9,10,11] (array)
15:24:30 [] onNext: [12,13,14,15] (array)
```

RxJS 5 has five different buffer operator variants.

Both lossy and loss-less operators are useful, and we'll use the `throttleTime()` operator in a moment when implementing the Server Manager application.

Implementing ProcessObservable

The application in this chapter is going to spawn subprocesses a lot so it makes sense to wrap this functionality into a self-sufficient Observable. This Observable will spawn a new subprocess, emit its output with onNext and also properly handle onError and onComplete notifications:

```php
// ProcessObservable.php
class ProcessObservable extends Observable {
  private $cmd;
  private $pidFile;

  public function __construct($cmd, $pidFile = null) {
    $this->cmd = $cmd;
    $this->pidFile = $pidFile;
  }

  public function subscribe($observer, $scheduler = null) {
    $process = new Process($this->cmd);
    $process->start();

    $pid = $process->getPid();
    if ($this->pidFile) {
      file_put_contents($this->pidFile, $pid);
    }

    $disposable = new CompositeDisposable();
    $autoObs = new AutoDetachObserver($observer);
    $autoObs->setDisposable($disposable);

    $cancelDisp = $scheduler->schedulePeriodic(function()
        use ($autoObs, $process, $pid, &$cancelDisp) {
      if ($process->isRunning()) {
        $output = $process->getIncrementalOutput();
        if ($output) {
          $autoObs->onNext($output);
        }
      } elseif ($process->getExitCode() === 0) {
        $output = $process->getIncrementalOutput();
        if ($output) {
          $autoObs->onNext($output);
        }
        $autoObs->onCompleted();
      } else {
        $e = new Exception($process->getExitCodeText());
        $autoObs->onError($e);
      }
```

```
    }, 0, 200);

    $disposable->add($cancelDisp);
    $disposable->add(new CallbackDisposable(
        function() use ($process) {

      $process->stop(1, SIGTERM);
      if ($this->pidFile) {
        unlink($this->pidFile);
      }
    }));

    return $disposable;
  }
}
```

This Observable internally uses the Symfony\Component\Process\Process class from Symfony3 components, which makes working with subprocesses easier.

It periodically checks for any available output from the subprocess and emits it. When the process terminates, we send proper onError or onComplete notifications. We can also optionally create a file with the process PID if we need to.

Notice that we used the AutoDetachObserver class to wrap the original observer and assigned it the $disposable object. For now it's just important to know that this class automatically calls dispose() on the disposable we passed it when it receives onError or onComplete notification.

We'll explain the AutoDetachObserver class in more detail in Chapter 10, *Using Advanced Operators and Techniques in RxPHP*.

We can test this Observable with a small script simulating a long-running process:

```
// sleep.php
$name = $argv[1];
$time = intval($argv[2]);
$elapsed = 0;

while ($elapsed < $time) {
    sleep(1);
    $elapsed++;
    printf("$name: $elapsed\n");
}
```

Then we use the `ProcessObservable` to spawn this process and re-emit all its output:

```
// process_observable_01.php
$loop = new React\EventLoop\StreamSelectLoop();
$scheduler = new Rx\Scheduler\EventLoopScheduler($loop);

$pid = tempnam(sys_get_temp_dir(), 'pid_proc1');
$obs = new ProcessObservable('php sleep.php proc1 3', $pid);
$obs->subscribe(new DebugSubject(), $scheduler);

$loop->run();
```

This will just print one line every second and then end:

```
$ php process_observable_01.php
11:59:05 [] onNext: proc1: 1
  (string)
11:59:06 [] onNext: proc1: 2
  (string)
11:59:07 [] onNext: proc1: 3
  (string)
11:59:07 [] onCompleted
```

Now let's start with the main application for this chapter.

Server Manager application

Finally, we can start writing the largest application so far. The Server Manager is going to be a CLI application that will be responsible for spawning WebSocket servers, where each server is a standalone application itself, with its own clients and chat history.

A typical use-case could be a Unix server that manages multiple instances of some game server. Each server needs to be isolated. If any of them crashed, we don't want all games servers on this machine to crash as well. At the same time, we want to be able to collect some status information from servers and monitor them in real time with the Server Manager.

We can describe the structure of this entire application and what role the Server Manager has with the following diagram:

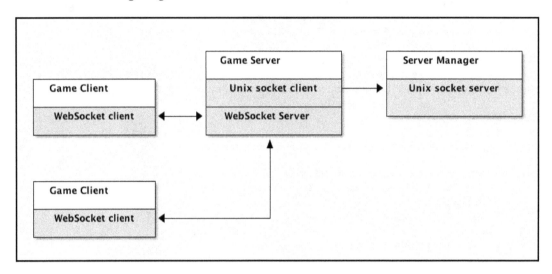

In this diagram, we can see the **Server Manager** application on the right. It communicates via Unix sockets with a single instance of **Game Server**. This instance of **Game Server** has two clients connected to it via WebSockets.

Communication between the **Server Manager** and the **Game Server** is only one way; the **Game Server** will actively send its status to the **Server Manager** itself. Communication between the **Game Server** and all its clients has to be two-way. When a user sends a message, we need to resend it to all other clients connected to the same **Game Server**.

We'll start with just creating a basic class stub that listens to user input via `stdin`, and, based on that, calls some action:

```
// ServerManager.php
class ServerManagerCommand extends Command {
  private $scheduler;
  private $loop;
  private $unixSocketFile;
  private $output;
  private $commands = [
    'n' => 'spawnNewServer',
    'q' => 'quit',
  ];

  protected function configure() {
    $this->setName('manager');
```

```
    $this->addArgument('socket_file',InputOption::VALUE_REQUIRED);
  }

  protected function execute($input, $output) {
    $this->output = $output;
    $this->unixSocketFile = $input->getArgument('socket_file');
    @mkdir(dirname($this->unixSocketFile), 0766, true);

    $loop = new React\EventLoop\StreamSelectLoop();
    $this->loop = $loop;
    $this->scheduler = new EventLoopScheduler($this->loop);

    $subject = new Subject();
    $stdin = $subject->asObservable();

    $stdinRes = fopen('php://stdin', 'r');
    $loop->addReadStream($stdinRes, function($s) use ($subject) {
      $str = trim(fgets($s, 1024));
      $subject->onNext($str);
    });

    foreach ($this->commands as $pattern => $method) {
      $stdin
        ->filter(function($string) use ($pattern) {
          return $pattern == $string;
        })
        ->subscribeCallback(function($value) use ($method) {
          $this->$method($value);
        });
    }

    // ... We'll continue here later

    $this->loop->run();
  }
}

$command = new ServerManagerCommand();
$application = new Application();
$application->add($command);
$application->setDefaultCommand($command->getName());
$application->run();
```

We created a stream from `php://stdin` and added it to the event loop. This is exactly what we've seen in the previous chapter when talking about the PHP Streams API. To make adding new commands easy, we created a `Subject` instance where we call `onNext()` on any user input.

We don't subscribe to the `Subject` instance directly, but rather to an Observable returned from its `asObservable()` method. Of course, we could subscribe directly to the `Subject` instance since it acts as an Observable and an observer at the same time. However, if anyone had access to the `Subject` instance, then we can't be sure that somebody won't call its `onNext()` or `onComplete()` by mistake, which might cause unpredictable behavior. For this reason, it's good practice to hide the fact that we're using `Subject` internally and expose only Observables using `asObservable()`.

We have two commands at this moment:

- n: This command spawns a new subprocess using `ProcessObservable` and adds its disposable to the list of running processes. We'll use these disposables to unsubscribe later. Each subprocess will be assigned a unique port number. This port will be used by the Game Server to start the WebSocket server.
- q: This command is used to quit this application. This means we need to call `dispose()` on all disposables from the array of active processes, close all Unix socket connections, and then stop the event loop.

We'll now implement creating new subprocesses and quitting the application. To quit the application, we'll need the array of all socket connections (`$processes` private property) that we don't have yet.

Creating new subprocesses with ProcessObservable

We don't need anything special to create a new subprocess, because we'll use the `ProcessObservable` class that we created previously. Each subprocess will have its own port number assigned, where it'll run its WebSocket server:

```
class ServerManager extends Command {
  /** @var DisposableInterface[] */
  private $processes = [];

  // ...

  private function spawnNewServer() {
    $port = $this->startPort++;
    $cmd = 'php GameServer.php game-server '
      . $this->unixSocketFile . ' ' . $port;
    $cmd = escapeshellcmd($cmd);
    $process = new ProcessObservable($cmd);
    $this->output->writeln('Spawning process on port '.$port);
```

```
    $this->processes[$port] = $process->subscribeCallback(
      null,
      function($e) use ($port) {
        $msg = sprintf('%d: Error "%s"', $port, $e);
        $this->output->writeln($msg);
      },
      function() use ($port) {
        $this->output->writeln(sprintf('%d: Ended', $port));
      }, $this->scheduler
    );
  }

  private function quit() {
    foreach ($this->servers as $server) {
      $server->close();
    }
    foreach ($this->processes as $process) {
      $process->dispose();
    }
    $this->loop->stop();
  }
}
```

We spawn a new subprocess and then subscribe to it to read its output. We're not, in fact, expecting to receive any output; we're doing this just in case the subprocess crashed and we want to see what happened.

Note that we're also passing the single instance of Scheduler to `subscribeCallback()` using `$this->scheduler`. We need to do this because `ProcessObservable` adds its own periodic timer to check for output from the subprocess. This is one of the cases where we need to be sure to use just a single event loop, as we were talking about in the previous chapter.

All disposables will be stored in the `$processes` array organized by their port numbers. It's important to keep references to all disposables so that we can end all subprocesses gently by just disposing them (`ProcessObservable` will send a `SIGTERM` signal).

Game Server application

We'll switch for a moment to the Game Server application. We'll only make the most essential part of it, the one that connects to the Unix socket server and periodically sends a value from `IntervalObservable`.

We want to do this to be able to test that the Server Manager receives and displays statuses correctly. This is the part where we'll use `switchMap()` and `combineLatest()` operators to work with higher-order Observables.

We won't bother with WebSocket implementation right now – that'll come later:

```php
// GameServer.php
class GameServer extends Command {
  /** @var StreamObservable */
  private $streamObservable;

  protected function configure() {
    $this->setName('game-server');
    $this->addArgument('socket_file',InputOption::VALUE_REQUIRED);
    $this->addArgument('port', InputOption::VALUE_REQUIRED);
  }

  protected function execute($input, $output) {
    $file = $input->getArgument('socket_file');
    $port = $input->getArgument('port');

    $client = stream_socket_client("unix://".$file, $errno, $err);
    stream_set_blocking($client, 0);

    $loop = new React\EventLoop\StreamSelectLoop();
    $this->streamObservable = new StreamObservable($client,$loop);
    $this->streamObservable->send('init', ['port' => $port]);
    $this->streamObservable->send('status', 'ready');
    $scheduler = new EventLoopScheduler($loop);

    Observable::interval(500, $scheduler)
      ->subscribeCallback(function($counter) {
        $this->streamObservable->send('status', $counter);
      });

    $loop->run();
    // WebSocket server will go here...
  }
}
```

Using the `stream_socket_client()` function, we connect to the Unix socket server.

Note that right after the connection is established we send two messages to the Server Manager. The first one is indicating that the subprocess is running with `init`, and it also indicates which port it's using (the port for the WebSocket server). The second message is `status` with just a string, `ready`". This is what we'll display in the Server Manager. Then we create `IntervalObservable`, which sends a status via the Unix socket stream every 500 ms.

We're using some mystery `StreamObservable` class that we haven't implemented yet. The Unix socket stream is, in fact, a two-way channel, so it makes sense to wrap its connection with an Observable for convenience. When it receives data, it calls `onNext()`, and when we close the connection, it calls `onComplete()`.

This Observable also sends data, so it might look like a `Subject` instance could better fit this purpose. Although it sends data via the `send()` method, it, in fact, writes directly to the stream with `fwrite()`. Subjects are designed to send data to observers, which is not our case.

The `StreamObservable` class is then a relatively simple Observable that adds its stream to the event loop and emits all the data it receives:

```
//  StreamObservable.php
class StreamObservable extends Observable {
  protected $stream;
  protected $subject;
  protected $loop;

  public function __construct($stream, LoopInterface $loop) {
    $this->stream = $stream;
    $this->loop = $loop;
    $this->subject = new Subject();

    $this->loop->addReadStream($this->stream, function ($stream) {
      $data = trim(fgets($stream));
      $this->subject->onNext($data);
    });
  }

  public function subscribe($observer, $scheduler = null) {
    return $this->subject->subscribe($observer);
  }

  public function send($type, $data) {
    $message = ['type' => $type, 'data' => $data];
    fwrite($this->stream, json_encode($message) . "\n");
  }
```

```
        public function close() {
          $this->loop->removeReadStream($this->stream);
          fclose($this->stream);
          $this->subject->onCompleted();
        }
    }
```

Now it should be obvious how the GameServer class works. After we implement the WebSocket server, we'll use the send() method on StreamObservable to report its status to the Server Manager. However, instead of using IntervalObservable and its incrementing counter, we'll send the number of clients connected and the number of messages in the chat history.

Let's go back to the Server Manager and implement the Unix socket server that is required to establish the connection between the Game Server and Server Manager.

Server Manager and the Unix socket server

In order to be able to use stream_socket_client() to connect to a socket server, we need to first create the server with stream_socket_server(). The principle is identical to what we saw in the previous chapter when explaining the example with a simple HTTP server, made just using stream_socket_server(), stream_socket_accept(), and StreamSelectLoop:

```
class ServerManager extends Command {
    // ...
    private $statusSubject;
    private $servers = [];

    protected function execute($input, $output) {
        // ...
        @unlink($this->unixSocketFile);
        $address = "unix://" . $this->unixSocketFile;
        $server = stream_socket_server($address, $errno, $errMsg);
        stream_set_blocking($server, 0);

        $this->loop->addReadStream($server, function() use ($server) {
          $client = stream_socket_accept($server);
          $server = new GameServerStreamEndpoint($client,$this->loop);

          $server->onInit()->then(function($port) use ($server) {
            $msg = sprintf('Sub-process %d initialized', $port);
            $this->output->writeln($msg);
            $this->addServer($port, $server);
```

```
      });
   });

   $this->statusSubject = new Subject();
   // ... We'll continue here later
}

private function addServer($port, $server) {
   $this->servers[$port] = $server;
   $this->statusSubject->onNext(null);
}
}
```

Accepting new connections via Unix sockets is analogous to TCP connections. In the GameServer class, we saw that the first status call it always makes after establishing the connection is "init", along with its port number to tell the Server Manager which Game Server is initialized and ready to start receiving WebSocket clients. We also said that we need to keep track of all active connections in order to be able to close them when we want to quit the application. Collecting statuses from each subprocess requires us to be able to distinguish which socket connection belongs to which subprocess (and which port we assigned to it).

This is why, when we accept a new connection, we wrap it with the GameServerStreamEndpoint class that has an onInit() method returning an instance of the Promise class. This Promise class is then resolved with the subprocess port number (see GameServer class) when the new connection sends its init status. After this, we finally add the connection into the array of connections (with port numbers as keys) using the addServer() method.

Note that we're keeping one array for processes (the $processes property) and another array for stream connections wrapped with GameServerStreamEndpoint (the $servers property).

Also note that at the end of the addServer() method, we call $statusSubject->onNext(null). This will trigger an update to the collection of subscriptions to subprocess statuses. We'll come to this in a moment.

Implementing the GameServerStreamEndpoint class

This class is going to combine the `StreamObservable` that we created a moment ago, Promises, the `Deferred` class, and Observables. This way, we can completely hide its internals where we decode the JSON strings received from the stream, and filter messages by their type:

```php
// GameServerStreamEndpoint.php
class GameServerStreamEndpoint {
  private $stream;
  private $initDeferred;
  private $status;

  public function __construct($stream, LoopInterface $loop) {
    $this->stream = new StreamObservable($stream, $loop);
    $this->initDeferred = new Deferred();

    $decodedMessage = $this->stream
      ->lift(function() {
        return new JSONDecodeOperator();
      });

    $unsubscribe = $decodedMessage
      ->filter(function($message) {
        return $message['type'] == 'init';
      })
      ->pluck('data')
      ->subscribeCallback(function($data) use (&$unsubscribe) {
        $this->initDeferred->resolve($data['port']);
        $unsubscribe->dispose();
      });

    $this->status = $decodedMessage
      ->filter(function($message) {
        return $message['type'] == 'status';
      })
      ->pluck('data')
      ->multicast(new ReplaySubject(1));
    $this->status->connect();
  }

  public function getStatus() {
    return $this->status;
  }
```

```
  public function onInit() {
    return $this->initDeferred->promise();
  }

  public function close() {
    return $this->stream->close();
  }
}
```

We subscribe to the `StreamObservable` instance to decode any incoming messages (the `$decodedMessage` variable). Then, with `filter()` operators, we pass through only messages of particular types.

If the message type is `init`, we resolve the `Promise` object returned from `onInit()`. We know there should never be multiple `init` calls, so we can unsubscribe right after that.

A slightly more complicated situation is when we receive the `status` message. We chain `$decodedMessage` with the `multicast()` operator. This is an operator we haven't met yet, and we'll look into it in more detail in the next chapter. For now, we just need to know that this operator subscribes to its source Observable using an instance of `Subject` that we provided, which in this case is `ReplaySubject`. Then, it returns a `ConnectableObservable` (see Chapter 3, *Writing a Reddit Reader with RxPHP*).

The important thing with `multicast()` is that it creates a single subscription to its source Observable. We're using `ReplaySubject` purposely because it remembers the last value it emitted, so if we subscribe to the Observable returned from `getStatus()` multiple times, we'll always receive the most recent value immediately.

There're multiple variants of the `multicast()` operator, each with a slightly different purpose, but more on that in Chapter 8, *Multicasting in RxPHP and PHP7 pthreads Extension*.

Displaying real-time statuses from subprocesses

In order to display the status of a single `GameServerStreamEndpoint`, we can subscribe to the Observable returned from `getStatus()`, which is, in fact, a `ConnectableObservable`.

However, our use-case isn't that simple. What if we spawn a new subprocess and want to subscribe to it as well? For *N* subprocesses, we need *N* subscriptions. Also, our requirement is to monitor all statuses in real time, so this looks like we could use the `combineLatest()` operator with an array of Observables (an array of Observables emitting statuses). The problem is that we don't know how many Observables we'll have because we're going to add them on the go by spawning new subprocesses.

One solution could be using `combineLatest()` to subscribe to all current status Observables and, when a new subprocess is created, unsubscribing and creating a new array of status Observables for the `combineLatest()` operator. This is, of course, doable, but there's a better and more elegant solution using the `switchLatest()` operator and higher-order Observables from `Chapter 6`, *PHP Streams API and Higher-Order Observables*.

We'll first demonstrate the principle on a separate example and then apply it to the `ServerManager` class.

Combining the switchLatest() and combineLatest() operators

Let's say we add a new server every 1000 ms, but one of the existing servers updates its status every 600 ms. This means we need to recreate a new Observable with `combineLatest()` every second from the current array of servers.

Consider the following example where we simulate this situation using two `IntervalObservables`:

```php
// switch_latest_01.php
$range = [1];
$loop = new StreamSelectLoop();
$scheduler = new EventLoopScheduler($loop);

$newServerTrigger = Observable::interval(1000, $scheduler);
$statusUpdate = Observable::interval(600, $scheduler)->publish();
$statusUpdate->connect(); // Make it hot Observable

$newServerTrigger
    ->map(function() use (&$range, $statusUpdate) {
        $range[] = count($range) + 1;
        $observables = array_map(function($val) {
            return Observable::just($val);
        }, $range);

        return $statusUpdate
            ->combineLatest($observables, function() {
                $values = func_get_args();
                array_shift($values);
                return $values;
            });
    })
    ->switchLatest()
    ->take(8)
```

```
    ->doOnCompleted(function() use ($loop) {
        $loop->stop();
    })
    ->subscribe(new DebugSubject());

$loop->run();
```

Instead of the array of servers, we use a `$range` variable that we're constantly expanding, and instead of real statuses, we just wrap values with `Observable::just()`.

The Observable `$statusUpdate` emits independently on the `$statusUpdate` Observable, which makes the `combineLatest()` operator sometimes re-emit the same values without any change, while being subscribed to the same array of Observables.

The core parts of this Observable chain are obviously `combineLatest()` and `switchLatest()`. Since `$newServerTrigger` represents adding a new server, we need to provide `combineLatest()` with a fresh array of Observables that we want to subscribe to. Then `switchLatest()` unsubscribes from the previous Observable returned by `combineLatest()` and subscribes to the new one.

You might wonder why we're using `func_get_args()` and `array_shift()` to get the values passed to the callable. The Operator `combineLatest()` passes values for each source Observable unpacked (*N* source Observables result in *N* function parameters), but we don't know how many source Observables we're going to have. That's why we take all arguments as a single array and then remove the first item. The first item is a value from `$statusUpdate` that is also included by `combineLatest()` as a source Observable, but for us it has no purpose, so we won't re-emit it.

 Note that the selector function for the `combineLatest()` is optional. If we don't provide it, the operator will just pass all values from all source Observables in a single array.

The output in the console will look as follows:

```
$ php switch_latest_01.php
12:18:32 [] onNext: [1,2] (array)
12:18:32 [] onNext: [1,2] (array)
12:18:33 [] onNext: [1,2,3] (array)
12:18:34 [] onNext: [1,2,3] (array)
12:18:34 [] onNext: [1,2,3,4] (array)
12:18:35 [] onNext: [1,2,3,4,5] (array)
12:19:25 [] onNext: [1,2,3,4,5] (array)
12:19:26 [] onNext: [1,2,3,4,5,6] (array)
22:54:16 [] onCompleted
```

The following is the timestamped order of events in this example:

- 1000 ms: The $newServerTrigger Observable fires for the first time and appends the second item to the $range array. The operator combineLatest() is now subscribed to two Observables created with Observable::just(). Since these are both cold, the combineLatest() re-emits their values immediately because it already has a value for each of them.
- 1200 ms: The $statusUpdate Observable fires (it's a hot Observable thanks to publish() and connect(), so it was emitting the event even though we weren't subscribed to it). This makes combineLatest() fire again.
- 1800 ms: The $statusUpdate Observable fires yet again, which makes combineLatest() emit for the third time. We get the same result as before because there're still only two Observables at this moment.
- 2000 ms: The $newServerTrigger Observable fires and appends a new item to $range. Now the combineLatest() operator subscribes to three Observables.

This goes on until we collect eight emissions in total (thanks to the take(8) operator). This was a really practical example of higher-order Observables in action.

We can reimplement it with the Server Manager application now:

```
class ServerManager extends Command {
  // ...
  protected function execute($input, $output) {
    // ...
    $this->statusSubject
      ->map(function() {
        $observables = array_map(function($server) {
          /** @var GameServerStreamEndpoint $server */
          return $server->getStatus();
        }, $this->servers);

        return Observable::just(true)
          ->combineLatest($observables, function($array) {
            $values = func_get_args();
            array_shift($values);
            return $values;
          });
      })
      ->switchLatest()
      ->map(function($statuses) {
        $updatedStatuses = [];
        $ports = array_keys($this->servers);
        foreach ($statuses as $index => $status) {
```

```
        $updatedStatuses[$ports[$index]] = $status;
      }
      return $updatedStatuses;
    })
    ->subscribeCallback(function($statuses) use ($output) {
      $output->write(sprintf("\033\143")); // clean screen
      foreach ($statuses as $port => $status) {
        $str = sprintf("%d: %s", $port, $status);
        $output->writeln($str);
      }
    });

  // ...
  }
}
```

This is exactly the same chain of operators, just a little enhanced by adding port numbers for each status.

When we add a new server in the `addServer()` method, we trigger `$statusSubject`, which recreates the array of Observables with statuses. Then, when the status of any of the servers is updated, it triggers `combineLatest()` directly because that's the only subscriber for them.

Now it should also make sense why we used `ReplaySubject` when writing `GameServerStreamEndpoint`. When we resubscribe to already existing status Observables, we want to have at latest one value always available, so that `combineLatest()` doesn't have to wait until all of its source Observables emit a value. They already did thanks to `ReplaySubject`, which emits the latest value right on subscription.

We can test how this works by running the `ServerManager.php` script. The `GameServer` instances will periodically emit values with `IntervalObservable` now, so we should already be getting status updates.

So let's start the `ServerManager.php` application:

```
$ php ServerManager.php manager ./var/server.sock
Listening on socket ./var/server.sock
Running ...
```

This command takes a path to the Unix socket file as an argument. It automatically passes this file path to all subprocesses so they know where they should try to connect. Now, we can press *n* characters followed by the *Enter* key to spawn a couple of subprocesses. Each subprocess first sends the `ready` status and then starts emitting values from the `IntervalObservable` class.

The output could look like the following:

```
8888: 28
8889: 15
8890: 14
8891: ready
```

Then you can press *Q* followed by the *Enter* key to gracefully quit the application.

 Notice that we used the operator chain `map(callback)->switchLatest()`. This combination of operators has a shortcut `flatMapLatest(callback)`. However, to make our code more explicit we'll typically use the longer and more obvious variant.

Finally, we can implement the WebSocket server and client.

Implementing a WebSocket server

To implement a WebSocket server, we'll use a library called `cboden/ratchet`:

```
$ composer require cboden/ratchet
```

A WebSocket server is represented by a class implementing the `MessageComponentInterface` interface with four methods `onOpen()`, `onClose()`, `onError()`, and `onMessage()`. How this class behaves on each of the events is up to the developer. Usually in chat applications, we want to keep all active connections in an array of clients and read messages, with `onMessage()` to resend them to all clients.

We'll first implement only the required methods and then add some custom ones as well:

```php
// ChatServer.php
use Ratchet\MessageComponentInterface;
use Ratchet\ConnectionInterface;

class ChatServer implements MessageComponentInterface {
  private $connections;
  private $history = [];
  private $subject;
```

```php
  public function __construct() {
    $this->subject = new Subject();
  }

  public function onOpen(ConnectionInterface $conn) {
    $this->connections[] = $conn;
    foreach (array_slice($this->history, -5, 5) as $msg) {
      $conn->send($msg);
    }
    $this->subject->onNext(null);
  }

  public function onMessage(ConnectionInterface $from, $msg) {
    $this->history[] = $msg;
    foreach ($this->connections as $conn) {
      if ($from !== $conn) {
        $conn->send($msg);
      }
    }
    $this->subject->onNext(null);
  }

  public function onClose(ConnectionInterface $conn) {
    foreach ($this->connections as $index => $client) {
      if ($conn !== $client) {
        unset($this->connections[$index]);
      }
    }
    $this->subject->onNext(null);
  }

  public function onError(ConnectionInterface $conn, $e) {
    $this->onClose($conn);
  }
}
```

It should be obvious what this code does without any further explanation. Just note that we're using $subject to signal that its status has changed and needs to be sent to the Server Manager via Unix sockets.

Now we can add more methods. In particular, we'll need `getObservable()`, where we'll subscribe to be notified with the current statuses:

```
class ChatServer implements MessageComponentInterface {
  // ...
  public function getObservable() {
    return $this->subject
      ->map(function() {
        return sprintf('clients: %d, messages: %d',
          $this->getClientsCount(),
          $this->getChatHistoryCount()
        );
      });
  }

  private function getClientsCount() {
    return count($this->connections);
  }

  private function getChatHistoryCount() {
    return count($this->history);
  }
}
```

This class itself isn't enough to start a WebSocket server.

The WebSocket connection is first established as a normal HTTP connection, and then it's upgraded to a WebSocket connection.

Back in the `GameServer` class, we subscribe to the Observable returned from the `getObservable()` method to be notified when the status for this chat server changes and needs to be sent to the Server Manager. The status of the chat server is represented by the current number of clients and the total number of messages in the chat history:

```
class GameServer extends Command {
  // ...
  protected function execute($input, $output) {
    // ...
    $webSocketServer = new ChatServer();
    $socket = new Reactor($loop);
    $socket->listen($port, '0.0.0.0');
    $server = new IoServer(
      new HttpServer(new WsServer($webSocketServer)),
      $socket,
      $loop
    );
```

```
$webSocketServer->getObservable()
  ->subscribeCallback(function($status) {
    $this->streamObservable->send('status', $status);
  });

$server->run();
  }
}
```

When we're already in the `GameServer` class, we can see how to use backpressure in practice. With multiple Game Servers, where each is emitting values multiple times a second, we might want to use `ThrottleTimeOperator` to limit emissions via the Unix socket stream:

```
Observable::interval(500, $scheduler)
  ->lift(function() {
    return new ThrottleTimeOperator(2000);
  })
  ->subscribeCallback(function($counter) {
    $this->streamObservable->send('status', $counter);
  });
```

Now, each `GameServer` class will send its status at most once every two seconds. In a real-world application, we'll obviously not use `IntervalObservable`, and leave emitting statuses to `$webSocketServer->getObservable()`. Either way, the use of backpressure and `ThrottleTimeOperator` remains the same.

Implementing a WebSocket client

To implement a WebSocket client, we're going to use another PHP library called `ratchet/pawl`:

> **$ composer require ratchet/pawl 0.2.2**

The client will read input from `php://stdin` and send it via WebSocket to the server. It'll also watch for any incoming messages and print them to the console:

```
// GameClient.php
use function Ratchet\Client\connect;

class GameClient extends Command {
  protected function configure() {
    $this->setName('chat-client');
    $this->addArgument('port', InputArgument::REQUIRED);
    $this->addArgument('address', InputArgument::OPTIONAL,
```

```
                  '', '127.0.0.1');
        }

        protected function execute($input, $output) {
           $port = $input->getArgument('port');
           $address = $input->getArgument('address');

           $stdin = fopen('php://stdin', 'r');
           $loop = new StreamSelectLoop();

           connect('ws://' . $address . ':' . $port, [], [], $loop)
              ->then(function($conn) use ($loop, $stdin, $output) {
                 $loop->addReadStream($stdin,
                    function($stream) use ($conn, $output) {
                       $str = trim(fgets($stream, 1024));
                       $conn->send($str);
                       $output->writeln("> ${str}");
                    });

                 $conn->on('message', function($str) use ($conn,$output){
                    $output->writeln("< ${str}");
                 });
              }, function ($e) use ($output) {
                 $msg = "Could not connect: {$e->getMessage()}";
                 $output->writeln($msg);
              });
        }
    }
```

The WebSocket client is created using the connect() function, where, as a protocol, we use ws. This method returns a Promise that's resolved with the WebSocket connection object when the connection is established or otherwise rejected. This function also requires an event loop where we have to provide our single instance of StreamSelectLoop. The same event loop is used to read from the fopen() stream.

If we didn't provide the event loop directly, the connect() function would create its own instance internally. This loop would cause exactly what we described in the previous chapter, and the inner loop reading from the php://stdin stream would never run.

We also use this connection object to set up event listeners with the on() method and to send data to the server with the send() method. All sent messages are prefixed with >, while all received messages are prefixed with <.

Now we can use this client to test the real usage of the Server Manager. If we run three instances of `GameClient` and send some example messages, the output might look like the following:

```
$ php GameClient.php chat-client 8890
Hello, World!
> Hello, World!
< Test!
```

Then, monitoring real-time statuses might look like this:

```
8888: ready
8889: clients: 1, messages: 0
8890: clients: 1, messages: 2
8891: ready
```

Any new WebSocket client or any new message causes an immediate update to this overview.

Summary

This chapter was really code intensive, with a lot of examples based on using Unix sockets and WebSockets. We also utilized a lot of what we've learned in this and the previous chapter, including higher-order Observables, with `swtichLatest()` and `combineLatest()`, backpressure and which operators we can use, using event loops with multiple streams, and using the `multicast()` operator to share a single subscription among multiple observers.

In the next chapter, we'll have a look at multicasting in Rx and start using the `pthreads` PHP extension to leverage true parallelism with threads that would normally be hardly achievable.

8
Multicasting in RxPHP and PHP7 pthreads Extension

To make use of multiple CPUs and multiple cores, we've been using subprocesses. This is, of course, a very easy and safe method to run code in parallel. In combination with Unix sockets, we can make inter-process communication happen with ease. In the previous chapter, we combined all of this with RxPHP to make applications that were completely separated and run in parallel.

In this chapter, we'll have a look at a very interesting PHP7 extension called `pthreads`, which allows multithreading in PHP using POSIX threads.

In particular, this chapter will cover the following topics:

- A deeper look into the `Subject` class and its variants.
- Multicasting operators in RxPHP and all its derivatives
- Examples of `ConnectableObservable` and `MulticastObservable`
- Using a single instance of the Subject with multiple source Observables
- Basics of multithreading in PHP
- Notes on today's state of the `pthreads` extension, its two major versions, and its current practical usage
- Writing a couple of multithreaded applications with the `pthreads` extension that'll demonstrate how to use the `Thread`, `Worker`, and `Poll` classes

Before we go parallel, we should have a look at yet another feature of Reactive Extensions called multicasting, which involves the `multicast()` operator and its derivates. Multicasting is build around Subjects so let's first have a better look at what different types of Subject are available to us.

Subjects

We've been using Subjects in this book since Chapter 2, *Reactive Programming with RxPHP*, but there're multiple different variants of the Subject class for more specific use cases where all of them are relevant to multicasting.

BehaviorSubject

The BehaviorSubject class extends the default Subject class and lets us set a default value that is passed to its observer right on subscription. Consider this very simple example of BehaviorSubject:

```
// behaviorSubject_01.php
use Rx\Subject\BehaviorSubject;

$subject = new BehaviorSubject(42);
$subject->subscribe(new DebugSubject());
```

When DebugSubject subscribes to the BehaviorSubject class, the default value 42 is emitted immediately. This is a similar functionality to using the startWith() operator.

The output is then just a single line:

```
$ php behaviorSubject_01.php
15:11:54 [] onNext: 42 (integer)
```

ReplaySubject

The ReplaySubject class internally contains an array of the last N values it received and automatically re-emits them to every new observer on subscription.

In the following example, we subscribe to RangeObservable, which immediately emits all its values to the ReplaySubject class. The last three values are always stored in an array and when we later subscribe with the DebugSubject class, it'll immediately receive all three of them:

```
// replaySubject_01.php
use Rx\Subject\ReplaySubject;
$subject = new ReplaySubject(3);

Observable::range(1, 8)
    ->subscribe($subject);
```

```
$subject->subscribe(new DebugSubject());
```

The output consists of the last three values that the `ReplaySubject` class received:

```
$ php replaySubject_01.php
15:46:30 [] onNext: 6 (integer)
15:46:30 [] onNext: 7 (integer)
15:46:30 [] onNext: 8 (integer)
15:46:30 [] onCompleted
```

Notice, that we also received the `complete` signal, which is correct because it was emitted by `RangeObservable`.

AsyncSubject

The last Subject type RxPHP offers out of the box is called `AsyncSubject`, which might seem a little confusing. The only thing this Subject does is that it emits only the last value it received before receiving the `complete` signal.

We'll demonstrate this Subject on a similar example to the previous one. We'll just switch the order of actions and we'll subscribe the `DebugSubject` class before subscribing to the source Observable to see that it silently suppresses all values except the last one:

```
// asyncSubject_01.php
use Rx\Subject\AsyncSubject;
$subject = new AsyncSubject();
$subject->subscribe(new DebugSubject());

Observable::range(1, 8)
    ->subscribe($subject);
```

The output is only the last value emitted by the source `RangeObservable`:

```
$ php asyncSubject_01.php
16:00:46 [] onNext: 8 (integer)
16:00:46 [] onCompleted
```

Now we know everything we need to start working with multicasting and the `multicast()` operator in particular.

Multicasting in RxPHP

In Reactive Extensions, multicasting means sharing a single subscription among multiple observers via an instance of a `Subject` class. All multicasting operators are internally based on the general `multicast()` operator that implements their most common functionality. Of course, we're not limited to only using the `Subject` class and we'll use `ReplaySubject` and `BehaviorSubject` as well.

Multicasting is common to all Rx implementations, so knowledge of how it works inside is generally useful.

The multicast() operator and ConnectableObservable

The `multicast()` operator returns `ConnectableObservable` or `MulticastObservable` based on what arguments we pass. We'll first have a look at how it works with `ConnectableObservable`, because this should be very familiar to us.

A typical use case could look like the following example:

```
// multicast_01.php
$observable = Rx\Observable::defer(function() {
        printf("Observable::defer\n");
        return Observable::range(1, 3);
    })
    ->multicast(new Subject());

$observable->subscribe(new DebugSubject('1'));
$observable->subscribe(new DebugSubject('2'));
$observable->connect();
```

Instead of instantiating `ConnectableObservable`, we used the `multicast()` operator to do it for us.

In this example, we created a single source Observable and subscribed two observers to it. Then, after calling `connect()`, the `ConnectableObservable` class subscribed to an instance of `AnonymousObservable` returned from the `Observable::defer` static method.

As we can see, the `multicast()` operator returns an instance of `ConnectableObservable`. The result from this example is as follows:

```
$ php multicast_01.php
Observable::defer
10:43:42 [1] onNext: 1 (integer)
10:43:42 [2] onNext: 1 (integer)
10:43:42 [1] onNext: 2 (integer)
10:43:42 [2] onNext: 2 (integer)
18:12:16 [1] onNext: 3 (integer)
18:12:16 [2] onNext: 3 (integer)
10:43:42 [1] onCompleted
10:43:42 [2] onCompleted
```

All observers subscribe to the same instance of the Subject that we passed. This is an important implication that we need to be aware of.

In a moment, we'll have a look at a slightly modified version of this example that passes different arguments to `multicast()`.

MulticastObservable

Another Observable used for multicasting is called `MulticastObservable`. Its usage is similar to `ConnectableObservable`, but its internal functionality is very different. Consider the following example:

```
// multicastObservable_01.php
$source = Rx\Observable::defer(function() {
    printf("Observable::defer\n");
    return Observable::range(1, 3);
});

$observable = new MulticastObservable($source, function() {
    return new Subject();
}, function (ConnectableObservable $connectable) {
    return $connectable->startWith('start');
});

$observable->subscribe(new DebugSubject('1'));
$observable->subscribe(new DebugSubject('2'));
```

When subscribing to `MulticastObservable`, it internally calls the `multicast()` operator on the source Observable (which returns `ConnectableObservable`, as we saw in the previous example) and runs the first callable to create an instance of the `Subject` class. This is the first major difference to using just `multicast()`, where we always shared the same instance of the `Subject` class. The `MulticastObservable`, in contrast, creates a new `Subject` for every subscriber.

So internally, we have an instance of `ConnectableObservable`. Then it calls the second callable with this `ConnectableObservable` passed as an argument, which means we can further chain operators to it, or we could even use a completely different Observable (just remember this method has to return an Observable because the operator will internally subscribe to it).

This callable is often called the **selector function** because it lets us select where we want to subscribe. After that, `MulticastObservable` subscribes to the Observable returned and calls the `connect()` method on the `ConnectableObservable`.

In our example, we create a new instance of the `Subject` class for every subscriber and then chain `startWith()` with the `ConnectableObservable`, which makes it emit a single value before emitting values from the source.

The output will look like the following:

```
$ php multicastObservable_01.php
12:54:20 [1] onNext: start (string)
Observable::defer
12:54:20 [1] onNext: 1 (integer)
12:54:20 [1] onNext: 2 (integer)
12:54:20 [1] onNext: 3 (integer)
12:54:20 [1] onCompleted
12:54:20 [2] onNext: start (string)
Observable::defer
12:54:20 [2] onNext: 1 (integer)
12:54:20 [2] onNext: 2 (integer)
12:54:20 [2] onNext: 3 (integer)
12:54:20 [2] onCompleted
```

Note that the deferred Observable was called twice, which is correct. Each observer has its own instances of the Subject and `ConnectableObservable`. We have full control of what Subjects we're using for multicasting instead of leaving it to the default `multicast()` behavior.

The question is, why does it matter whether we're using the same instance of the Subject or not?

Subjects and their internal state

We know how to use Subjects. We also know what the `next`, `complete`, and `error` signals do. So what happens if we use a single `Subject` and subscribe to a cold Observable multiple times? Consider the following example:

```
// subject_01.php
$subject = new Subject();

$subject->subscribe(new DebugSubject('1'));
$subject->onNext(1);
$subject->onNext(2);
$subject->onNext(3);
$subject->onCompleted();

$subject->subscribe(new DebugSubject('2'));
$subject->onNext(4);
$subject->onCompleted();
```

We'll run this example and talk about what happens inside the `Subject` instance. Note that we subscribed to the `Subject` twice where the first observer (represented by `DebugSubject`) receives the first three values and then emits the `complete` signal.

However, what happens with the second observer?

```
$ php subject_01.php
13:15:00 [1] onNext: 1 (integer)
13:15:00 [1] onNext: 2 (integer)
13:15:00 [1] onNext: 3 (integer)
13:15:00 [1] onCompleted
13:15:00 [2] onCompleted
```

The second observer received just the `complete` signal, and none of the observers received the value `4`.

It's very important to understand what happens internally inside a `Subject` class when it receives a `complete` signal (this means it receives a `complete` signal or we call the `onCompleted()` method manually):

1. The `Subject` class checks whether it's already been marked as stopped. If it has, then the method returns immediately. If it's not stopped, then it marks itself as stopped.
2. The complete signals are then sent to all observers.
3. The array of observers is emptied.

So now it should make sense. The first three values were emitted as usual. Then we called `onComplete()`, which did exactly what we described in these bullet points. At this point, this `Subject` instance has no observers (see step 4). Then we subscribe with another observer, which is added to the array of observers. This observer immediately receives a `complete` signal because the Subject is already stopped and didn't end with an error.

At this point, calling `onNext(4)` does nothing because the `Subject` instance is already stopped (see step 1).

This principle might be a problem in situations where we purposely want to defer creating Observables with, for example, the `Observable::defer` static method that will be called multiple times. Once it sends the `complete` signal, all consecutive values will be ignored by the `Subject` instance for the reasons we explained. We'll have another example featuring this issue later in this chapter.

This is a very important principle we need to be aware of when using `multicast()` operators and the `ConnectableObservable`.

Whether this applies to `MulticastObservable` is up to us, depending on what we return from its first callable. We can use the same instance of `Subject` or we can create a new one depending on what we want to achieve.

 If this all looks confusing, just remember that Subjects have an internal state. When they receive `complete` or `error` notification, they'll never re-emit any value further.

The multicast() operator and MulticastObservable

So let's go back to the `multicast()` operator and see how `MulticastObservable` is related to all this. We said that `multicast()` returns `ConnectableObservable` or `MulticastObservable` depending on the arguments we use. This is true when we use the second argument to `multicast()`.

Consider the following example, where we also pass a selector function to the `multicast()` operator:

```
// multicast_02.php
use Rx\Observable;
use Rx\Subject\Subject;

$subject = new Subject();
```

```
$source = Observable::range(1, 3)
    ->multicast($subject, function($connectable) {
        return $connectable->concat(Observable::just('start'));
    })
    ->concat(Observable::just('concat'));

$source->subscribe(new DebugSubject());
$source->subscribe(new DebugSubject());
```

If we use the second argument to multicast(), it wraps the $subject variable with a callable before it's passed to MulticastObservable. In fact, multicast() is internally implemented as the following:

```
function multicast($subject, $selector=null, $scheduler=null){
    return $selector ?
      new MulticastObservable($this, function () use ($subject) {
        return $subject;
      }, $selector) :
      new ConnectableObservable($this, $subject, $scheduler);
}
```

This always guarantees that we're using the same Subject. The only thing that decides which Observable we'll receive is whether we use the selector function or not. The preceding example also adds the startWith() and concat() operators to see what effect this selector function can have.

The output for this example is affected by the issue we showed earlier:

```
$ php multicast_02.php
13:41:23 [] onNext: start (string)
13:41:23 [] onNext: 1 (integer)
13:41:23 [] onNext: 2 (integer)
13:41:23 [] onNext: 3 (integer)
13:41:23 [] onNext: concat (string)
13:41:23 [] onCompleted
13:41:23 [] onNext: start (string)
13:41:23 [] onNext: concat (string)
13:41:23 [] onCompleted
```

The second subscriber hasn't received any value, even though we subscribed twice to the source Observable.

Comparing ConnectableObservable and MulticastObservable

To be extra clear about the difference between these two use cases and
`ConnectableObservable` and `MulticastObservable`, let's have a look at these two
diagrams:

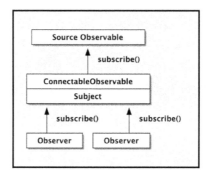

Diagram representing a ConnectableObservable with two observers

In this diagram, we have a single `ConnectableObservable` that internally contains one
`Subject`. Both observers are subscribed to the same `Subject`.

On the other hand, with `MulticastObservable` we'll get the following structure:

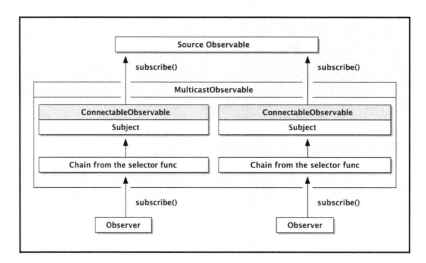

Diagram representing a MulticastObservable with two observers

The two `ConnectableObservables` inside the grey boxes mean we have no control over them (these are created automatically by the internal `multicast()` call, as mentioned earlier).

As we can see from the examples, with `MulticastObservable` created via the `multicast()` call, we won't be able to achieve the same result as we see in this image because `multicast()` always forces us to use a single Subject instance. Of course, we could always create an instance of `MulticastObservable` ourselves, as we saw earlier in this chapter, but there's also an operator for this purpose that we can use.

The multicastWithSelector() operator

To simplify creating instances of `MulticastObservable`, we have the `multicastWithSelector()` operator, which takes two callables as arguments that have the same purpose as calling `MulticastObservable` itself.

Consider the following example:

```
// multicastWithSelector_01.php
$source = Observable::range(1, 3)
    ->multicastWithSelector(function() {
        return new Subject();
    }, function(ConnectableObservable $connectable) {
        return $connectable->concat(Observable::just('concat'));
    });

$source->subscribe(new DebugSubject());
$source->subscribe(new DebugSubject());
```

This example illustrates the diagram we saw previously. We have two observers where each has its own instance of `Subject`. We also made use of the selector function that appends a `concat` string at the end of the chain.

The output is then easily predictable:

```
$ php multicastWithSelector_01.php
15:05:56 [] onNext: 1 (integer)
15:05:56 [] onNext: 2 (integer)
15:05:56 [] onNext: 3 (integer)
15:05:56 [] onNext: concat (string)
15:05:56 [] onCompleted
15:05:56 [] onNext: 1 (integer)
15:05:56 [] onNext: 2 (integer)
15:05:56 [] onNext: 3 (integer)
```

```
15:05:56 [] onNext: concat (string)
15:05:56 [] onCompleted
```

This was an introduction to multicasting in Rx and the `multicast()` operator in RxPHP. Since there're a few other operators based on `multicast()`, we'll talk about them now when we know how `multicast()` behaves internally.

The publish*() and share*() operator groups

There're multiple other operators internally using the `multicast()` operator, and we can split them into two basic groups:

- `publish*()`: Operators starting with the word "publish" wrap the `multicast()` operator and call it with one of the `Subject` classes. All `publish*` variants accept an optional argument, which is the selector function that we talked about earlier. Therefore, all of them can return `ConnectableObservable` or `MulticastObservable` just like `multicast()`.
- `share*()`: Operators starting with the word "share" internally use the same `publish*` equivalent and chain it with the `refCount()` operator. All `share*` operators don't allow any selector function.

To understand the difference between the two groups, we need to first understand what the `refCount()` operator is.

The refCount() operator

We already know this very basic usage of `ConnectableObservable`. Let's consider the following example, and first see how we can call the `connect()` method manually and then switch to the `refCount()` operator:

```
// refCount_01.php
$source = Observable::create(function($observer) {
    $observer->onNext(1);
    $observer->onNext(2);
    $observer->onNext(3);
});
$conn = new Observable\ConnectableObservable($source);
$conn->subscribe(new DebugSubject('1'));
$conn->subscribe(new DebugSubject('2'));
$conn->connect();
```

This is simple. We have two observers subscribed to the `ConnectableObservable` waiting to call `connect()`, which subscribes to the source Observable (in this case `AnonymousObservable` with a custom subscribe function) and emits all values to both observers at the same time.

Note that we're purposely not using `RangeObservable` because we don't want to emit the `complete` signal:

```
$ php refCount_01.php
17:20:41 [1] onNext: 1 (integer)
17:20:41 [2] onNext: 1 (integer)
17:20:41 [1] onNext: 2 (integer)
17:20:41 [2] onNext: 2 (integer)
17:20:41 [1] onNext: 3 (integer)
17:20:41 [2] onNext: 3 (integer)
```

This is pretty simple, but we had to call `connect()` ourselves, which is sometimes alright. However, other times we can leave this logic to the `refCount()` operator.

Well, actually it's not an operator (it's not lifted to an Observable chain with the `lift()` method). It's just a method on `ConnectableObservable` that returns an instance of `RefCountObservable`.

This Observable internally subscribes and unsubscribes to the source Observable. When the first observer subscribes, it also calls `connect()` on the `ConnectableObservable`. Then when another observer subscribes, it does nothing because we've already subscribed. When unsubscribing, the procedure is exactly the opposite. If even the last observer unsubscribes, then `RefCountObservable` also unsubscribes the `ConnectableObservable`.

This has some interesting consequences. We can use `refCount()` to automatically subscribe when there's at least one observer, as we can see in this example:

```php
// refCount_02.php
$source = Rx\Observable::create(function ($observer) {
    $observer->onNext(1);
    $observer->onNext(2);
    $observer->onNext(3);
});
$conn = (new Rx\Observable\ConnectableObservable($source))
    ->refCount();

$conn->subscribe(new DebugSubject('1'));
$conn->subscribe(new DebugSubject('2'));
```

We have two observers again, but this time we're not calling `connect()` by ourselves. Instead, we're using `refCount()` to call the `connect()` method for us. Since we're sharing the same subscription to the source, only the first observer will receive values. The second observer doesn't cause another subscription to the source (as we can see from the preceding explanation):

```
$ php refCount_02.php
17:52:05 [1] onNext: 1 (integer)
17:52:05 [1] onNext: 2 (integer)
17:52:05 [1] onNext: 3 (integer)
```

However, if we unsubscribe after receiving values for the first observer (which causes unsubscription from `ConnectableObservable` inside `RefCountObservable`) and then subscribe again with the second observer, it'll make the source emit all its values because we have subscribed to it again:

```
// refCount_03.php
// ...
$sub = $conn->subscribe(new DebugSubject('1'));
$sub->dispose();
$conn->subscribe(new DebugSubject('2'));
```

When we called `dispose()`, we made `RefCountObservable` unsubscribe from its source because there are no more observers.

This example prints all values twice:

```
$ php refCount_03.php
17:53:29 [1] onNext: 1 (integer)
17:53:29 [1] onNext: 2 (integer)
17:53:29 [1] onNext: 3 (integer)
17:53:29 [2] onNext: 1 (integer)
17:53:29 [2] onNext: 2 (integer)
17:53:29 [2] onNext: 3 (integer)
```

Of course, we need to be sure we don't stop the inner `Subject` in `ConnectableObservable` as we talked about before. The `ConnectableObservable` class uses a single instance of `Subject`, so if it received a complete signal, then no unsubscription or subscription would change this.

The publish() and share() operators

Now we know what the `multicast()` and `refCount()` operators do, we can finally understand what `publish()` and `share()` do.

Using `publish()` is just a shortcut to calling `multicast()` with the `Subject` instance as a parameter. If we rewrote the very first example on the `multicast()` operator, it would look almost the same:

```
// publish_01.php
use Rx\Observable;
$observable = Observable::defer(function() {
        printf("Observable::defer\n");
        return Observable::range(1, 3);
    })
    ->publish();

$observable->subscribe(new DebugSubject('1'));
$observable->subscribe(new DebugSubject('2'));
$observable->connect();
```

The output for this demo is exactly the same as for `multicast_01.php`, so we don't need to reprint it here.

The `share()` Operator uses the `publish()->refCount()` chain internally, so we don't need to call `connect()` any more. However, the output is not the same.

The `RangeObservable` sent the complete signal, which marked the internal `Subject` in `ConnectableObservable` as stopped, so the second observer won't receive anything except the `complete` signal that is emitted by the `Subject` class right at the point of subscription (it's not emitted by the source Observable):

```
// share_01.php
use Rx\Observable;
$observable = Observable::defer(function() {
        printf("Observable::defer\n");
        return Observable::range(1, 3);
    })
    ->share();

$observable->subscribe(new DebugSubject('1'));
$observable->subscribe(new DebugSubject('2'));
```

From the output, we can see that the source Observable is really created just once:

```
$ php share_01.php
Observable::defer
18:17:12 [1] onNext: 1 (integer)
18:17:12 [1] onNext: 2 (integer)
18:17:12 [1] onNext: 3 (integer)
18:17:12 [1] onCompleted
18:17:12 [2] onCompleted
```

These two basic operators have many variants, but are based on the same principle.

The publishValue() and shareValue() operators

These operators are based on `BehaviorSubject` instead of just `Subject`. The principle is then exactly the same. The `publishValue()` operator calls `multicast()` with an instance of `BehaviorSubject`. Then the `shareValue()` operator calls `publishValue()->refCount()`.

Using `BehaviorSubject` allows us to set the default value that is emitted to all observers when they subscribe.

We can test this operator on the same example as before:

```
// publishValue_01.php
$source = Observable::defer(function() {
        printf("Observable::defer\n");
        return Observable::range(1, 3);
    })
    ->publishValue('default');

$source->subscribe(new DebugSubject());
$source->subscribe(new DebugSubject());
$source->connect();
```

The output always starts with the default string because it's emitted by `BehaviorSubject` as the first value:

```
$ php publishValue_01.php
18:47:17 [] onNext: default (string)
18:47:17 [] onNext: default (string)
Observable::defer
18:47:17 [] onNext: 1 (integer)
18:47:17 [] onNext: 1 (integer)
18:47:17 [] onNext: 2 (integer)
```

```
18:47:17 [] onNext: 2 (integer)
18:47:17 [] onNext: 3 (integer)
18:47:17 [] onNext: 3 (integer)
18:47:17 [] onCompleted
18:47:17 [] onCompleted
```

Using `shareValue()` is the same as using `share()`, so we don't need to include it here.

The replay(), shareReplay(), and publishLast() operators

All these share exactly the same principle as the previous two operators, just based on `ReplaySubject` (`replay()` and `shareReplay()`) or `AsyncSubject` (the `publishLast()` operator).

We don't need to include examples for those operators here because there would be nothing new for us to see.

PHP pthreads extension

Since the year 2000, PHP can be compiled as **thread safe**, which allows any process to run multiple instances of the PHP interpreter in multiple threads (one thread per PHP interpreter). Each PHP interpreter has its own isolated context which doesn't share any data (the "share nothing" philosophy) with others.

This is commonly used in web servers such as Apache (depending on its modules). Apache creates multiple subprocesses where each subprocess runs multiple threads with multiple PHP interpreters. Running interpreters in threads instead of subprocesses has its advantages and disadvantages.

Creating only threads is significantly faster and doesn't consume as much memory as creating subprocesses.

An obvious disadvantage is isolation. Even though all PHP interpreters run independently in threads, if any of them causes, for example, a "segmentation fault" error, then the entire process and all of its threads are terminated immediately. This even includes threads that didn't cause any error and that might be processing an HTTP request from another client at that moment.

This so-called **Server API** (**SAPI**) isn't very helpful to us. We need to be able to run our own pieces of code in threads ("user land multithreading"). The PHP extension pthreads is an object-oriented API that does exactly this. It takes our code and creates a new PHP interpreter, which then starts executing it.

Note that the PHP pthreads are based on POSIX threads, which means that when we create a thread using pthreads, we're creating a real thread and not forking or creating subprocesses underneath.

In some languages, such as Python, there are threads that behave like they're executing code in parallel, but in fact there's still just one single threaded Python interpreter switching from one "thread" to another. So there's no real parallelism.

However, PHP pthreads come with a cost, and it's important to understand at least a little of what's going on inside.

Prerequisites

In this chapter, we'll use the new pthreads v3, which means we need to use PHP7+. There's also the older pthreads v2, which is designed for PHP5. Since there are major differences in the internal implementations with these two versions, we'll stick only to the new one.

As we said earlier, in order to use the pthreads extension, PHP has to be compiled with the **Thread Safety** option enabled. This needs to be enabled when compiling PHP and can't be enabled later (if you're only downloading the PHP executable, make sure you're downloading the correct one, usually marked as ZTS).

A universal way to install pthreads is with the PECL tool, which should work on all platforms:

```
$ pecl install pthreads
```

Alternatively, if you're running OS X, you can use a homebrew tool that also enables it in PHP config files for you:

```
$ brew install php70-pthreads
```

 The current pthreads v3 can be enabled only when running PHP code in a standalone script. This means pthreads can't be part of any PHP application ran using for example php-fpm. In other words, we can use pthreads only in console applications and not it web applications.

Introduction to multithreading with pthreads in PHP7

The most basic example of pthreads in PHP can simply be the spawning of multiple threads and printing their results. We'll make random pauses with `sleep()` functions to simulate multiple long running tasks. Remember that in PHP the `sleep()` function is always blocking (it blocks the interpreter execution for a certain number of seconds):

```php
// threads_01.php
class MyThread extends Thread {
    protected $i;
    public function __construct($i) {
        $this->i = $i;
    }
    public function run() {
        sleep(rand(1, 5));
        printf("%d: done\n", $this->i);
    }
}

$threads = [];
foreach (range(0, 5) as $i) {
    $thread = new MyThread($i);
    $thread->start();
    $threads[] = $thread;
}

foreach ($threads as $thread) {
    $thread->join();
}
echo "All done\n";
```

A task is represented by a class extending the base `Thread` class and implementing its `run()` method. This `run()` method contains code that'll be run in a separate thread when we call `start()`. Note that we need to implement the `run()` method and not the `start()` method. The `start()` method is an internal method written in C that calls `run()` for us.

After we create and start each thread, we use the `join()` method, which blocks the current interpreter and waits until that particular thread finishes. If it's already finished, then it'll continue. By looping over all threads and calling `join()`, we effectively wait until all of them finish.

When we run this example, we'll get the following result (you'll get a different order since we're using random sleep intervals):

```
$ php threads_01.php
0: done
2: done
1: done
5: done
3: done
4: done
All done
```

We won't go into much depth when using the `pthreads` extension in this chapter. There are primarily three reasons for this, as of April 2017:

- **Documentation on pthreads is very insufficient**: Documentation on most of the classes and methods in pthreads contains very little information. There's at most one sentence, usually without any example, so it's mostly up to the developer to guess what it does.
- **Documentation, examples, and other sources of information are often obsolete**: The new pthreads v3 works only with PHP7. However, the official documentation at `http://php.net/manual/en/book.pthreads.php` covers only `pthreads` v2. In the meantime, `pthreads` internals have changed, so you might be surprised that some examples won't work at all. For example, the `Mutex` and `Cond` classes don't exist at all now.
- **Documentation is non-existent**: The new classes coming with pthreads v3 aren't documented at all. The official homepage `https://github.com/krakjoe/pthreads` mentions differences between the two versions, but doesn't contain any information on how to effectively use them. For example, the PHP documentation found at `http://php.net/manual/en/book.pthreads.php` doesn't mention the `Volatile` class at all.

This all means that using pthreads is a pain at this moment, and getting any relevant information is hard.

There are also caveats regarding having multiple PHP contexts that need to share data while staying completely isolated. Since we need to be aware of these issues, it's worth spending some time explaining what this means for us.

Getting/setting data from/to threads

In PHP, all objects are passed by reference by default. Consider the following example, where we pass an instance of `stdClass` to another object, where we modify it:

```php
// references_01.php
$obj = new stdClass();
$obj->prop = 'foo';

$obj2 = $obj;
printf("%d\n", $obj === $obj2);

class TestClass {
    public $obj;
    public $objCopy;

    public function copyObj() {
        $this->objCopy = $this->obj;
        $this->objCopy->prop2 = 'bar';
    }
}

$testObj = new TestClass();
$testObj->obj = $obj;
$testObj->copyObj();
printf("%d\n", $obj === $testObj->objCopy);
print_r($obj);
```

We created an instance of `stdClass` called `$obj`. Then we reassigned it to `$obj2` and compared the two with an identity operator (three equal signs ===). Then we pass the `$obj` to an instance of `TestClass`, where we do the same and also add one more property to it called `prop2`.

The output from this example is what we might expect:

```
$ php7 references_01.php
1
1
stdClass Object (
    [prop] => foo
    [prop2] => bar
)
```

All the variables reference the same object. This is what we're used to and what we're using in PHP all the time.

However, this can't work with `pthreads`. We're not allowed to share objects (memory addresses) among different PHP contexts. These have to always be isolated, which is the very basic premise for thread-safe execution. We can test this with a very simple example, following on from the previous one:

```php
// threads_02.php
class MyThread extends Thread {
    public $obj;
    public $objCopy;

    public function run() {
        $this->objCopy = $this->obj;
        $this->objCopy->prop2 = 'bar';
        printf("%d\n", $this->obj === $this->obj);
    }
}

$obj = new stdClass();
$obj->prop = 'foo';

$thread = new MyThread($obj);
$thread->obj = $obj;
$thread->start();
$thread->join();

printf("%d\n", $obj === $thread->objCopy);
print_r($obj);
```

In this example, we're using the identity operator to compare `$this->obj` with another variable that should be referencing the same object.

Now let's see what happens when we run this example:

```
$ php threads_02.php
0
0
stdClass Object (
    [prop] => foo
)
```

All the comparisons return `false`. Even the most obvious one, `$this->obj === $this->obj`, returns `false`.

In `pthreads`, it has to work like this because PHP interpreters are isolated, and thus all read and write operations from the parent and other contexts need to be performed via copying data. However, there's an exception to this rule. Classes coming from the `pthreads` extension (including all their descendants) aren't copied, and are just referenced, as we'll see in a later example.

So in this example, we actually copied the object multiple times. Every call to `$this->obj` made a copy to the current context, as well as to the last `$thread->objCopy` statement.

The consequence of this principle is that we have to gather results from threads manually; we can't just pass an object to its constructor that will be populated with results by the thread itself.

A modified version of the first example would look like this:

```php
// threads_08.php
class MyThread extends Thread {
    protected $i;
    public $result;

    public function __construct($i) {
        $this->i = $i;
    }

    public function run() {
        sleep(rand(1, 5));
        printf("%d: done\n", $this->i);
        $this->result = pow($this->i, 2);
    }
}

$threads = [];
foreach (range(5, 7) as $i) {
    $thread = new MyThread($i);
    $thread->start();
    $threads[] = $thread;
}

foreach ($threads as $i => $thread) {
    $thread->join();
    printf("%d: %d\n", $i, $thread->result);
}
echo "All done\n";
```

This is basically the same demo as before; we're just storing results for each thread in a public property that we can later read after calling `join()`.

The output for this example is as follows:

```
$ php threads_08.php
7: done
5: done
6: done
0: 25
1: 36
2: 49
All done
```

Although creating threads is simple, if we had multiple threads it'd be hard to keep track of which threads are running and which are already finished. In real-world applications, it's usually not required to spawn many threads to be executed just once. Creating so many threads is inefficient and, most importantly, unnecessary.

Using Thread, Worker, and Pool classes

The `Thread` class represents a single interpreter context and a single task. When we want to run the same task multiple times, we need to create multiple instances of the same class and then join all the results (to wait until they're done).

There's also the `Worker` class. Similar to the `Thread` class, it represents a single interpreter context, but instead of doing a single job, it can stack jobs and execute them one after another.

We can take the previous `MyThread` class and this time we'll execute all tasks on a single `Worker`:

```
// threads_03.php

class MyThread extends Thread {
    protected $i;
    public $result;

    public function __construct($i) {
        $this->i = $i;
    }

    public function run() {
        sleep(rand(1, 5));
        printf("%d: done\n", $this->i);
```

```
            $this->result = pow($this->i, 2);
        }
    }

$worker = new Worker();
$threads = [];
foreach (range(1, 4) as $i) {
    $thread = new MyThread($i);
    $worker->stack($thread);
    $threads[] = $thread;
}

$worker->start();
echo "Starting worker\n";

// Add another task after the worker has started
$thread = new MyThread(42);
$worker->stack($thread);
$threads[] = $thread;
$worker->shutdown();

foreach ($threads as $i => $thread) {
    printf("%d: %d\n", $i, $thread->result);
}
echo "All done\n";
```

Since we have a single interpreter context, all tasks will be executed one after another. With the call to shutdown(), we make the Worker class wait until all stacked tasks are done. We can also add tasks to the worker after it's started the execution:

```
$ php7 threads_03.php
Starting worker
5: done
6: done
7: done
42: done
0: 25
1: 36
2: 49
3: 1764
All done
```

Note that tasks are run one after another and not in parallel.

We used the default `Worker` class provided by `pthreads`, but we can make our own class extending from `Worker` as well. For example, consider the following class:

```
class MyWorker extends Worker {
    public function run() {
        // ... Initialize this Worker and its context.
    }
}
```

This class extends the `run()` method just like the `Thread` class. The `Worker` class's `run()` method, however, is called only once when initializing the PHP interpreter context, and allows us to set up the `Worker` class.

We can, of course, create multiple `Worker` instances and stack tasks on them, but handling which workers are available and which workers are busy would be tedious.

For this reason, `pthreads` have the `Pool` class. It can contain a number of workers and distribute tasks among them. We don't need to worry about selecting the correct worker, and can leave everything to the `Pool` class.

Now let's consider the following example, where we'll use a `Pool` of three `Worker` classes to perform six tasks in total:

```
// threads_04.php
class MyWorker extends Worker {
    public function run() {
        printf("%s: starting worker\n", date('H:i:s'));
    }
}
class Task extends Threaded {
    public function run() {
        sleep(3);
        printf("%s: done\n", date('H:i:s'));
    }
}
printf("%s: start\n", date('H:i:s'));
$pool = new Pool(3, MyWorker::class);

foreach (range(0, 5) as $i) {
    $pool->submit(new Task());
}

$pool->shutdown();
echo "All done\n";
```

Each `Task` instance makes a three-second-long sleep. Since we're using three `Worker` classes, we can run three tasks at the same time, so running this demo should take exactly six seconds. Just as we did with the `Worker` class, we call `shutdown()`, which waits until all the tasks are processed and then shuts down all the workers. This is like calling `join()` on each task.

The `Pool` class takes three arguments: the number of workers to run simultaneously, the `Worker` class name that it'll instantiate (we can obviously use the default `Worker::class` as well), and an array of parameters passed to the `Worker` class's constructor.

The output from this example is as follows:

```
$ php threads_04.php
22:50:51: start
22:50:51: starting worker
22:50:51: starting worker
22:50:51: starting worker
22:50:54: done
22:50:54: done
22:50:54: done
22:50:57: done
22:50:57: done
22:50:57: done
All done
```

The main difference from the developer's perspective is that we're scheduling six tasks to be executed on three threads. In our very first example of pthreads, we executed six tasks as well, but on six threads.

The general rule of thumb is to use as few threads as we need. Creating threads requires some resource allocations (mostly creating a new PHP interpreter), and with tasks that actually do some heavy computing, the code will reach a point where the creation of additional threads will no longer produce any performance benefit. It's very effective to run in parallel tasks that spend most of their time waiting, such as system calls, or downloading data via HTTP. We can create many threads for these tasks, and they will all run in parallel and won't require practically any CPU time.

On the other hand, if we had tasks that do require CPU time, then at some point adding more threads won't have any effect because there will be no more CPUs/cores to run the interpreters, so it'll need to switch from one execution context to another. All the threads will run in parallel, but it'll take a long time to finish all of them. Whether it's worth it or not depends on what we want to achieve, but usually it's better to use a lower number of threads and execute tasks in smaller chunks.

A good number of threads for computationally intensive tasks is usually calculated as *(number of CPUs) * (number of cores per CPU)*.

So this is why we might want to use the `Pool` class. Also, an important aspect we haven't seen in the previous example is how we can grab results from the finished tasks.

Retrieving results from thread pools

The easiest way to get processed data from threads is by keeping their references and then iterating them to get results. The most obvious example could look like the following:

```
// threads_12.php
class MyThread extends Thread {
    protected $i;
    public $result;
    public function __construct($i) {
        $this->i = $i;
    }
    public function run() {
        $this->result = pow($this->i, 2);
    }
}

$pool = new Pool(3);
$threads = [];
foreach (range(1, 7) as $i) {
    $thread = new MyThread($i);
    $pool->submit($thread);
    $threads[] = $thread;
}
$pool->shutdown();

$results = [];
foreach ($threads as $thread) {
    $results[] = $thread->result;
}
print_r($results);
```

This is very simple and works as expected. However, it's not very practical. We used the shutdown() method to wait for all scheduled tasks to finish and then collected all the results from all threads. This would get more complicated if we didn't want to wait until all threads have finished and wanted to collect results as they're ready. We'd have to go back to something like an event loop that periodically checks all threads for their results.

Of course this is doable, but pthreads proposes another and more elegant way of doing this.

For this reason, the Pool class has a method called collect(). This method takes as an argument a callable that is called on every thread. This callable has to decide whether the thread has already finished or not. If it is finished, we can grab its result right inside the callable and return true, which means this thread can be disposed.

Unfortunately, there's one large BUT. In the current pthreads v3, the behavior of Pool::collect() has most likely changed. In most examples, you'll see the collect() method being used as follows:

```php
// threads_10.php
$pool = new Pool(3);

while (@$i++ < 6) {
    $pool->submit(new class($i) extends Thread {
        public $id;
        private $garbage;

        public function __construct($id) {
            $this->id = $id;
        }
        public function run() {
            sleep(1);
            printf("Hello World from %d\n", $this->id);
            $this->setGarbage();
        }
        public function setGarbage() {
            $this->garbage = true;
        }
        public function isGarbage(): bool {
            return $this->garbage;
        }
    });
}
while ($pool->collect(function(Collectable $work){
    printf("Collecting %d\n", $work->id);
    return $work->isGarbage();
})) continue;
```

```
$pool->shutdown();
```

This example is using an anonymous class (a PHP7 feature) to extend `Thread` to represent a single task.

Although this example seems simple and is used in many resources (including the `stackoverflow.com` answers by the author of pthreads), it doesn't collect all the results. We wanted to include this example here to show how it should work and most likely will work in the updated version of pthread.

The output of PHP7 and pthreads v3 looks like the following (you'll probably get these lines in a different order):

```
$ php threads_10.php
Hello World from 1
Collecting 1
Hello World from 2
Collecting 2
Hello World from 3
Collecting 3
Hello World from 4
Hello World from 5
Hello World from 6
```

As you can see, the last three threads weren't collected at all.

There are a couple of possible reasons why this doesn't work:

- With prior versions of pthreads, we had to extend the `Collectable` class instead of the `Thread` class. The `Collectable` class used to be a class originally, but this has changed, and it's now an interface. This change is documented on the pthreads readme page (`https://github.com/krakjoe/pthreads#php7`). Now, the `Thread` class implements `Collectable` automatically. In most resources, you'll find `Collectable` used as a class.
- The official documentation on `Pool::collect()` is insufficient. It doesn't mention at all that the callables need to return `Boolean` determining whether the thread should be disposed. Also, the documentation is for the older `pthreads` v2 where the `collect()` method is said to return void. This is not (or maybe never was) true since it's always used in a `while` loop (see `http://stackoverflow.com/questions/28416842/how-does-poolcollect-works` or `https://gist.github.com/krakjoe/9384409`).

- Changes to `Pool::collect()` are mentioned in the official readme at `https://github.com/krakjoe/pthreads#php7`. Quote: *"The `Pool::collect` mechanism was moved from `Pool` to `Worker` for a more robust `Worker` and simpler `Pool` inheritance."* What this means remains a mystery.

- In some examples, you'll see developers extending the `Pool` class and looping with `while (count($this->work))`. This was probably meant to loop while there is work scheduled. In pthreads v3, the `work` property doesn't exist on the `Pool` class. The official readme page listing the breaking changes we mentioned already has no record of this change.

So our biggest problem is the lack of any reliable information.

It looks desperate, but there is, in fact, a sane way of collecting all the results. We'll make use of yet another undocumented class called `Volatile` and pass it to all our threads. As we said earlier when talking about sharing data between interpreter contexts, all data needs to be copied. In contrast, classes coming from the pthreads extension (and all classes extending them) are referenced directly, and we're going to use this to our advantage.

Let's have a look at this example using the `Volatile` class to collect the results from the threads:

```php
// threads_05.php
class Task extends Thread {
  public $result;
  private $i;

  public function __construct($i, Volatile $results) {
    $this->i = $i;
    $this->results = $results;
  }
  public function run() {
    sleep(1);
    $result = pow($this->i, 2);
    printf("%s: done %d\n", date('H:i:s'), $result);

    $this->results->synchronized(function($results,$result){
      $results[] = (array)['id' => $this->i,'result' => $result];
      $results->notify();
    }, $this->results, $result);
  }
}

$pool = new Pool(2);
$results = new Volatile();
foreach (range(0, 3) as $i) {
```

```
    $pool->submit(new Task($i, $results));
}

$results->synchronized(function() use ($results) {
  while (count($results) != 4) {
    $results->wait();
  }
});

while ($pool->collect()) continue;
$pool->shutdown();
print_r($results);
echo "All done\n";
```

The first part looks very familiar. We created a class extending the Thread class, and then an instance of Pool where we'll schedule four tasks. Each task in its constructor takes the same instance of Volatile. That's the object where we'll append results for all our threads.

With the Volatile class, we're also using three new methods that are useful only when executing multithreaded code where we need some sort of synchronization between threads:

- synchronized(): This method runs the callable while holding the access lock for this object. We need to use this method in our example to be sure that only one thread is able to append results at a time. Note that the pthreads are using POSIX threads underneath, so the operator [] is not an atomic operation at all. If we didn't use locks, then multiple threads might try to modify the resulting array, which would lead to completely unpredictable behavior.
- wait(): This method makes the current interpreter context wait until notify() is called on the same object (it's a blocking operation). Note that calling wait() will release the access lock while it is waiting, and then it'll be reacquired after awakening with notify(). Therefore, this method needs to be called inside synchronized().
- notify(): This method wakes the waiting interpreter context after calling the wait() method.

Using wait() and notify() might be very dangerous if used inappropriately. If the thread containing notify() called this method before the first thread arrived at wait(), then the first context would be stuck at wait() forever because there'd be no other notify() call to awaken it.

So we run `wait()` calls in a loop because we know that only one thread can acquire the lock, and therefore each thread will append to `$results` one after the other.

All threads will share the same reference to `Volatile` because, as we said, it's a class from the pthreads extension (or its derivate extending the `Threaded` class), so it won't be copied on read/write attempts.

When we run this example, we'll get the expected output:

```
$ php threads_05.php
17:21:42: done 0
17:21:42: done 1
17:21:43: done 9
17:21:43: done 4
Volatile Object (
    [0] => Array (
            [id] =>
            [result] => 0
        )
    [1] => Array (
            [id] =>
            [result] => 1
        )
    [2] => Array (
            [id] =>
            [result] => 9
        )
    [3] => Array (
            [id] =>
            [result] => 4
        )
)
All done
```

Note one last thing. When appending our results, we used the following line:

```
$results[] = (array)['id' => $this->i, 'result' => $result];
```

We're using typecasting with `(array)`, which seems redundant. In fact, we have to do this in order not to lose the reference to this array. When setting an array to a property of the `Thread` class, it's automatically converted into a `Volatile` object unless we typecast it beforehand to an array. Without typecasting, the `Volatile` object representing the array would be deallocated when this context is shut down, so we need to force typecast it to an array in order to be copied.

There's actually one more solution to the problem described above with `Pool` class not collection all results correctly (although this solution is not as elegant as using `synchronized()` methods). Instead of using the `collect()` method to control how long we want to run the while loop, we can manually count the threads that have finished, in a similar way to the following example:

```
// threads_13.php
$pool = new Pool(3);
// populate $pool with 6 tasks...
$remaining = 6;
while ($remaining !== 0) {
  $pool->collect(function(Collectable $work) use (&$remaining) {
    $done = $work->isGarbage();
    if ($done) {
      printf("Collecting %d\n", $work->id);
      $remaining--;
    }
    return $done;
  });
}
```

Now the responsibility to run the while loop as long as necessary lies on us and not the `collect()` method (that might be bugged).

When we run this example with the same anonymous class instances as shown previously, we'll correctly collect all the results.

```
$ php threads_13.php
Hello World from 1
Collecting 1
Hello World from 2
Collecting 2
Hello World from 3
Collecting 3
Hello World from 4
Hello World from 5
Hello World from 6
Collecting 6
Collecting 4
Collecting 5
```

RxPHP and pthreads

A good question is how is all this about pthreads related to RxPHP and to Rx in general.

In PHP, we're typically not used to work with asynchronous tasks and if we do, the implementation details are well hidden from us. This is for example the case with event loops and RxPHP, where we don't need to care what's going on inside RxPHP classes under the hood.

In the next chapter, we'd like to achieve the same state where we'll have a general purpose Observable or an operator that runs tasks in parallel using pthreads. Since working with asynchronous code in RxPHP is easy, pthreads is a perfect candidate that could add very interesting functionality which can be easily reused anywhere.

Summary

In this chapter, we went through two larger topics. We'll use both of them in the next chapter, where we'll write multithreaded applications with pthreads, as well as distributed applications with Gearman.

The two topics we covered were multicasting in RxPHP and all operators related to it, and using the PHP7 pthreads v3 extension to write multithreaded PHP7 applications.

Multicasting in Rx is very useful in order to share a single connection to source Observables without resubscribing. This comes with the `refCount()` operator to work more easily with `ConnectableObservables`.

Multithreaded programming in PHP is possible with the pthreads extension. However, it's not as simple as it seems, and there are multiple caveats, most importantly insufficient documentation and an overall unintuitive approach. In the next chapter, we'll use just the most basic functions from pthreads to avoid confusion and eventual inconsistency with future updates of pthreads. The goal for the next chapter is to write an extendable code quality tool, based on the `nikic/php-parser` project (`https://github.com/nikic/PHP-Parser`), which will allow adding custom rules using RxPHP operator chains. We'll base the application on what we've covered in this chapter.

Multithreaded and Distributed Computing with pthreads and Gearman

9

We've spent quite some time with pthreads in the previous chapter. However, we haven't seen them used in any practical applications. That's what we're going to do in this chapter where we'll wrap pthreads with RxPHP to hide their internal implementation details and to make thread pools easily reusable in any RxPHP application.

Apart from pthreads, we'll take a look at distributing jobs across multiple workers locally or on multiple machines. We'll use the Gearman framework and its PHP bindings to make the same application as we'll do with pthreads, just instead of running it in multiple threads we'll use multiple workers (independent processes).

In this chapter, we're going to write an extendable code quality tool to test various style checks in PHP scripts. For example, this can be not using assignments in conditions, or just variable names following certain coding standard. PHP projects tend to grow very large these days. If we wanted to analyze every file in a single thread, it would take a very long time, so we want to run the analyzer part in parallel if possible.

In particular, this chapter will cover the following topics:

- Quick introduction to the PHP Parser library and how can we wrap its parser with an RxPHP operator
- Wrap pthreads `Pool` class with our custom operator that'll receive `Thread` classes and run them in parallel automatically
- Write a `Thread` class that'll run PHP Parser in a separate thread

- Introduce the Gearman framework and write a very basic client and worker in PHP. We'll also see how to run clients and workers using just Gearman's CLI options
- Distribute PHP Parser tasks across multiple Gearman workers
- Compare single process multithreaded applications with a distributed Gearman application

We'll go through the PHP Parser library very quickly because our main interest is mostly in pthreads and the Gearman framework.

However, we'll spend some time writing the `PHPParserOperator` class, which will combine many of the things we've learned in the previous chapters.

Introduction to the PHP Parser library

PHP Parser is a library that takes a source code written in PHP, passes it through a lexical analyzer, and creates its respective syntax tree. This is very useful for static code analysis, where we want to check our own code not only for syntactic errors but also for satisfying certain quality criteria.

In this chapter, we'll write an application that takes a directory, iterates all its files and subdirectories recursively, and runs each PHP file through the PHP Parser. We will check only for one specific pattern; that is enough for this demo.

We want to be able to find any statement where we use the assignment inside a condition. This could be any of the following examples (this time we're also including line numbers for clarity):

```
// _test_source_code.php
1. <?php
2. $a = 5;
3. if ($a = 1) {
4.     var_dump($a);
5. } elseif ($b = 2) {}
6. while ($c = 3) {}
7. for (; $d = 4;) {}
```

All this is of course a valid PHP syntax, but let's say we want to make our code easy to understand. When your application is not behaving as you'd expect and you don't know how you might spot any of the preceding examples, then you would not be able to say at first sight whether this is intentional or you're just missing one equals sign. Maybe you wanted to write a condition such as if ($a == 1) and you just forgot one =.

This can be easily spotted and reported by the static code analyzer.

So, let's start by first trying the PHP Parser library itself and then wrap it with the RxPHP operator.

Using the PHP Parser library

Before we start, we need to install the PHP Parser library. As usual, we'll use the `composer` for this:

```
$ composer require nikic/php-parser
```

The easiest use case is just taking the source code we want to analyze and process it with the parser:

```php
// php_parser_01.php
use PhpParser\ParserFactory;

$syntax = ParserFactory::PREFER_PHP7;
$parser = (new ParserFactory())->create($syntax);

$code = file_get_contents('_test_source_code.php');
$stmts = $parser->parse($code);
print_r($stmts);
```

The output from this script is going to be a very long nested tree structure representing the code we passed to the parser:

```
$ php php_parser_01.php
...
[2] => PhpParser\Node\Stmt\If_ Object
    (
      [cond] => PhpParser\Node\Expr\Assign Object (
        [var] => PhpParser\Node\Expr\Variable Object (
          [name] => a
            [attributes:protected] => Array (
              [startLine] => 4
              [endLine] => 4
            )
        )
      [expr] => PhpParser\Node\Scalar\LNumber Object (
        [value] => 1
        ...
```

We can see that the `if` statement has a property called `cond` that contains the parsed condition, which is an instance of `Expr\Assign`. In fact, all the statements we're going to test have the `cond` property, so testing whether they contain an assignment in condition is going to be relatively simple. The only exception is the `for` loop, where the condition might have multiple expressions separated by the comma , character.

Since the syntax tree is a nested structure, we'll need some way to iterate it recursively. Fortunately, this is supported by the library out of the box via the `NodeTraverser` class and by registering custom visitors. Visitors are classes with multiple callbacks that are called when the tree traverser starts/ends processing the entire tree or enters/leaves a single node.

We will make a very simple node visitor that checks for the node type and eventually the `cond` property. This is a way we can spot all the assignments inside conditions and print their respective line number from the source PHP script.

Consider the following code. This will also be part of the custom operator that we'll write later:

```php
// php_parser_02.php
use PhpParser\NodeTraverser;
use PhpParser\ParserFactory;
use PhpParser\Node;
use PhpParser\Node\Stmt;
use PhpParser\Node\Expr;
use PhpParser\NodeVisitorAbstract;

class MyNodeVisitor extends NodeVisitorAbstract {
  public function enterNode(Node $node) {
    if (($node instanceof Stmt\If_ ||
          $node instanceof Stmt\ElseIf_ ||
          $node instanceof Stmt\While_
       ) && $this->isAssign($node->cond)) {

      echo $node->getLine() . "\n";
    } elseif ($node instanceof Stmt\For_) {
      $conds = array_filter($node->cond, [$this, 'isAssign']);
      foreach ($conds as $cond) {
        echo $node->getLine() . "\n";
      }
    }
  }

  private function isAssign($cond) {
    return $cond instanceof Expr\Assign;
  }
```

```
}

$syntax = ParserFactory::PREFER_PHP7;
$parser = (new ParserFactory())->create($syntax);
$code = file_get_contents('_test_source_code.php');

$traverser = new NodeTraverser();
$traverser->addVisitor(new MyNodeVisitor());
$stmts = $parser->parse($code);
$traverser->traverse($stmts);
```

As you can see, we're checking each node type with multiple `instanceof` statements and their respective `cond` properties. With the `for` statement, we need to check the array of the `cond` statements but the rest is analogous.

Every time we spot our tested style check, we just print the line number so that the preceding example will print the following:

```
$ php php_parser_02.php
3
5
6
7
```

We can see that the line numbers really match the source file we presented earlier. This is all nice but not very helpful when we want to use it with RxPHP or, even more interestingly, with pthreads.

Implementing PHPParserOperator

If we wanted to process multiple files, we could just run the parser multiple times. But what if we wanted to have better control over what files are going in, or we wanted to make the preconfigured parser with our custom node visitor easily embeddable into any RxPHP application.

For example, let's assume we want to use the PHP Parser library in the following way:

```
// php_parser_observer_01.php
Observable::fromArray(['_test_source_code.php'])
  ->lift(function() {
    $classes = [AssignmentInConditionNodeVisitor::class];
    return new PHPParserOperator($classes);
  })
  ->subscribe(new DebugSubject());
```

We have a typical RxPHP chain of operators where we lifted `PHPParserOperator`. This class takes in its constructor an array of classes that will be added as node visitors to its internal `NodeTraverser`.

As an input, we're using a primitive array of filenames that'll be emitted by the source Observable. The observer will then receive just an array of code style violations reported by each of the visitor classes.

Before writing the operator itself, we should first take a look at how to modify the visitor class from the previous example. Since we want to be able to add any number of custom node visitors that can check anything they want, we need to be able to collect all their results and re-emit them as a single value by `PHPParserOperator`.

Writing AssignmentInConditionNodeVisitor

We can start by defining an interface that all our node visitors have to implement:

```php
// ObservableNodeVisitorInterface.php
interface ObservableNodeVisitorInterface {
    public function asObservable();
}
```

The one requirement for a node visitor is to return an Observable where it'll emit all code style violations:

```php
// AssignmentInConditionNodeVisitor.php
use PhpParser\NodeVisitorAbstract as Visitor;
use PhpParser\Node;
// We're omitting the rest of use statements ...

class AssignmentInConditionNodeVisitor
    extends Visitor implements ObservableNodeVisitorInterface {
  private $subject;
  private $prettyPrinter;

  public function __construct() {
    $this->subject = new Subject();
    $this->prettyPrinter = new PrettyPrinter\Standard();
  }
  public function enterNode(Node $node) {
    // Remains the same as above just instead of echoing the
    // line numbers we call $this->emitNext(...) method.
  }
  public function afterTraverse(array $nodes) {
    $this->subject->onCompleted();
```

```
  }
  public function asObservable() {
    return $this->subject->asObservable();
  }
  private function isAssign($cond) {
    return $cond instanceof Expr\Assign;
  }
  private function emitNext(Node $node, Expr\Assign $cond) {
    $this->subject->onNext([
      'line' => $node->getLine(),
      'expr' => $this->prettyPrinter->prettyPrintExpr($cond),
    ]);
  }
}
```

This node visitor uses a Subject internally and in the `emitNext()` method it emits every code style violation as a single item. This item is an associative array itself that contains the line number and the well formatted expression that caused the violation (to make it obvious to the user why it's reported). The `PrettyPrinter` class is a part of the PHP Parser library.

This `Subject` class also needs to emit a `complete` signal when we're done with this syntax tree. That's in the `afterTraverse()` method. Calling the `complete` signal is very important to let other operators work with this `Subject` properly.

Since we need to expose this `Subject`, we need to be sure nobody else can manipulate with it so we wrap it using the `asObservable()` operator.

Writing PHPParserOperator

This operator will hold a single reference to the PHP Parser that we'll invoke for every file that comes to this operator. This also means that we'll need to create a new instance of the `NodeTraverser` class for each file and add new instances of each custom node visitor to it.

From the operator's point of view, all node visitors are just Observables that emit style violations. The operator needs to collect all values from all of them and then reemit this collection as a single item.

We'll split this example into two smaller chunks. First, we'll have a look at the creation of the `NodeTraverser` instances filled with node visitors:

```
// PHPParserOperator.php
use Rx\ObservableInterface;
use Rx\ObserverInterface;
use Rx\SchedulerInterface;
use Rx\Operator\OperatorInterface;
```

```
use Rx\Observer\CallbackObserver;
use PhpParser\NodeTraverser;
use PhpParser\ParserFactory;

class PHPParserOperator implements OperatorInterface {
  private $parser;
  private $traverserClasses;

  public function __construct($traverserClasses = []) {
    $syntax = ParserFactory::PREFER_PHP7;
    $this->parser = (new ParserFactory())->create($syntax);
    $this->traverserClasses = $traverserClasses;
  }

  private function createTraverser() {
    $traverser = new NodeTraverser();
    $visitors = array_map(function($class) use ($traverser) {
      /** @var ObservableNodeVisitorInterface $visitor */
      $visitor = new $class();
      $traverser->addVisitor($visitor);

      return $visitor->asObservable()
        ->toArray()
        ->map(function($violations) use ($class) {
          return [
            'violations' => $violations,
            'class' => $class
          ];
        });
    }, $this->traverserClasses);
    return [$traverser, $visitors];
  }
  // ...
}
```

We keep an array of class names for node visitors in the $traverserClasses property.
When we want to create a new NodeTraverser, we iterate this array with the
array_map() function and instantiate each class. Then we not only add it to the traverser
but we also take its Observable (returned from the asObservable() method) and chain it
with the toArray() and map() operators.

The `toArray()` operator collects all items emitted by the source Observable and re-emits them as a single array when the source completes. This is why we had to be sure we properly called complete in the `AssignmentInConditionNodeVisitor` class. We also used `map()` to emit the final collection of violations with the class name that generated them. This isn't necessary, but for practical reasons we want to be able to tell what node visitor generated these results (or, in other words, what style violations are in this collection).

The `createTraverser()` method returns two values: the `NodeTraverser` instance and an array of Observables returned from each node visitor.

The rest of `PHPParserOperator` is where the actual subscription happens:

```php
class PHPParserOperator implements OperatorInterface {
  // ...
  public function __invoke($observable, $observer, $sched=null) {
    $onNext = function($filepath) use ($observer) {
      $code = @file_get_contents($filepath);
      if (!$code) { /* ... emit error message */ }

      list($traverser, $visitors) = $this->createTraverser();
      (new ForkJoinObservable($visitors))
        ->map(function($results) use ($filepath) {
          // $results = all results from all node visitors.
          $filtered = array_filter($results, function($result) {
            return $result['violations'];
          });
          return [
            'file' => $filepath,
            'results' => $filtered,
          ];
        })
        ->subscribeCallback(function($result) use ($observer) {
          $observer->onNext($result);
        });

      $stmts = $this->parser->parse($code);
      $traverser->traverse($stmts);
    };

    $callbackObserver = new CallbackObserver(
      $onNext,
      [$observer, 'onError'],
      [$observer, 'onCompleted']
    );
    return $observable->subscribe($callbackObserver, $sched);
  }
```

```
}
```

First of all, we're using `CallbackObserver`, which just passes through all `error` and `complete` signals. The interesting things happen only in the anonymous function `$onNext`:

1. We're expecting each item to be a string representing a file path. We read the content of the file with the `file_get_contents()` function to get the source code we want to analyze.

2. Then, we call `createTraverser()`, which returns a new instance of `NodeTraverser` and also an array of Observables, where we'll get all the style violations. These are already wrapped with `toArray()` and `map()` as we saw earlier.

3. We're creating a new `ForkJoinObservable` and passing it the array of Observables from the previous call. We implemented this Observable in Chapter 5, *Testing RxPHP Code*. The `ForkJoinObservable` class subscribes to all its source Observables and remembers only the latest value emitted by each one of them. When all the source Observables are complete, it reemits all the values as a single array. We know all the sources will emit just one value and then complete, thanks to the `toArray()` operator.

4. We're not interested in node visitors that didn't emit any violations, so we remove them from the result in the `map()` operator.

5. In the end, we just subscribe the observer itself to this chain. Note that we're purposely not using just `subscribe($observer)` because this would reemit everything including errors and complete signals. The Observable chain we created will complete immediately after emitting its single value thanks to `ForkJoinObservable`, which is what we don't want. Have a look at the previous chapter where we talked about sharing a single instance of Subject and what unexpected results it might produce. The same reasons apply here as well.

After all this, we just run the `traverse()` method that analyzes the source code and, thanks to our custom node visitors with Observables, will emit all violations that'll be gathered in `ForkJoinObservable`.

This was a pretty complex operator with a sophisticated behavior. If we go back to the example where we showed how we want to use this operator, we can see that all this logic is effectively hidden from us.

When we run the original example that we used earlier, we'll get the following result:

```
$ php php_parser_observer_01.php
Array (
    [file] => _test_source_code.php
    [results] => Array (
      [0] => Array (
        [violations] => Array (
          [0] => Array (
            [line] => 3
            [expr] => $a = 1
          )
          [1] => Array (
            [line] => 5
            [expr] => $b = 2
          )
          [2] => Array (
            [line] => 6
            [expr] => $c = 3
          )
          [3] => Array (
            [line] => 7
            [expr] => $d = 4
          )
        )
        [class] => AssignmentInConditionNodeVisitor
      )
    )
)
```

Each item coming from this operator is a series of nested arrays. We can see the filename we analyzed and the array of results, where each items is generated by one node visitor. Since we have just one result, we also have just one array here. Each result is marked by the node visitor class name and a list of violations. Each violation contains the line number and the exact expression where it occurred.

This is all nice but how long would it take to analyze a larger project such as the Symfony3 framework? Right now, Symfony3 (without third-party dependencies) has over 3200 files. If processing a single file would take just 1ms, then analyzing the entire project would take over 3s (in fact, processing would take much longer just because of so many filesystem operations).

So, this looks like a prime example where we could utilize our knowledge of multithreaded programming in PHP with pthreads.

Implementing ThreadPoolOperator

We're going to write a universal operator that receives jobs represented by `Thread` class instances from its source Observable. Then, it'll submit them to an internal instance of the `Pool` class that we saw in the previous chapter.

In fact, this example with pthreads is going to be entirely built on all the things we've learned in the previous chapter, so we won't recap them here.

 This example is also going to use PHP7 syntax in some situations since pthreads v3 works only with PHP7 anyway.

For this operator, well internally use an event loop. In RxPHP, this means we'll use the `StreamSelectLoop` class wrapped with a `Scheduler` class. Let's see the source code for `ThreadPoolOperator` and then talk about why it's implemented like this:

```php
// ThreadPoolOperator.php
class ThreadPoolOperator implements OperatorInterface {
  private $pool;

  public function __construct($num = 4,
      $workerClass = Worker::class, $workerArgs = []) {

    $this->pool = new Pool($num, $workerClass, $workerArgs);
  }

  public function __invoke($observable, $observer, $sched=null) {
    $callbackObserver = new CallbackObserver(function($task) {
        /** @var AbstractRxThread $task */
        $this->pool->submit($task);
      },
      [$observer, 'onError'],
      [$observer, 'onCompleted']
    );

    $dis1 = $sched->schedulePeriodic(function() use ($observer) {
      $this->pool->collect(function($task) use ($observer) {
        /** @var AbstractRxThread $task */
        if ($task->isDone()) {
          $observer->onNext($result);
          return true;
        } else {
          return false;
        }
      }
```

```
        });
    }, 0, 10);

    $dis2 = $observable->subscribe($callbackObserver);
    $disposable = new BinaryDisposable($dis1, $dis2);
    return $disposable;
    }
}
```

The constructor for `ThreadPoolOperator` takes the same arguments as the constructor for the `Pool` class that is created right away. The interesting things take place in the `__invoke()` method.

Every item that arrives to this operator is sent to the thread pool with the `submit()` method. This means that `ThreadPoolOperator` can only work with items represented by the `Thread` class from the pthreads extension (and of course all classes extending this class).

Internally, we use the `Scheduler` class to periodically call a callable that will check the thread pool for threads that have finished and are ready to be collected. This is the same `collect()` method we saw in the previous chapter. However, in this implementation we're making only a single check in every iteration of the callable. There's one very important reason why we want to use it this way. We know that we can use the `collect()` method in a loop that runs as long as there are tasks scheduled to be run.

The loop typically looks like this:

```
$remaining = N;
while ($remaining !== 0) {
    $pool->collect(function(Thread $work) use (&$remaining) {
        $done = $work->isDone();
        if ($done) {
            $remaining--;
        }
        return $done;
    });
}
```

This is of course correct. The only problem is that this call is blocking. The interpreter is stuck in this loop and doesn't let us do anything else. If we wanted to use such a loop and at the same time read data from a stream via `StreamSelectLoop` (see `Chapter 6`, *PHP Streams API and Higher-Order Observables*), we wouldn't be able to receive anything as long as this loop is running. Another example that wouldn't work if we used just this `while` loop could be `IntervalObservable` , which needs to schedule timers itself. These wouldn't be triggered until this loop is ended.

That's why we're periodically scheduling a 10ms timer to run `collect()` just once and then let other timers or streams be handled. The finished threads are kept in the `Pool` class until we read and reemit their results.

This implementation has one very important behavior. Since it is running all tasks in parallel and completely independently of the rest of the Observable chain, we need to be aware when we send the `complete` signal.

Consider the following code:

```
Observable::fromArray([1,2,3])
    ->map(function($val) {
        return new MyThread($val);
    })
    ->lift(function() {
        return ThreadPoolOperator(...);
    })
    ...
```

In this example, the `ThreadPoolOperator` class receives three instances of `MyThread` that'll be submitted to the `Pool` instance, but it also receives a complete signal. This complete signal is immediately passed to its observer that unsubscribes before any of the threads are finished and emit any value.

At the same time, `ThreadPoolOperator` can't decide for itself when you want to send the `complete` signal. Sometimes when the thread pool is empty and there are no tasks running. Other times we might want to start threads based on PHP stream activity that can happen at any time.

That's why we don't send `complete` signals automatically.

Implementing PHPParserThread

Now we can take a look at how the actual parser task is going to be implemented. We already know that it needs to be represented by a class extending the default `Thread` class from the pthreads extension and we also know that we're going to process files using the PHP Parser, so we can reuse the `PHPParserOperator` class.

Before we do that, we should define some common behavior for all `Thread` objects:

```
// AbstractRxThread.php
abstract class AbstractRxThread extends Thread {
    private $done = false;
    protected $result;
```

```
    public function getResult() {
        return $this->result;
    }
    public function isDone() {
        return $this->done;
    }
    protected function markDone() {
        $this->done = true;
    }
}
```

All tasks we want to run with `ThreadPoolOperator` need to extend this abstract class that defines some common methods.

Notice that we don't have a setter method for the `$result` property. This is intentional and we'll see why when we look at the implementation of `PHPParserThread` that we will use in this application:

```
class PHPParserThread extends AbstractRxThread {
  private $filenames;

  public function __construct($filename) {
    $this->filenames =
        (array)(is_array($filename) ? $filename : [$filename]);
    /** @var Volatile result */
    $this->result = [];
  }

  public function run() {
    $last = 0;
    Observable::fromArray($this->filenames)
      ->lift(function() {
        $classes = ['AssignmentInConditionNodeVisitor'];
        return new PHPParserOperator($classes);
      })
      ->subscribeCallback(function ($results) use (&$last) {
        $this->result[$last++] = (array)[
          'file' => $results['file'],
          'results' => $results['results'],
        ];
      }, null, function() {
        $this->markDone();
      });
  }
}
```

As you can see, we're using typecasting for the exact same reasons as described in the previous chapter. Also notice that we're wrapping the input file with an array. Since we want to make this class reusable, we'll support both passing a single file and an array of files. We're initializing the `$result` property with an empty array that's automatically converted to a `Volatile` object by pthreads (again, for more information refer to the previous chapter). For this reason, we need to keep track of the number of items already persistent by ourselves with the `$last` variable. Also, notice that our result is always going to be an array, even when processing just a single file.

At this point, we need to be aware why not to use any setter method for `$result`. In the previous chapter, when talking about `Volatile` objects, we said that pthreads automatically convert arrays to `Volatile` when assigning to a property in any class extending the `Threaded` class. For this reason, we can't use a setter because we wouldn't be able to force typecasting to array with `(array)`. This automatic conversion happens on assignment, so we'd have to force all results in `AbstractRxThread` to be arrays or leave it to the automatic conversion, which is something we definitely don't want.

To be extra clear about this issue, let's consider the following setter method:

```
public function setResult($result) {
    $this->result = $result;
}
```

The assignment happens inside this function where we don't want to force using arrays with `(array)` typecast. We might want to use a simple string or an integer, for example.

So this was our `PHPParserThread` class that we'll use in this example. There's actually one more issue.

Creating a new thread with pthreads means we're internally creating a new PHP interpreter context. The only classes and functions this new context knows are those built into the PHP interpreter itself. This new context has no idea what `Observable` or `PHPParserOperator` classes are.

Just like we include the `autoload.php` Composer autoloader script when running any PHP application, we need to do this for every new thread we create. Since we don't want to do this every time we use `PHPParserThread`, we can make use of a custom worker that'll do it for us in its `run()` method. This `run()` method is called when spawning a new interpreter context and lets us initialize it by, for example, including the `autoload.php` script.

Implementing PHPParserWorker

For the sake of simplicity, we're not defining our classes in namespaces and usually just including them with the require_once keyword, such as in the following example:

```
require_once __DIR__ . '/../Chapter 02/DebugSubject.php';
```

For this reason, we need to tell the autoloader created inside each worker where to find such classes ideally without relying on the require_once statements.

Our worker will be a simple class (based on the official example on how to use Composer's autoloader with pthreads at
https://github.com/krakjoe/pthreads-autoloading-composer):

```php
// PHPParserWorker.php
class PHPParserWorker extends \Worker {
  protected $loader;
  public function __construct($loader) {
    $this->loader = $loader;
  }

  public function run() {
    $classLoader = require_once($this->loader);
    $dir = __DIR__;
    $classLoader->addClassMap([
      'DebugSubject' => $dir . '/../Chapter 02/DebugSubject.php',
      'ThreadWorkerOperator' => $dir.'/ThreadWorkerOperator.php',
      'PHPParserThread' => $dir . '/PHPParserThread.php',
      'PHPParserWorker' => $dir . '/PHPParserWorker.php',
      'PHPParserOperator' => $dir . '/PHPParserOperator.php',
    ]);
  }

  public function start(int $options = PTHREADS_INHERIT_ALL) {
    return parent::start(PTHREADS_INHERIT_NONE);
  }
}
```

This worker uses require_once to register the autoloader, where we add a few class paths. The initialized interpreter context will be used by all Thread instances ran by this worker.

Finally, we can put all this into a single Observable chain.

Running PHP Parser in a multithreaded application

First, we will test all the classes we made right now on processing the same sample file as earlier and then move to recursively processing directories from the Symfony3 project:

```
// threads_php_parser_01.php
$loop = new StreamSelectLoop();
$scheduler = new EventLoopScheduler($loop);

Observable::create(function(ObserverInterface $observer) {
    $observer->onNext('_test_source_code.php');
  })
  ->map(function($filename) {
    return new PHPParserThread($filename);
  })
  ->lift(function() {
    $args = [__DIR__ . '/../vendor/autoload.php'];
    return new ThreadPoolOperator(2,PHPParserWorker::class,$args);
  })
  ->flatMap(function($result) {
    return Observable::fromArray((array)$result);
  })
  ->take(1)
  ->subscribeCallback(function($result) {
    print_r($result);
  }, null, null, $scheduler);

$loop->run();
```

This example is using all three classes for multithreading that we created in this chapter. Let's see what happens in this operator chain step by step:

1. We have a single source Observable that emits the filename as its value. Notice that we're purposely not sending the complete signal.
2. Then we use map to turn all filenames to instances of the PHPParserThread class.
3. The ThreadPoolOperator class is fed with tasks it has to run.
4. We've mentioned already that all results from ThreadPoolOperator are returned as arrays even when we processed just a single file. For this reason, we use flatMap() to reemit its values and flatten the result. Also we need to typecast the result from Volatile to an array.

5. We didn't send the `complete` signal from the source on purpose. However, we know that we processed only one file and therefore we're expecting only one item to be emitted. So we can use `take(1)` to send the `complete` signal for us and the observer will unsubscribe successfully, which will stop the event loop as well.

We can run this example and see that it returned exactly the same result as the original version with just `PHPParserOperator`:

```
$ php threads_php_parser_01.php
Array (
  [file] => _test_source_code.php
  [results] => Array (
    [0] => Array (
      [violations] => Array (
        ...
```

 Although most of our CLI applications in this book are based on the Symfony Console component, this time we don't even need it since the entire application can be written as a single operator chain.

In this example, we spawned two workers even though we wanted to process just a single file.

The question is what will be the difference if we try to process multiple files in parallel. For this reason, we'll create a Symfony3 test project that contains literally thousands of PHP files we can test:

```
$ composer create-project symfony/framework-standard-edition testdir
```

The following example will work just like the previous one. This time, however, we'll make a recursive iterator that walks through all subdirectories and emits all PHP files it finds. We can write this all as one large operator chain:

```
// threads_php_parser_02.php
const MAX_FILES = 500;
Observable::create(function($observer) use ($loop) {
    $start = microtime(true);
    $src = __DIR__ . '/../symfony_template';
    $dirIter = new \RecursiveDirectoryIterator($src);
    $iter = new \RecursiveIteratorIterator($dirIter);

    while ($iter->valid()) {
        /** @var SplFileInfo $file */
        $file = $iter->current();
        if ($file->getExtension() === 'php' && $file->isReadable()){
```

```
            $observer->onNext($file->getRealPath());
        }
        $iter->next();
    }

    return new CallbackDisposable(function() use ($loop, $start) {
        echo "duration: ".round(microtime(true) - $start, 2)."s\n";
        $loop->stop();
    });
}) // End of Observable::create()
->bufferWithCount(20)
->map(function($filenames) {
    return new PHPParserThread($filenames);
})
->lift(function() {
    $args = [__DIR__ . '/../vendor/autoload.php'];
    return new ThreadPoolOperator(4,PHPParserWorker::class,$args);
})
->flatMap(function($result) {
    return Observable::fromArray((array)$result);
})
->take(MAX_FILES)
->filter(function($result) {
    return count($result['results']) > 0;
})
->subscribeCallback(function($result) {
    print_r($result);
}, null, null, $scheduler);
```

This is the longest operator chain we've written in this book. The main thing that has changed is the source emitting filenames that we want to analyze. We have two different iterators, where both of them return `SplFileInfo` objects. We know how many files we want to test in total, so we can avoid emitting redundant values with the `take()` operator.

When we spoke about backpressure in the previous chapters, we mentioned the `bufferWithCount()` operator that stacks values and then reemits them in a single array. This comes very handy now where we don't want to create a task on the thread pool for every single file and rather emit them in batches.

In the end, we also used `filter()` to ignore all the results that don't have any violations. Of course, we're interested only in files that have at least one violation.

An important part of this example is that it measures how long it took to run this entire application (from the initial subscription until disposing `CallbackDisposable`).

If we run this code, we'll see a large list that looks similar to the following:

```
$ php threads_php_parser_02.php
...
Array (
    [file] => ...vendor/symfony/src/Symfony/Bridge/Twig/AppVariable.php
    [results] => Array (
      [0] => Array (
        [violations] => Array (
          [0] => Array (
            [line] => 101
            [expr] => $request = $this->getRequest()
          )
        )
        [class] => AssignmentInConditionNodeVisitor
      )
    )
)
...
```

The line reported contains the following code:

```
if ($request = $this->getRequest()) {
```

This is really a code style that we wanted to be able to report.

Now comes the important question, what is the effect of running the analyzer in multiple-threads? We can make a couple of reruns with settings such as 1, 2, 4, and 6 threads. To get more relevant results, we can increase the number of files processed to 1,000 and also disable the `xdebug` extension that otherwise slows down the execution significantly. On average, the times were as follows:

```
1 thread = 5.60s
2 threads = 3.52s
4 threads = 3.08s
6 threads = 4.80s
```

As we can see, increasing the number of threads starts to be counterproductive. These times were measured on 2, 5 GHz Intel Core i5, which is a dual-core processor with an SSD hard drive. The result for a higher number of threads would probably be better with a non-SSD hard drive because each thread would have to spend more time loading file contents, which would allow other threads to execute in the meantime.

We almost reached half the time of running just a single thread, which is a realistic expectation. On a dual-core processor and with the overhead generated by RxPHP and PHP itself, this is an expected result.

We can have a look at the output of the `htop` command that shows the current CPU usage to prove that both cores are fully utilized:

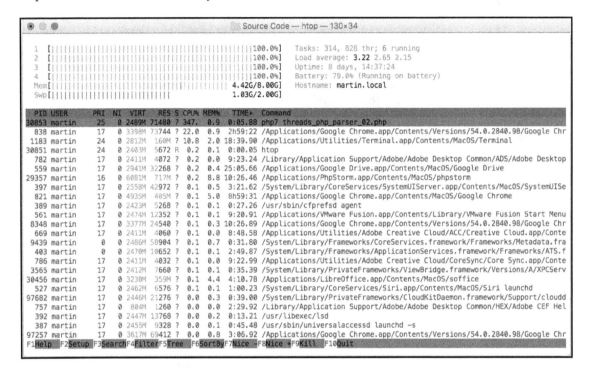

Current CPU usage when running threads_php_parser_02.php example

The `htop` tool is showing four cores because there are two hardware threads per core (it's in fact just a dual-core processor).

Running the parser in parallel in a single process by just utilizing pthreads is pretty efficient.

Our use case can be generalized as simply splitting a job among multiple workers. We don't really care what protocols we'll use or how the distribution is going to happen. We don't even care about what worker will process a particular batch. We just need to get the job done.

This is an ideal use case for Gearman.

Introduction to Gearman

Gearman is a framework for distributing work among multiple processes and machines. Due to its functionality, it can serve as a manager, load balancer, or interface between different languages with no single point of failure.

Since this book is about Rx/reactive/asynchronous programming, we're going to cover Gearman fairly quickly. Needless to say, Gearman is very easy to set up and use.

The Gearman PHP extension is written in the C language, so we need to install it via PECL or a package manager relevant to your platform (refer to `http://gearman.org/download/` for more information).

Gearman's name is an anagram of the word "Manager" and it pretty well captures its purpose. Gearman doesn't do the work itself. It just receives a task (also referred to simply as a job) from a client and delegates it to an available worker.

The structure of any Gearman application is easily understood from the following diagram:

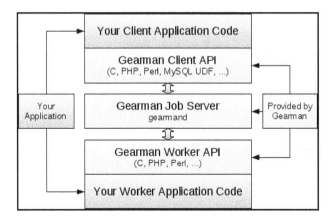

Diagram from the official Gearman documentation (http://gearman.org/)

Every Gearman application has the following three main components:

- **Gearman Job Server**: This is usually run as a daemon that accepts tasks from clients and delegates them to workers. It's written in C (originally in Perl) and doesn't do any work by itself. It's also able to keep the current tasks queue persisted in a database so it can be restored on failure.
- **Client**: This is any application in any language that needs some job to be done. This can be a web application that needs to send an e-mail or a CLI application that needs to run static analysis on a couple of files. The client doesn't do the job by itself. It sends a message to the job server and either waits until it's done or just waits for confirmation from the job server that it was added to the queue.
- **Worker**: This is the part that actually does the job delegated by the job server. It can be written in any language as well. It contains a list of functions that it's able to perform and based on that the job server assigns the work it needs to do.

So in order to start using Gearman, we need to have the job server part installed and running on our system; it's usually called **gearman** or **gearmand**. You can find the instructions how to install and run Gearman for your platform at `http://gearman.org/download/`.

String strlen client and worker

We can create a very simple application, where we'll have a worker that takes a string and returns its length. The client in this case will just send a string to the job server requesting to get the length back.

Our client is going to be pretty simple. It'll just request a job, `strlen`, to be done and then wait until it receives a response from the job server:

```
// gearman_client_01.php
$client = new GearmanClient();
$client->addServer('127.0.0.1');
$client->setTimeout(3000);

$length = @$client->doNormal('strlen', 'Hello World!');
if (empty($length)) {
    echo "timeout\n";
} else {
    var_dump(intval($length));
}
```

Our client connects to a single job server and sets a three-second timeout. If it doesn't receive a response within this time, then it continues executing the rest of the script. We're using a single server, but we can have multiple job servers running on different machines, and if any of them crash, clients will continue with the other ones. This makes the system fault tolerant. Also, notice that our client is blocking.

We're requesting a job to be done using the doNormal() method, where we need to specify the name of the job we want to do and all the data the worker needs in order to complete it. Apart from doNormal(), there are also methods such as doLow() and doHigh() that request the job with a different priority.

Typically, when we want to run a job, we want to know its result. For example, in this case, we wanted to wait to get the string length back. In some situations, we just want to schedule a job, but we're not interested in when it happens and what its result is. A typical use case is a web application where a user registers and we want to send them a confirmation e-mail. We don't want to slow down the page load by waiting until the e-mail is sent.

For this reason, the Client class also has the doBackground() method (with their higher and lower priority variants). This method sends the request to a job server and only waits for confirmation that it was received. The client is not interested in when it'll be executed and with what result. If we refer to the previous use case with a web application and sending confirmation e-mails, it doesn't matter whether the e-mail is sent right now or after 10 seconds.

The worker script will wait for jobs from the job server, execute them, and return the result:

```
// gearman_worker_01.php
$worker = new GearmanWorker();
$worker->addServer('127.0.0.1');
$worker->addFunction('strlen', function(GearmanJob $job) {
    echo 'new job: ' . $job->workload()
        . ' (' . $job->workloadSize() . ")\n";
    return strlen($job->workload());
});

while ($worker->work()) { }
```

Usually, the worker runs in a loop and therefore is blocking as well. We connect to the same job server as the client and define a single function called strlen. This is the same name that the client specified when requesting a job. The value returned from the callable will be sent back to the client automatically.

Now, we can test this example. Before running either the client or the worker, we need to start the Gearman job server:

```
$ gearmand --verbose DEBUG
```

We can use the verbose option to make the process more talkative. Without specifying any other options, the job server will listen on port 4730, which is used by the PHP extension as well, so we don't need to configure anything.

Then, we'll run both the worker and the client. It doesn't matter which one we run first. Our client waits for three seconds before the timeout expires, so we can run it first and the pending job will be queued by the job server until there's at least one worker available to execute this job.

The console output after we run both the client and the worker will look like the following:

```
$ php gearman_worker_01.php
new job: Hello World! (12)
```

The worker is, in fact, running in a loop, so after processing this job, it'll wait for another one:

```
$ php gearman_client_01.php
int(12)
```

The client just receives the response and ends.

What's sometimes useful is that the Gearman CLI also contains a gearman application that can run as a client or worker. In our example, we didn't have to write a worker at all and could simply run the following command:

```
$ gearman -w -f strlen -- wc -c
```

This command creates a worker that connects to its default settings (localhost on port 4730). With -w, we told Gearman that we want to start a worker, and with -f strlen, we defined what function it handles. Then, when it receives a new job, it spawns a new subprocess and runs wc -c, where it feeds the workload as a standard input. So, this command is a drop-in replacement for our PHP worker.

Of course we can run multiple workers at the same time on the same machine. Each worker can handle multiple different functions. The job server is responsible for deciding what worker is going to process each job.

Running PHP Parser as a Gearman worker

We've already seen how to run our `PHPParserOperator` in multiple threads. We can, however, run it in multiple processes more easily than in threads by writing a Gearman worker that runs `PHPParserOperator` internally.

The worker will be very simple. It'll just receive the filename it needs to load and analyze, and then return the result:

```
// gearman_worker_02.php

$worker = new GearmanWorker();
$worker->addServer('127.0.0.1');

$worker->addFunction('phpparser', function(GearmanJob $job) {
    Observable::just($job->workload())
        ->lift(function() {
            $classes = ['AssignmentInConditionNodeVisitor'];
            return new PHPParserOperator($classes);
        })
        ->subscribeCallback(function($results) use ($job) {
            $job->sendComplete(json_encode($results));
        });
});
while ($worker->work()) { }
```

The main difference is that we're not using any return statement in the callable for the `phpparser` function. Since everything is asynchronous in RxPHP, we need to use the `sendComplete(...)` method to send the result to the client and mark the job as done.

When we run this worker, it won't print any output to the console:

```
$ php gearman_worker_02.php
```

Then we can test it right away, without writing any client application, and just use the CLI command as a client:

```
$ gearman -f phpparser -s "_test_source_code.php" | json_pp
{
   "results" : [
      {
         "violations" : [
            {
               "expr" : "$a = 1",
               "line" : 3
            },
            ...
```

```
            ],
            "class" : "AssignmentInConditionNodeVisitor"
          }
      ],
      "file" : "_test_source_code.php"
  }
```

We can see that the console output is the same as we saw previously when testing the `PHPParserOperator` operator.

The `-f phpparser` tells `gearman` what function we want to run, and with `-s` we can skip reading from the standard input and just pass the string as a workload. At the end, we used `json_pp` to pretty print the output to make it more readable.

Of course, we're running this example on the same machine and in the same directory, so we don't need to worry about correct file paths. In a real-world application, we'd probably send the file content instead.

This was a fairly quick introduction to Gearman. As we can see, using Gearman is very easy. Actually, in PHP it's much easier to use Gearman than using the pthreads extension to run jobs in parallel.

From our perspective, it's important to know that Gearman applications are usually blocking, so everything we mentioned about running multiple even loops in Chapter 6, *PHP Streams API and Higher-Order Observables*, is very relevant here as well.

If you want to read more about Gearman, head over to their official documentation with examples at `http://gearman.org/manual/`.

Comparing pthreads and Gearman

The main difference between using pthreads and Gearman is obviously whether we're running a single process with multiple threads or just one process multiple times.

The advantages and disadvantages of pthreads were partly covered in the previous chapter and also here. Having completely separated PHP interpreter contexts makes things a little non-intuitive (for example, using autoloaders and yet again sharing data between contexts) and definitely requires more debugging than the same single-threaded equivalent. However, if we're willing to spend the necessary time with it, the performance benefits are significant and at the end running a single process is always easier than taking care of multiple processes.

Gearman is designed to delegate work from clients to workers and send the results back to clients, if necessary. It's not supposed to be a general message exchanging framework. Thanks to this very specific focus, using Gearman is very easy. With workers, we don't care who, where, and sometimes not even when the work will be done. This is all up to the job server to decide.

In terms of scaling, threads are not a real option here. On the other hand, scaling with Gearman is simple. Just add more workers and Gearman will distribute the load evenly between them.

If we wanted to use some more adaptable frameworks, then RabbitMQ or ZMQ would be some good options. These are designed to be easily optimizable, for example by disabling acknowledge messages or using the publish/subscribe pattern, and overall provide more flexibility than Gearman. However, more effort is definitely required to implement these properly.

Summary

The purpose of this chapter was to use multithreaded and distributed computing on a practical example that also involves RxPHP.

We used PHP Parser library to make static code analysis of PHP scripts. We wrapped the parser with the RxPHP operator and ran it in parallel in multiple threads using the pthreads extension and in multiple workers with Gearman.

We also saw how we can make thread pools reusable in RxPHP by wrapping them with `ThreadPoolOperator`.

The next chapter will cover topics that didn't fit into any of the previous ones, and show some interesting and advanced use cases for RxPHP.

10
Using Advanced Operators and Techniques in RxPHP

This is the last chapter dedicated to explaining new RxPHP operators. There are few topics that didn't fit into any of the preceding chapters, so we'll cover them now. A couple of times we'll revisit Observable multicasting from `Chapter 8`, *Multicasting in RxPHP and PHP7 pthreads Extension*, in practical examples and also four new operators, `zip()`, `window()`, `materialize()`, and `dematerialize()`, which are more advanced techniques for modifying Observable chains.

In particular, in this chapter we'll cover the following topics:

- The `zip()` and `window()` operators that work with higher-order Observables
- The `materialize()` and `dematerialize()` operators
- Error propagation in Observable chains and how to properly catch exceptions from user-defined callbacks
- Theory around creating hot/cold Observables and the difference in unsubscribing and completing Observable chains
- Creating anonymous operators
- Writing a recursive `DirectoryIteratorObservable` that emits all files in a directory and all its subdirectories
- Writing a variant of `DirectoryIteratorObservable` based on multicasting
- Writing an FTP client based on RxPHP
- Using RxPHP in blocking and synchronous applications

We've seen so many RxPHP operators throughout this entire book. All of them worked with values in some way or another.

However, there are also operators that are, in principle, similar to those used by hot Observables or cold Observables when testing the RxPHP code that we saw in Chapter 5, *Testing RxPHP Code*.

The zip() operator

The zip() operator is similar to the ForkJoinObservable that we implemented ourselves in Chapter 5, *Testing RxPHP Code*. The main difference is that it internally stores all emissions for each source Observable in a separate queue and then re-emits their values when all sources have a value at a specific index.

This will be understood better by looking at the following example:

```
// zip_01.php
$obs1 = Observable::range(1, 7);
$obs2 = Observable::fromArray(['a', 'b']);
$obs3 = Observable::range(42, 5);

$obs1->zip([$obs2, $obs3])
    ->subscribe(new DebugSubject());
```

We have three source Observables where each of them emits a different number of items. Then the zip() operator emits an array of values only when all the sources have emissions at the same index. So we know that DebugSubject will receive only two items because the $obs2 Observable emits only two items.

In other words, the zip() operator can't make the third emission because it doesn't have a third value for the second $obs2 Observable.

The output from this example is as follows:

```
$ php zip_01.php
07:26:16 [] onNext: [1,"a",42] (array)
07:26:16 [] onNext: [2,"b",43] (array)
07:26:16 [] onCompleted
```

Notice that it contains only the first two values for each source Observable.

We can have a look at another and more complicated example that simulates asynchronous emission from multiple source Observables:

```php
// zip_02.php
$loop = new StreamSelectLoop();
$scheduler = new EventLoopScheduler($loop);

$obs1 = Observable::interval(1000, $scheduler)
  ->map(function($i) { return chr(65 + $i); });

$obs2 = Observable::interval(500, $scheduler)
  ->map(function($i) { return $i + 42; });

Observable::interval(200, $scheduler)
  ->zip([$obs1, $obs2])
  ->subscribe(new DebugSubject());

$loop->run();
```

Since each source Observable emits with a different interval, the `zip()` operator will have to emit according to the slowest one, which emits every 1000ms. Values for the rest of the Observables are then stacked internally in queues.

This example will print the following output:

```
$ php zip_02.php
08:48:47 [] onNext: [0,"A",42] (array)
08:48:48 [] onNext: [1,"B",43] (array)
08:48:49 [] onNext: [2,"C",44] (array)
08:48:50 [] onNext: [3,"D",45] (array)
...
```

Notice that we're actually not losing values. All values that weren't re-emitted yet are kept inside the `zip()` operator.

The window() operator

The `window()` operator belongs among the more advanced higher-order Observables. We've seen the `switchLatest()` operator in Chapter 6, *PHP Streams API and Higher-Order Observables*, and we know that it automatically subscribes to the latest Observable emitted from its source Observable.

The exact opposite is the `window()` operator that takes a so called "window boundary" Observable as an argument and splits the source emissions into separate Observables based on emission from the "window boundary" Observable.

An example will definitely make this more obvious:

```php
// window_01.php
$source = Observable::range(1, 10)->publish();
$windowBoundary = $source->bufferWithCount(3);

$source->window($windowBoundary)
  ->doOnNext(function() {
    echo "emitting new window Observable\n";
  })
  ->switchLatest()
  ->subscribe(new CallbackObserver(function($value) {
    echo "$value\n";
  }));

$source->connect();
```

We have a source Observable emitting 10 items in total. The `window()` operator splits them into chunks of three items because of the Observable in the `$windowBoundary` variable that we pass as an argument to `window()`. This means that we'll make four Observables in total where the first three emit three items (and then complete) and the last one just a single item (and then it completes as well).

To make this even more obvious, we added the `doOnNext()` operator to print a log every time we create a new Observable.

The `switchLatest()` operator is then used to always subscribe only to the latest Observable emitted by `window()`.

So in the console it'll look like we split the source into chunks of three items. In other words, we split the source into windows of three times:

```
$ php window_01.php
emitting new window Observable
1
2
3
emitting new window Observable
4
5
6
emitting new window Observable
```

```
7
8
9
emitting new window Observable
10
```

You're probably wondering what's this all good for. The `window()` operator, optionally takes a selector function. This function receives as an argument the current window before pushing it to its observers. For us this means that we can further chain operators to it before it's passed further, which can be very useful.

Imagine we're in a situation where we're receiving messages of many different types, but we want to be able to guarantee that we pass through only one message of each type every 100 messages.

We can simulate such a situation by creating a source Observable with 500 items where we repeat only three different characters. Then split it into windows with 100 items each and use the selector function to chain the new window Observables with the `distinct()` operator:

```php
// window_02.php
$chars = [];
for ($i = 0; $i < 500; $i++) {
  $chars[] = chr(rand(65, 67));
}
echo 'Source length: ' . count($chars) . "\n";

$source = Observable::fromArray($chars)->publish();
$windowBoundary = $source->bufferWithCount(100);

$source->window($windowBoundary, function($observable) {
    return $observable->distinct();
  })
  ->doOnNext(function() {
    echo "emitting new window Observable\n";
  })
  ->switchLatest()
  ->subscribe(new CallbackObserver(function($value) {
    echo "$value\n";
  }));

$source->connect();
```

Every Observable emitted by the `window()` operator has its own instance of the `distinct()` operator, so after every 100 items we start comparing distinct items all over again.

This example prints the following output:

```
$ php window_02.php
Source length: 500
emitting new window Observable
A
C
B
emitting new window Observable
C
A
B
emitting new window Observable
B
C
A
emitting new window Observable
C
B
A
emitting new window Observable
B
C
A
emitting new window Observable
```

Note that the order of characters is always going to be different because the source is generated randomly.

We can see that even though each window contains 100 items, these are always filtered by the `distinct()` operator that we chained to the window Observable in the selector function.

 The `window()` operator definitely falls into the group of more advanced and not so common operators in practice. In RxJS 5 there're even more variants of this operator for more specific use cases.

The materialize() and dematerialize() operators

In Chapter 5, *Testing RxPHP Code*, when we talked about testing in RxPHP, we weren't using real values, and instead were passing some special recorded objects that wrapped the actual value with OnNextNotification (or its error or complete variants). We did this because of the TestScheduler class and because we had to be able to uniquely identify each value in order to compare object references and not just their values. Comparing just values wouldn't guarantee that they are identical because primitive types such as strings or integers aren't passed by reference by default.

There are two operators that use a similar principle. These are materialize() and dematerialize().

The first one takes each value, wraps it with a notification object, and re-emits it as a typical onNext signal. This includes error and complete signals as well. These are wrapped and re-emitted like any other value, and after that a complete signal is sent.

This means we can completely ignore error signals or handle them as regular values. Before we talk more about what we can do with all this, let's consider the following example where we'll see what the materialize() operator actually does:

```
// materialize_01.php
Observable::range(1, 3)
    ->materialize()
    ->subscribe(new DebugSubject());
```

This is just a RangeObservable that emits three values and then sends complete signals. The materialize() operator converts each signal into an object, so this example will print the following output to the console:

```
$ php materialize_01.php
20:15:48 [] onNext: OnNext(1) (Rx\Notification\OnNextNotification)
20:15:48 [] onNext: OnNext(2) (Rx\Notification\OnNextNotification)
20:15:48 [] onNext: OnNext(3) (Rx\Notification\OnNextNotification)
20:15:48 [] onNext: OnCompleted() (...\OnCompletedNotification)
20:15:48 [] onCompleted
```

We can see that DebugSubject received five signals in total. The first three are just numbers emitted by the source RangeObservable. Then follows the complete signal from the source, wrapped as well, and after that another complete signal, but this time emitted by the materialize() operator itself.

Now let's have a look at another example where we emit an error:

```
// materialize_02.php
Observable::create(function(\Rx\ObserverInterface $observer) {
        $observer->onNext(1);
        $observer->onNext(2);
        $observer->onError(new \Exception("It's broken"));
        $observer->onNext(4);
    })
    ->materialize()
    ->subscribe(new DebugSubject());
```

This is very similar to the previous example, but this time we're forcing one error signal among normal emissions. As we said, the materialize() operator wraps the error and then calls complete.

When we run this example, we'll see that the wrapped value 4 never arrived to DebugSubject since it has already unsubscribed because of the complete signal:

```
$ php materialize_02.php
20:25:59 [] onNext: OnNext(1)  (Rx\Notification\OnNextNotification)
20:25:59 [] onNext: OnNext(2)  (Rx\Notification\OnNextNotification)
20:25:59 [] onNext: OnError(Exception)  (...\OnErrorNotification)
20:25:59 [] onCompleted
```

So what's all this actually good for when we can't, in fact, skip either the error or the complete signals?

While materialize() wraps signals with a notification object, there's also the exact opposite operator called dematerialize(). And, of course, we can use these two operators independently of each other.

Customizing error bubbling with dematerialize()

Imagine that we have an Observable chain that needs to emit multiple errors, but it can't decide which of these are severe and need to be propagated further down the chain and which can be safely ignored. In a normal Observable chain, the first error would cause immediate unsubscription.

With clever usage of notification objects and the `dematerialize()` operator, we can let the error pop up when we want.

In the following example, we generate a series of nine numbers. Every third number is then converted into an error notification. The errors aren't important and can be safely ignored. But the sixth number is different, and when it appears we always want to signal an error.

Consider the following example that generates multiple error signals and wraps them with notifications:

```php
// materialize_03.php
Observable::range(1, 9)
  ->materialize()
  ->map(function(Notification $notification) {
    $val = null;
    $notification->accept(function($next) use (&$val) {
      $val = $next;
    }, function() {}, function() use (&$val) { $val = -1; });

    if ($val % 3 == 0) {
      $msg = "It's really broken";
      $e = $val==6 ? new LogicException($msg) : new Exception();
      return new OnErrorNotification($e);
    } else {
      return $notification;
    }
  })
  ->subscribe(new DebugSubject());
```

This example uses `materialize()` at the beginning to convert all values to notifications. Then, inside the `map()` operator, we unwrap all notifications with their `accept()` method that propagates their value to the appropriate callable (it's like calling `subscribe()` on an Observable). This way we can see its value and just return it as it is or eventually return `OnErrorNotification` instead.

When we run this example, we'll get the following output:

```
$ php materialize_03.php
21:05:42 [] onNext: OnNext(1) (Rx\Notification\OnNextNotification)
21:05:42 [] onNext: OnNext(2) (Rx\Notification\OnNextNotification)
21:05:42 [] onNext: OnError(Exception) (...\OnErrorNotification)
21:05:42 [] onNext: OnNext(4) (Rx\Notification\OnNextNotification)
21:05:42 [] onNext: OnNext(5) (Rx\Notification\OnNextNotification)
21:05:42 [] onNext: OnError(LogicException)
(...\OnErrorNotification)
21:05:42 [] onNext: OnNext(7) (Rx\Notification\OnNextNotification)
21:05:42 [] onNext: OnNext(8) (Rx\Notification\OnNextNotification)
```

```
21:05:42 [] onNext: OnError(Exception) (...\OnErrorNotification)
21:05:42 [] onNext: OnCompleted() (...\OnCompletedNotification)
21:05:42 [] onCompleted
```

This is what we wanted to get. None of the errors actually did anything, and they were all emitted as a normal onNext signal. Note that instead of number six we have a LogicException. Now the last thing is to filter out all errors that are unimportant for us. This means all errors except the single LogicException.

We'll prepend the filter() and dematerialize() operators before the subscribe() call. We have to use dematerialize() to turn notifications to their respective signals. So the preceding example will look like the following:

```
// materialize_04.php
// the preceding chain from materialize_03.php
->filter(function(Notification $notification) {
    if ($notification instanceof OnErrorNotification) {
        $e2 = new OnErrorNotification(new LogicException());
        return (string)$notification == (string)$e2;
    } else {
        return true;
    }
})
->dematerialize()
->subscribe(new DebugSubject())
```

If we rerun this finalized example, we'll get the following output:

```
$ php materialize_04.php
21:09:33 [] onNext: 1 (integer)
21:09:33 [] onNext: 2 (integer)
21:09:33 [] onNext: 4 (integer)
21:09:33 [] onNext: 5 (integer)
21:09:33 [] onError (LogicException): It's really broken
```

All the other errors were ignored by the filter() operator and the only one that was preserved and unwrapped with dematerialize() is the LogicException.

This method of handling errors is obviously a hack that we typically don't want to do, but it's good to know that even this is possible with RxPHP out of the box, without creating custom observers or Observables.

Error handling in RxPHP operator chains

You may be wondering why we can't just emit multiple errors from an Observable and then use `materialize()` to wrap them.

Consider the following example with `Observable::create` that emits two errors:

```
// materialize_05.php
Observable::create(function($observer) {
    $observer->onNext(1);
    $observer->onNext(2);
    $observer->onError(new Exception());
    $observer->onNext(4);
    $observer->onError(new Exception());
    $observer->onNext(6);
})
->materialize()
->subscribe(new DebugSubject());
```

It might look like this example should wrap all the values and errors into notifications because we put the `materialize()` operator right after the `Observable::create`. Let's see what happens when we run this:

```
$ php materialize_05.php
21:14:53 [] onNext: OnNext(1)  (Rx\Notification\OnNextNotification)
21:14:53 [] onNext: OnNext(2)  (Rx\Notification\OnNextNotification)
21:14:53 [] onNext: OnError(Exception)  (...\OnErrorNotification)
21:14:53 [] onCompleted
```

So why can we only see the emissions up to the first error even though we used `materialize()`?

Every time we use `lift()`, we're actually creating a new instance of `AnonymousObservable`. This Observable creates an instance of `AutoDetachObserver` internally on subscription, and after that, it calls its subscription callable. This `AutoDetachObserver` class automatically calls `dispose()` on its internal disposable object (which unsubscribes from the source) when it receives the `error` or `complete` signal.

Since almost all operators internally use `lift()`, they are also using `AutoDetachObserver`.

This includes `Observable::create()`, which is just a static method that creates a new `AnonymousObservable`.

So this is why an Observable can never emit more than one `error` or `complete` signal. They will always be ignored because the `AutoDetachObserver` class has already unsubscribed when it received the first one.

The default error handler

We know that each observer can take as an optional parameter an error handler that is called on error notification. Although the default behavior is different than we might expect. If we do specify the error callable, we can handle the error however we want to.

For example, consider the following example where we specify only the error handler:

```php
// error_01.php
Observable::range(1, 5)
  ->filter(function($val) {
    if ($val === 3) {
      throw new \Exception("It's broken");
    }
  })
  ->subscribe(new CallbackObserver(
    null,
    function(\Exception $e){
      $msg = $e->getMessage();
      echo "Error: ${msg}\n";
    })
  );
```

When we run this example we'll see that the handler is called properly:

```
$ php error_01.php
Error: It's broken
```

Now what happens if don't set any error handler at all? We can see this situation in the following example:

```php
// error_02.php
Observable::range(1, 5)
  ->filter(function($val) {
    if ($val === 3) {
      throw new \Exception("It's broken");
    }
  })
  ->subscribe(new CallbackObserver());
```

We're using the `CallbackObserver` without any parameter, so the following output is what we'll get:

```
$ php error_02.php
PHP Fatal error:  Uncaught Exception: It's broken in /.../Chapter
10/error_02.php:12
Stack trace:
#0 [internal function]: {closure}(3)
#1 /.../reactivex/rxphp/lib/Rx/Operator/FilterOperator.php(40):
call_user_func(Object(Closure), 3)
#2 [internal function]:
Rx\Operator\FilterOperator->Rx\Operator\{closure}(3)
   ...
```

The exception was simply rethrown. We didn't set any error callable, so this is probably something we didn't expect to happen. It's good to be aware of this behavior because it means that if we don't handle error notifications they might cause unexpected script termination.

> The default error handling is the same in RxJS 5; however, there's an ongoing discussion whether this is the correct way Rx should behave. It's likely that in the future versions of RxJS this behavior will change.

Catching exceptions inside operators

A similar principle applies also when calling any user defined functions inside an Observable or an operator. For example, when using the `map()` operator the callable is wrapped with a try-catch block. Any exception thrown inside our callable is then sent as an error notification.

This means that neither Observables nor operators are supposed to throw exceptions unless something unexpected occurs that shouldn't happen under normal circumstances. Throwing an exception inside a user defined callable is a valid use case.

We can test the difference on these two examples. First we'll throw an exception inside the selector function to the `zip()` operator from the same example we saw previously:

```
// error_03.php
$obs1 = Observable::range(1, 7);
$obs2 = Observable::fromArray(['a', 'b']);
$obs3 = Observable::range(42, 5);

$obs1->zip([$obs2, $obs3], function($values) {
```

```
        throw new \Exception("It's broken");
    })
    ->subscribe(new DebugSubject());
```

The exception will be caught and sent as an error notification:

```
$ php error_03.php
09:41:05 [] onError (Exception): It's broken
```

In this example, we will see what happens when we try to use a regular object instead of a source Observable:

```
// error_04.php
$obs1 = Observable::range(1, 7);
$obs2 = Observable::fromArray(['a', 'b']);
$object = new stdClass();

$obs1->zip([$obs2, $object])
    ->subscribe(new DebugSubject());
```

Note that this type of error is catchable in PHP7:

```
$ php error_04.php
PHP Fatal error:  Uncaught Error: Call to undefined method
stdClass::subscribe() in /.../lib/Rx/Operator/ZipOperator.php:110
...
```

The exception was left to terminate the script execution because this is a situation that shouldn't happen. It probably means that we have a bug in our code where we unintentionally wanted to use an stdClass instance instead of an Observable.

The Observable::create() method versus the Subject class

Apart from creating custom Observables, we know that we can use the Observable::create() static method or an instance of the Subject class to emit items by ourselves, but so far we haven't talked about which one we should choose over the other and why.

As a rule of thumb it's usually better to use Observable::create(). It's not always possible, but it has its advantages.

For the next couple of examples, let's consider that we want to work with an API that implements the following interface. This could be any Facebook/Twitter/WebSocket or system API:

```
interface RemoteAPI {
    public function connect($connectionDetails);
    public function fetch($path, $callback);
    public function close();
}
```

Hot/cold Observables and Observable::create()

In the most general sense an Observable is just a function that connects an observer with the producer of values. By producer we understand any source of values that is unrelated to RxPHP. For example, this can be any class implementing our `RemoteAPI` interface.

We'll see that this works well with our definitions of hot/cold Observables from Chapter 2, *Reactive Programming with RxPHP*. A cold Observable creates its producer (in our case, connects to the remote API) on subscription. This means that we don't want to make any remote calls to the API until we have at least one observer.

So a cold Observable internally using the RemoteAPI interface could look like the following:

```
// observable_create_01.php
class RemoteServiceAPI implements RemoteAPI {
  ...
}

Observable::create(function(ObserverInterface $observer) {
  $producer = new RemoteServiceAPI();
  $producer->connect('...');

  $producer->fetch('whatever', function($result) use ($observer){
    $observer->onNext($result);
  });

  return new CallbackDisposable(function() use ($producer) {
    $producer->close();
  });
});
```

This fulfills our expectations from a cold Observable. The producer doesn't exist until we subscribe and it automatically also closes the connection when unsubscribing because we returned the `CallbackDisposable` instance from the callback to the `Observable::create()` method.

If we wanted to create a hot Observable with the `Observable::create()` method it would be similar, but this time the Observable is not responsible for neither creating nor closing the producer:

```php
// observable_create_02.php
$producer = new RemoteServiceAPI();
$producer->connect('...');

Observable::create(function($observer) use ($producer) {
    $producer->fetch('whatever', function($result) use ($observer){
        $observer->onNext($result);
    });
});

// somewhere later...
$producer->close();
```

The producer is created independently on the hot Observable and subscribing/unsubscribing to it has no effect on the producer.

You might be wondering how is this all related to comparing `Observable::create()` and the `Subject` class?

The point is that we can't simply do the same with Subjects. We could of course use a Subject in this scenario, but than we'd have to handle all subscription and unsubscription logic ourselves (including creating/closing the producer). Nonetheless, in Chapter 8, *Multicasting in RxPHP and PHP7 pthreads Extension*, we talked about the internal states in Subjects, which is also very relevant here.

As a rule of thumb, every time you end up using a Subject think whether you could achieve the same with `Observable::create()` instead.

Call stack length and EventLoopScheduler

When developing PHP applications, it's handy to enable the Xdebug extension that we can use to debug our code. However this comes with the cost of reduced performance, higher memory usage, and a limited number of possible nested function calls.

The last issue is relevant to us in particular. For example, in RxPHP when we make a long operator chain and use the `ImmediateScheduler` method. Consider the following very long chain of operators:

```
// stack_length_01.php
Observable::range(1, 10)
  ->doOnNext(function($val) { /* do whatever */ })
  ->startWithArray([12, 15, 17])
  ->skip(1)
  ->map(function($val) {
    return $val * 2;
  })
  ->filter(function($val) {
    return $val % 3 === 0;
  })
  ->doOnNext(function($val) { /* do whatever */ })
  ->takeLast(3)
  ->sum()
  ->doOnNext(function($val) { /* do whatever */ })
  ->subscribe(new CallbackObserver(function() {
    $backtrace = debug_backtrace();
    $len = count($backtrace);

    foreach ($backtrace as $item) {
      $args = count($item['args']);
      $func = $item['function'];
      if (isset($item['file'])) {
        $file = substr($item['file'],
            strrpos($item['file'], '/') + 1);
        echo "${file}#${item['line']} ${func} ${args} arg/s\n";
      } else {
        echo "${func} ${args} arg/s\n";
      }
    }
    echo "=============\n";
    echo "Stack length: ${len}\n";
  }));
```

This example chains nine operators and then in the observer prints the entire call stack. We know that the call stack will start at the subscriber's `onNext` handler and traverse upwards via `onNext()` calls to the `RangeObservable` where it starts emitting values. Then the stack goes back to the bottom via `subscribe()` calls.

The shortened output looks as follows:

```
$ php stack_length_01.php
{closure} 1 arg/s
CallbackObserver.php#45 call_user_func_array 2 arg/s
AbstractObserver.php#38 next 1 arg/s
AutoDetachObserver.php#53 onNext 1 arg/s
AbstractObserver.php#38 next 1 arg/s
DoOnEachOperator.php#34 onNext 1 arg/s
...

DoOnEachOperator.php#51 onCompleted 0 arg/s
Rx\Operator\{closure} 0 arg/s
CallbackObserver.php#35 call_user_func 1 arg/s
AbstractObserver.php#19 completed 0 arg/s
RangeObservable.php#59 onCompleted 0 arg/s
ImmediateScheduler.php#39 Rx\Observable\{closure} 1 arg/s
...

TakeLastOperator.php#55 subscribe 2 arg/s
Observable.php#740 __invoke 3 arg/s
AnonymousObservable.php#33 Rx\{closure} 2 arg/s
ReduceOperator.php#73 subscribe 2 arg/s
Observable.php#740 __invoke 3 arg/s
AnonymousObservable.php#33 Rx\{closure} 2 arg/s
DoOnEachOperator.php#55 subscribe 2 arg/s
Observable.php#740 __invoke 3 arg/s
AnonymousObservable.php#33 Rx\{closure} 2 arg/s
stack_length_01.php#39 subscribe 1 arg/s
=============
Stack length: 103
```

We can see that this call stack contains 103 nested function calls. This would be obviously hard to debug, so we can reduce its length by using `EventLoopScheduler` instead of default `ImmediateScheduler`. This will make every callback to the `schedule()` method run as a separate event by `EventLoopScheduler`.

We'll set the Scheduler right in the `Observable::range()` call as follows:

```
// stack_length_02.php
$loop = new StreamSelectLoop();
$scheduler = new EventLoopScheduler($loop);
Observable::range(1, 10, $scheduler)
    ...
    ->subscribe(new CallbackObserver(function() {
      ...
    }));
$loop->run();
```

Now when we run this example the call stack will contain only 65 nested calls:

```
$ php stack_length_02.php
{closure} 1 arg/s
CallbackObserver.php#45 call_user_func_array 2 arg/s
AbstractObserver.php#38 next 1 arg/s
. . .
Timers.php#90 call_user_func 2 arg/s
StreamSelectLoop.php#177 tick 0 arg/s
stack_length_02.php#45 run 0 arg/s
============
Stack length: 65
```

This obviously comes with a cost, so using the `EventLoopScheduler` class is always going to be slower than using the default `ImmediateScheduler`. Also the emissions that are wrapped with `schedule()` are called from the event loop and not from the place the `schedule()` method was invoked.

This can make debugging even harder, but the `EventLoopScheduler` class is especially useful when we don't want to block the execution thread and also want to let other code be executed (thanks to its event loop). In Chapter 6, *PHP Streams API and Higher-Order Observables*, we talked about even loops in great detail and how it's important not to block the execution thread. In such cases, using `EventLoopScheduler` is a very good choice.

 Using an asynchronous Scheduler is also relevant to RxJS because in a JavaScript environment the call stack length is limited.

Unsubscribing versus completing an Observable

We know that when we have an observer we'll stop receiving items when the source Observable completes or when we manually unsubscribe. However, we haven't talked about why we might choose one over the other.

There're basically two ways to stop receiving items:

- Unsubscribe from the source Observable
- Using an operator that completes the chain (such as the `takeUntil()` operator)

By unsubscribing we usually mean that we don't want to be receiving items any more. This obviously doesn't mean that the source Observable stopped sending items or sent the complete notification. We're just no longer interested in the items coming from the source.

As an important consequence to manually unsubscribing, the complete handler is never called. Consider the following example where we unsubscribe after receiving a few items:

```php
// unsubscribe_01.php
$loop = new StreamSelectLoop();
$scheduler = new EventLoopScheduler($loop);

$subscription = Observable::range(1, 10, $scheduler)
  ->subscribe(new CallbackObserver(
    function($val) use (&$subscription) {
      echo "$val\n";
      if ($val === 3) {
        $subscription->dispose();
      }
    },
    null, // no error handler
    function() {
      echo "completed!\n";
    })
  );

$loop->run();
```

Note that we had to use the `EventLoopScheduler` class instead of the default one because we need to run the observer callables as separate events in the loop. If we used the `ImmediateScheduler` class then the `$subscription` variable would always be null because all the callables would be called within the `subscribe()` call. In other words, the `$subscription` variable would be unassigned.

When we run this demo we can see that it prints the first three items and then ends and no complete handler was called:

```
$ php unsubscribe_01.php
1
2
3
```

But what if we're in a situation where the complete handler is important and we always want to call it when we unsubscribe? In such cases we can use any operator that sends a complete notification, for example, `takeUntil()` and an instance of the `Subject` class:

```
// unsubscribe_02.php
$subject = new Subject();

$subscription = Observable::range(1, 10)
  ->takeUntil($subject)
  ->subscribe(new CallbackObserver(
    function($val) use ($subject) {
      echo "$val\n";
      if ($val === 3) {
        $subject->onNext(null);
      }
    },
    null, // no error handler
    function() {
      echo "completed!\n";
    })
  );
```

We're using the `$subject` variable to notify the `takeUntil()` operator that we want to complete and then manually call the `onNext()` method inside a callable passed to the `CallbackObserver` class.

This way we ensured that apart from just unsubscribing the observer, we'll also call the complete handler, as we can see from the console output:

```
$ php unsubscribe_02.php
1
2
3
completed!
```

Whether we want to simply unsubscribe or send the complete notification is up to us. A big advantage of using a `Subject` class and the `takeUntil()` operator is that we can easily complete multiple chains by using a single `onNext()` call.

If we wanted to just unsubscribe multiple chains, then we'd have to collect and keep all their disposables and then call `dispose()` on all of them manually.

Anonymous operators

We've been using the lift() method to use custom operators in Observable chains a lot. In RxPHP v1, it's also the only way to implement custom operators. This method takes as a parameter the so called **operator factory**, which is a callable that returns an instance of the operator we want to use. This method is called every time we subscribe, so it might be called just once in total.

When using operators, we're making use of PHP's magic __invoke() method that allows us to use any object just as if it were a function.

Let's consider this simple example that shows the __invoke() method:

```php
// func_01.php
class MyClass {
    public function __invoke($a, $b) {
        return $a * $b;
    }
}
$obj = new MyClass();
var_dump($obj(3, 4));
```

We make an instance of MyClass that we used as if it was a regular function with $obj(3,4). If we run this example, we'll get the correct result:

```
$ php func_01.php
int(12)
```

Operators in RxPHP use the same principle. In fact the lift() method is deep inside the Observable class, defined as the following:

```php
public function lift(callable $operatorFactory) {
    return new AnonymousObservable(
        function($observer, $schedule) use ($operatorFactory) {

        $operator = $operatorFactory();
        return $operator($this, $observer, $schedule);
    });
}
```

The callable $operatorFactory doesn't need to return an operator object at all. It can just return another callable that'll take three arguments and do whatever it wants to. This is useful when we want to do a one-time operation where it doesn't make sense to make it reusable and write a custom operator for it.

For example, we can make the same operations on the source Observable and the observer just like in any other operator class:

```php
// anonymous_02.php
Observable::range(1, 5)
  ->map(function($val) {
    return $val * 2;
  })
  ->lift(function() {
    return function($observable, $observer, $scheduler) {
      $prevValue = 0;
      $onNext = function($value) use ($observer, &$prevValue) {
        $observer->onNext($value * $prevValue);
        $prevValue = $value;
      };
      $innerObs = new CallbackObserver(
        $onNext,
        [$observer, 'onError'],
        [$observer, 'onCompleted']
      );

      return $observable->subscribe($innerObs);
    };
  })
  ->subscribe(new DebugSubject());
```

Note that we have a $prevValue variable that is kept in this context, and we can use it among all invocations of the onNext signals.

Writing a custom DirectoryIteratorObservable

In the previous chapter, we used a couple of DirectoryIterators to recursively get all files in a directory and all its subdirectories. When iterating files, we might want to filter not only by filenames, but also by file size or access restrictions. Ideally, we could have a custom Observable that just checks the files names to match a certain pattern and then emits SplFileInfo objects so we can implement our filtering logic ourselves.

For this purpose, we'll write our own `DirectoryIteratorObservable` that does all this and has some extra options on top of that. We can split the implementation into two smaller chunks:

```php
// DirectoryIteratorObservable.php
class DirectoryIteratorObservable extends Observable {
  private $iter;
  private $scheduler;
  private $selector;
  private $pattern;

  public function __construct($dir, $pattern = null,
      $selector = null, $recursive = true, $scheduler = null) {

    $this->scheduler = $scheduler;
    $this->pattern = $pattern;
    if ($recursive) {
      $dirIter = new RecursiveDirectoryIterator($dir);
      $iter = new RecursiveIteratorIterator($dirIter);
    } else {
      $iter = new DirectoryIterator($dir);
    }
    $this->iter = $iter;

    if ($selector) {
        $this->selector = $selector;
    } else {
      $this->selector = function(SplFileInfo $file) {
        return $file;
      };
    }
  }
  // ...
}
```

We're still using `RecursiveIteratorIterator` internally; however, we have full control over it and won't let other developers fiddle with it. Somebody could, for instance, use `rewind()` or `seek()` methods and unintentionally move the inner pointer, not to mention that using three different iterators to traverse a directory structure is a little too much and not easily reusable.

That's why our Observable hides all this from the user and has just a couple of input parameters. We definitely want to be able to set a pattern to filter files right away. Sometimes we might want to traverse several directories recursively and other times just a single directory, so we'll have a separate parameter for this. The last behavior we want to be able to modify is what this operator is going to emit. By default, it's the `SplFileInfo` object, but if we set a custom selector function we can emit, for example, just the file names.

The main logic is in the `subscribe()` method, which is built around a `scheduleRecursive()` method from the `Scheduler` class:

```php
// DirectoryIteratorObservable.php
class DirectoryIteratorObservable extends Observable {
  // ...
  public function subscribe($observer, $scheduler = null) {
    if ($this->scheduler !== null) {
      $scheduler = $this->scheduler;
    }
    if ($scheduler === null) {
      $scheduler = new ImmediateScheduler();
    }
    $this->iter->rewind();

    return $scheduler->scheduleRecursive(
        function($reschedule) use ($observer) {
      /** @var SplFileInfo $current */
      $current = $this->iter->current();
      $this->iter->next();
      if (!$this->pattern || preg_match($this->pattern,$current)){
        try {
          $processed = call_user_func($this->selector, $current);
          $observer->onNext($processed);
        } catch (\Exception $e) {
          $observer->onError($e);
        }
      }

      if ($this->iter->valid()) {
        $reschedule();
      } else {
        $observer->onCompleted();
      }
    });
  }
}
```

Note that in RxPHP v2 the `subscribe()` method doesn't take the `Scheduler` as a parameter. This means that we'd access the `Scheduler` class directly with the `Scheduler::getImmediate()` static method instead.

We're looping over all values produced by the iterator and emitting them until we reach the end, where we emit just the complete signal. Note that we're wrapping the call to the selector function, so if it throws an exception we'll emit it as an `error` signal.

We can test this Observable on the same directory structure from the Symfony3 template, as we did in the previous chapter:

```
// directory_iterator_01.php
$dir = __DIR__ . '/../symfony_template';
(new DirectoryIteratorObservable($dir, '/.+\.php$/'))
    ->subscribeCallback(function(SplFileInfo $file) {
        echo "$file\n";
    });
```

This will print a very long list of file names (when `SplFileInfo` objects are type-casted to strings they return only filenames).

Note that, internally, this Observable works similarly to, for example, `RangeObservable`. In fact, it doesn't keep an array of observers and instead immediately emits all values to the observer that subscribed (we also move the iterator's inner pointer to the start with `rewind()`). The consequences are obvious.

If we subscribe twice to this Observable, it'll loop the entire iterable twice as well.

DirectoryIteratorSharedObservable

So this looks like a good use-case for multicasting. Of course, we could append the `publish()` operator every time we use `DirectoryIteratorObservable`, but this would be error prone as we could easily forget to use it. Instead, we can make another Observable that wraps `DirectoryIteratorObservable`, and appends the `publish()` operator to it every time:

```
// DirectoryIteratorSharedObservable.php
class DirectoryIteratorSharedObservable extends Observable {
    private $inner;
    public function __construct() {
        $args = func_get_args();
        // PHP7 array unpacking with "..."
        $this->inner = (new DirectoryIteratorObservable(...$args))
```

```
                ->publish();
    }
    public function subscribe($observer, $scheduler = null) {
        $this->inner->subscribe($observer, $scheduler);
    }
    public function connect() {
        return $this->inner->connect();
    }
    public function refCount() {
        return $this->inner->refCount();
    }
}
```

This Observable is just a wrapper around the original DirectoryIteratorObservable, which is internally instantiated and then chained with publish(). We're purposely using publish() and not share(). The share() operator also appends the refCount() operator, which automatically subscribes/unsubscribes based on the number of observers.

This is useful with Observables that need to perform some asynchronous operation, such as downloading data (our CURLObservable) or running code in parallel (our ThreadPoolOperator). With Observables that emit all their values immediately on subscription, such as RangeObservable or our fresh DirectoryIteratorObservable, it wouldn't work as we expect. All values would be emitted to the first observer because of the immediate call to the connect() method inside the refCount() operator.

Now we can test this operator by subscribing multiple observers and then calling the connect() method:

```
// directory_iterator_shared_01.php
$src = new DirectoryIteratorSharedObservable('.', '/.+\.php$/');
$src->subscribe(new DebugSubject('1'));
$src->subscribe(new DebugSubject('2'));
$src->subscribe(new DebugSubject('3'));
$src->connect();
```

The output for this demo will be a list of file names where each of the observers will receive a single item at a time from the current directory:

```
$ php7 directory_iterator_shared_01.php
09:52:55 [1] onNext: ./materialize_01.php (SplFileInfo)
09:52:55 [2] onNext: ./materialize_01.php (SplFileInfo)
09:52:55 [3] onNext: ./materialize_01.php (SplFileInfo)
09:52:55 [1] onNext: ./materialize_02.php (SplFileInfo)
09:52:55 [2] onNext: ./materialize_02.php (SplFileInfo)
09:52:55 [3] onNext: ./materialize_02.php (SplFileInfo)
...
```

We avoided reemitting the same directory structure for each observer and multicasted items from the source with the `public()` operator and manually called the `connect()` method.

FTP client with RxPHP

For this example, let's imagine that we're running an FTP server where we want to perform a couple of operations. PHP has built-in support for FTP connections, so we don't need to install any extra libraries.

Our goal is to be able to do some basic operations with an FTP connection while utilizing what we know from RxPHP. When working with Observables, most of the time we've been using them in operator chains, but Observables can be used as asynchronous inputs or outputs as well. When returning a value from an asynchronous function, we'd usually use a Promise, but the same principles work with Observables too, and we can also benefit from chaining them.

Note that all FTP calls in PHP are blocking. Some functions have their non-blocking variants, such as functions to upload or download files, but others, such as functions that change or list a directory, are always blocking. For this reason, we'll stay only with their blocking variants. This way we can handle their correct and error states with Observables. This is also going to be a nice example where we can use multicasting.

So this is going to be an example of how to use RxPHP in a synchronous and blocking application.

We'll split our first `FTPClient` class into two smaller chunks and see how we can implement RxPHP in this use-case:

```php
// FTPClient.php
class FTPClient {
  private $conn;
  private $cwd = '/';

  public function __construct($host, $username, $pass, $port=21) {
    $this->conn = ftp_connect($host, $port);
    if (!$this->conn) {
      throw new \Exception('Unable to connect to ' . $host);
    }
    if (!ftp_login($this->conn, $username, $pass)) {
      throw new \Exception('Unable to login');
    }
  }
}
```

```
    public function chdir($dir) {
      $this->cwd = '/' . $dir;
      if (!ftp_chdir($this->conn, $dir)) {
        throw new \Exception('Unable to change current directory');
      }
    }

    public function listDir() {
      return Observable::defer(function() {
        $files = ftp_nlist($this->conn, $this->cwd);
        return Observable::fromArray($files)
          ->shareReplay(PHP_INT_MAX);
      });
    }

    public function close() {
      ftp_close($this->conn);
    }
    // ...
  }
```

These are the most basic methods we need. Many FTP functions in PHP return just true or false based on whether they succeeded or not. We used this in the constructor to throw exceptions if any of these cases fail.

Then there's the first method that returns an Observable. When we want to get a list of all the files and directories in a directory, we'll call the `listFiles()` method. This method returns an Observable from the array of files it received. As we said, FTP functions in PHP are blocking, so we're not calling `ftp_nlist()` asynchronously and need to wait until it finishes. The fact that we're returning an Observable means that we can feed this Observable into another method in this `FTPClient` class that takes an Observable as an argument.

We're purposely using `Observable::defer` in order to postpone the actual network request until we subscribe to it. We'll see why this is important when we start writing a test application for `FTPClient`.

We can now have a look at three more methods that'll get the file size, download files from the FTP server, or upload files to the server:

```
class FTPClient {
  // ...
  public function size(Observable $files) {
    return Observable::create(function($obs) use ($files) {
      $files->subscribeCallback(function($filename) use ($obs) {
        $size = ftp_size($this->conn, $filename);
```

```
        $obs->onNext(['filename' => $filename, 'size' => $size]);
      });
    });
  }

  public function upload(Observable $files, $m = FTP_ASCII) {
    $subject = new Subject();
    $files->subscribeCallback(function($file) use ($subject, $m) {
      $fp = fopen($file, 'r');
      $filename = basename($file);

      if (ftp_fput($this->conn, $filename, $fp, $m)) {
        $subject->onNext($filename);
      } else {
        $e = new Exception('Unable to upload ' . $filename);
        $subject->onError($e);
      }
    });
    return $subject->asObservable();
  }

  public function download(Observable $files, $dir, $m=FTP_ASCII){
    $subject = new Subject();
    $files->subscribeCallback(
        function($file) use ($subject, $m, $dir) {

      $dest = $dir . DIRECTORY_SEPARATOR . $filename;
      if (ftp_get($this->conn, $dest, $filename, $mode)) {
        $subject->onNext($filename);
      } else {
        $e = new Exception('Unable to download ' . $filename);
        $subject->onError($e);
      }
    });
    return $subject->asObservable();
  }
}
```

The last two methods are very similar in principle. They both take an Observable as an argument and subscribe to it. Then they create an internal Subject that is used to emit successful uploads/downloads and errors. The same Subject is then turned into an Observable with an asObservable() operator and returned.

What's interesting with this approach is that we don't need to know which files we want to download/upload in advance. In other words, we can call these methods with instances of Subject and just carry on executing our code. Then, sometime later, we can start pushing items to these Subjects, which will cause the files to be downloaded/uploaded. We'll see this in a moment.

We also implemented the `size()` method that takes as an argument an Observable and subscribes to it. This method is internally implemented with `Observable::create()` for the same reason as `listDir()`. We want to defer emitting any values until there's at least one subscription.

Now we can start using this class in a simple demo application that'll first just connect to an FTP server, list all files and directories, and then try to change the current directory to the last one in the list:

```
// ftp_01.php
$ftp = new FTPClient('...', 'user', 'password');
echo "List content...\n";
$ftp->listDir()
    ->takeLast(1)
    ->subscribeCallback(function($dir) use ($ftp) {
        echo "Changing directory to "$dir"...\n";
        $ftp->chdir($dir);
    });
```

We're using `listDir()` to get the content of the current directory, which is the root directory for this user. Then we take just the last item and try to go inside that directory. We used the `ftp_nlist()` function internally in `listDir()` where it returns all files and directories together, so how do we know that the last item in the list is really a directory and not a file?

If it was a file, then the call to `chdir()` would throw an exception. A simple way to distinguish files from directories is by checking their size. Directories always have a size of −1, while ordinary files have a real size that is always greater or equal to 0:

```
// ftp_01.php
// ...
echo "File sizes...\n";
$getFileSizesSubject = new Subject();

$fileSizes = $ftp
  ->size($getFileSizesSubject->asObservable())
  ->doOnNext(function($file) {
    echo "Size of ".$file['filename']." is ".$file['size']."\n";
  })
```

```
    ->filter(function($file) {
      return $file['size'] != -1;
    })
    ->subscribe(new DebugSubject());

  $ftp->listDir()->subscribe($getFileSizesSubject);
```

This demonstrates very well what we talked about. We have a Subject that we pass as an argument to the `size()` method. This method is not going to subscribe to it until its own chain has an observer, which happens on the last line with `DebugSubject`.

We're still not calling any `ftp_size()` because the `Subject` class in the `$getFileSizesSubject` variable hasn't emitted any items yet. This happens when we call `listDir()`, which itself first calls `ftp_nlist()` to get a list of all files and directories and then starts emitting items to the `Subject` class, which then simply takes the item and re-emits it to its own observer, which is the callable inside the `size()` method.

Since `size()` is based on `Observable::create()` and `subscribe()` methods, it doesn't make any network calls until we start sending it items. This might happen any time after we called it.

This all might look a little confusing, but all we're doing is just passing items between a couple of Observables.

Another obvious use-case could be listing only files in a directory and then downloading all of them. We have two methods that require an Observable as a source of files. With `size()` they will be checked for their file size (to see whether they're files at all) and for `download()` to download them. Of course, we don't want to make two separate calls for each of these methods, so we'll use the output from the Observable with only files (that is, the `$fileSizes` variable) as the source Observable for the `download()` method.

In order to make this example a little more complicated, we'll assume that we want to use the list of files once more and, for example, just print the file names and their sizes:

```
// ftp_01.php
// ...
$fileSizes = $ftp
  ->size($getFileSizesSubject->asObservable())
  ->doOnNext(function($file) {
    echo "Size of ".$file['filename']." is ".$file['size']."\n";
  })
  ->filter(function($file) {
    return $file['size'] != -1;
  })
  ->publish();
```

```
$destDir = './_download';
@mkdir($destDir);

echo "Downloading files ...\n";
$filesToDownload = $fileSizes
  ->map(function($file) {
    return $file['filename'];
  });

$ftp->download($filesToDownload, $destDir)
  ->subscribeCallback(function($file) use ($destDir) {
    echo "$file downloaded";
    $fileDest = $destDir . DIRECTORY_SEPARATOR . $file;
    if (file_exists($fileDest)) {
      echo " - OK\n";
    } else {
      echo " - failed\n";
    }
  });

$fileSizes->subscribeCallback(function($file) {
  echo $file['filename'] . ' - ' . $file['size'] . "B\n";
});

$fileSizes->connect();
$ftp->listDir()->subscribe($getFileSizesSubject);
echo "Done\n";
```

In the `$filesToDownload` variable, we're storing a predefined chain of operators that emits only file names coming from `$fileSizes`.

If we run this demo application, we'll get the following output (depending on the FTP server we are connected to):

```
$ php ftp_01.php
List content...
Changing directory to "web"...
File sizes...
Downloading files ...
Size of . is -1
Size of .. is -1
Size of app is -1
Size of blog is -1
Size of cache is -1
Size of composer.json is 522
composer.json downloaded - OK
composer.json - 522B
Size of composer.lock is 23690
```

```
composer.lock downloaded - OK
composer.lock - 23690B
Size of log is -1
Size of src is -1
Size of stats is -1
Size of vendor is -1
Size of www is -1
Done
```

We can see that both Observables based on emissions from $fileSizes are sharing the same connection (the doOnNext() operator is called just once for each item).

We could also create methods listing only files or only directories. This could look like the following:

```
class FTPClient {
  // ...
  public function listFiles() {
    return $this->size($this->listDir())
      ->filter(function($file) {
        return $file['size'] != -1;
      });
  }

  public function listDirectories() {
    return $this->size($this->listDir())
      ->filter(function($dir) {
        return $dir['size'] == -1
          && $dir['filename'] != '.'
          && $dir['filename'] != '..';
      })
      ->map(function($dir) {
        return $dir['filename'];
      });
  }
}
```

These both use the same principle as postponing subscriptions, as we explained previously.

Summary

This chapter covered a couple of slightly unusual examples that are possible with RxPHP, and which didn't fit into any of the previous chapters. These aren't things that we use on a daily basis, but it's good to know that features such as these are possible.

In particular, we went through the operators `zip()`, `window()`, `materialize()`, and `dematerialize()`. We saw how to propagate and handle errors in Observable chains and what role `AutoDetachObserver` has. Also, we compared the `Observable::create()` static method and the `Subject` class and when unsubscribing and completing an Observable chain. Apart from this, we created anonymous operators and wrote the `DirectoryIteratorObservable` class that recursively iterates a directory structure. Finally, we used RxPHP to make a simple FTP client that uses Observables for inputs and outputs.

In the last chapter, we're going to talk about implementations of Reactive Extension in languages other than PHP. Most notably, we'll have a look at RxJS-what it is, how it's related to RxPHP, and what differences we can encounter in a JavaScript environment from PHP.

11
Reusing RxPHP Techniques in RxJS

Throughout this entire book, we've mentioned very often that certain functionality (such as operators or certain Observables) work differently in RxPHP and RxJS. Some operators from RxJS aren't even available in RxPHP yet. There're also features of RxJS that aren't even possible to make in RxPHP because of the nature of PHP interpreter.

We've referred to RxJS a lot even though Reactive Extensions were first developed for .NET as Rx.NET.

In this chapter, we're going to focus on the differences between current RxPHP and RxJS. Also, the knowledge of RxJS is very useful today because its popularity is still rising thanks to JavaScript frameworks such as Angular 2 that heavily rely on RxJS.

Topics covered in this chapter are going to be a little unusual because these will combine PHP and JavaScript (ECMAScript 6 – ES6, in particular):

- We'll see what RxJS is, and we'll talk about where it stands in today's world of JavaScript
- We'll write a few very simple demos of RxJS, introducing us to synchronous and asynchronous code in JavaScript
- We'll talk about asynchronous events in JavaScript and how we can benefit from them in RxJS
- We'll see how and why higher order Observables behave differently in RxJS and RxPHP
- We'll talk about operators that aren't available in RxPHP right now but are fully functional in RxJS

We expect you to know at least the basics of JavaScript and ideally the new ES6 standard (aka ES2015) as well. This isn't required of course since RxJS can be used with plain old JavaScript (ES5.1 to be precise), but it's very relevant to RxJS and its development process.

Also, ES6 is already very well supported by Node.js, so we don't have any reason not to use it.

Don't worry if you can't get your head around the new ES6 syntax that we'll use in this chapter. If you want to know more about ES6, you can have a look at a quick summary of the new functionalities it provides at `https://github.com/lukehoban/es6features`.

We're going to run all examples in this chapter by Node.js runtime (`https://nodejs.org`). If you're not familiar with Node.js, it's basically an environment that uses Chrome's V8 JavaScript engine and lets us run JavaScript code from a console.

What is RxJS?

Very simply, RxJS is an implementation of Reactive Extensions in JavaScript.

Now, get ready to get super confused.

Until December 2016, there were two major implementations of RxJS:

- **RxJS 4**: This is the older implementation most people are familiar with. Its source code is available at `https://github.com/Reactive-Extensions/RxJS`, and it's written in JavaScript (ES5). As we said at the beginning of this chapter, RxPHP refers at this moment mostly to this older RxJS 4 version that'll become obsolete in the near future.
- **RxJS 5**: The newer and completely rewritten RxJS that will replace the older RxJS 4. Its source code is available at `https://github.com/ReactiveX/rxjs`, and it's completely written in TypeScript 2.0.

Because we've mentioned yet another programming language called TypeScript, we should quickly look at what JavaScript versions are actually out there and where (and also if) we can use them:

- **ES5.1**: The good old JavaScript that probably everybody has encountered at some point.
- **ES6** (also named **ES2015**): This is the newer standard of JavaScript. It's backward compatible with ES5.1, and it brings features such as classes, generators, arrow functions, and the `let` keyword to create block scoped variables.

- **ES7** (**ES2016**): This is the even newer standard of JavaScript that brings in yet more features such as the `async`/`await` keyword to avoid creating callback hells.
- **TypeScript**: This is a superset of ES6 specification supplemented with type checking and is in the latest versions, also with features from ES7 such as the `async`/`await` keyword.

So TypeScript was the language of choice for RxJS 5 because of its compatibility with ES6 and type checking that helps prevent a lot of bugs in compile time.

Well, while speaking of compiling, we should probably mention where we can actually run any of these new and fancy languages:

- ES5.1 is supported by every current browser including mobile browsers and Node.js.
- ES6 can already be used with the two major JavaScript engines: Chrome's V8 and SpiderMonkey (used by FireFox). Although current compatibility with ES6 is pretty good (as we can see at `http://kangax.github.io/compat-table/es6/`), it's still not possible to rely only on ES6 for browser-based applications. We obviously need to also support older browsers and mobile devices. For this reason, any code written in ES6 needs to be compiled to ES5 using a compiler such as babel (`https://babeljs.io/`) or traceur (`https://github.com/google/traceur-compiler`). This doesn't apply to Node.js where we can freely use ES6 since Node.js v4 is already pretty old, and the penetration of different Node.js versions isn't such a problem like those we're used to from web browsers (there's one important exception with ES6 module imports that we'll mention later).
- ES7 brings some features that are already implemented natively in JavaScript engines (see `http://kangax.github.io/compat-table/es2016plus/`); however, this is still music of the future. We're not going to use ES7 features in Node.js in this chapter, to avoid compiling our code from ES7 to ES6.
- TypeScript is a relatively new language made by Microsoft and the community around it. It's not going to be natively supported by any JavaScript engines. It uses different syntax and new keywords that aren't compatible with either ES6 or ES7. This means that TypeScript code always needs to be compiled to ES6 or more commonly to ES5.

On the other hand, it's important to note that TypeScript is a superset of ES6. This means that any ES5 or ES6 code is also a valid TypeScript code that makes reusing already existing JavaScript very easy.

This is in contrast to other languages that can be compiled to ES5, such as Dart made by Google. Dart isn't compatible with JavaScript at all, and basically, all code needs to be rewritten to Dart. This might be one of the reasons why TypeScript is so popular today despite the fact that it came later than Dart.

So for this chapter, we're going to use Node.js (ideally, v6.9+, but basically, any v4+ should be fine) and ES6.

JavaScript module systems

To add to the confusion when talking about current JavaScript standards, we should also mention different module systems used today to define dependencies between JavaScript files.

Working with JavaScript was always tedious because there was never any unified way to split code into multiple files and load it on demand or even to bundle it.

So now we have nice ES6 syntax for ES6 modules available, let's consider the following code:

```
import * as lib from 'lib';
console.log(lib.square(42));
```

Can you tell in what environment we can run this code natively today?

This was a trick question. We can't run it anywhere because no JavaScript engine supports ES6 modules yet, not even Node.js.

 If you want to know more about why implementing ES6 modules into Node.js is so complicated, read this article by one of the Node.js developers at
https://hackernoon.com/node-js-tc-39-and-modules-a1118aecf95e.

Node.js at this moment supports only using the `require()` function to load modules in the CommonJS format (in fact, it's not exactly the CommonJS format; it's just very close to it). The `require()` function is natively available only in Node.js. If we wanted to use `require()` also in the browser, we'd need a polyfill or a bundler to merge multiple JavaScript files linked via `require()` calls into a single bundle.

If we really wanted to use ES6 module definitions right now, this would be another reason we'd have to compile our code. Note that we could actually compile ES6 code into another ES6 code, only to transform ES6 imports to one of the current module formats, such as UMD, CommonJS, AMD, SystemJS, or globals.

This has been resolved by various bundling tools, such as Browserify, webpack, SystemJS-Builder, or rollup.js. However, this just added yet another layer of complexity. Moreover, these tools just bundle multiple files into a single bundle. If we have a more complicated application where we need to load third-party libraries (that can be bundled in any format, which includes even the most basic Angular2 or React applications) we need to also care about module loaders.

Module loaders are, for example, SystemJS, require.js, require1k, curl.js, and probably dozens more.

This all means that when we start working on a JavaScript project today, we need to plan ahead the following four different things:

- What language I'm going to use? this has an effect on the features available and also on the compiler you have to use
- To what module format am I going to compile my source code?
- What bundling tool I'm going to use?
- How I am going to require my bundled project (by just including it via the `<script>` tag or do I need a module loader)?

So, RxJS 4 avoided almost all of this because it's written in ES5. The only necessary task is bundling it into a single file that can be loaded as easily as just using the `<script>` tag.

With RxJS 5, it gets more complicated.

The deployment process of RxJS 5

The entire RxJS 5 project is written in TypeScript. This means that it needs to be compiled to ES5, so we can use it in a browser or in Node.js.

The process goes as follows:

- The entire source code is first compiled to ES6 using the TypeScript compiler with the ES6 module resolution.
- The ES6 code is then compiled again using `closure-compiler-js` made by Google, which generates ES5 code.

- This ES5 code is bundled using rollup.js (before rollup.js, they were using Browserify) to create a single UMD bundle.
- This bundled file together with ES5 versions of each file along with their source maps and .d.ts files (TypeScript declaration file) are then uploaded to an npm repository. When we use RxJS 5 in, for example, Node.js, we will usually require only this single UMD bundle. When using RxJS 5 in a browser, we can just include it via the <script> tag thanks to the UMD module format.

 Universal Module Definition (**UMD**) is a universal module format that acts as AMD, CommonJS, SystemJS, or global depending on the environment loading it.

As we can see, developing applications in today's JavaScript is no joke. We'll see that it also has some benefits. In particular, prototypical-based inheritance can ease extending the existing Observables, which isn't possible in PHP for instance.

But before that, let's see how we can use RxJS 5 in Node.js.

A quick introduction to RxJS 5 in Node.js

We're already pretty experienced reactive developers, so none of these examples should surprise us.

We'll start by installing RxJS 5 via npm (basically, a dependency management tool similar to Composer in PHP):

```
$ npm install rxjs
```

As we said earlier, we're going to use ES6 syntax, but we want to avoid recompiling our code because of ES6 imports. That's why we'll always use the require() function to load dependencies. This example should be very simple:

```
// rxjs_01.js
const Rx = require('rxjs/Rx');

Rx.Observable.range(1, 8)
    .filter(val => val % 2 == 0)
    .subscribe(val => console.log('Next:', val));
```

We loaded RxJS 5 with `rxjs/Rx` under the Rx constant. Node.js knows where to find the `rxjs` package (it automatically looks for packages into the `node_modules` directory). The full name `rxjs/Rx` means that it'll load file from `./node_modules/rxjs/Rx.js`. It is like the entry point of this library. It contains a lot of `require()` calls and then it exports all the classes we as developers are allowed to use. All these classes are then accessible with the Rx prefix (for example, `Rx.Subject` or `Rx.TestScheduler`).

The arrow syntax `val => val % 2 == 0` we're using is just a shortcut to declare an anonymous function with a return statement:

```
function(val) {
    return val % 2 == 0;
}
```

The arrow => also makes the inner closure take the `this` context from its parent, but we're not going make use of this a lot here.

To run this demo, we'll just need Node.js runtime:

```
$ node rxjs_01.js
Next: 2
Next: 4
Next: 6
Next: 8
```

Even with this very primitive example, we can already see how different it is from PHP. When using Composer, we don't need to worry about where our dependencies come from because they're always loaded by the SPL autoloader usually generated by Composer.

Asynchronous calls in RxJS

Every time we wanted to make code in PHP asynchronous, we had to stick to event loops: in particular, `StreamSelectLoop` and `EventLoopScheduler`, and there was no way around it. Every `IntervalObservable` had to take as an argument a Scheduler (however, in RxPHP 2 this is done automatically for us so we usually don't need to worry about it).

This is in RxJS, and in general, any JavaScript environment completely different from PHP.

Consider the following example:

```
// interval_01.js
const Rx = require('rxjs/Rx');
const Observable = Rx.Observable;

Observable.interval(1000)
    .subscribe(val => console.log('#1 Next:', val));
Observable.interval(60)
    .subscribe(val => console.log('#2 Next:', val));
```

Note that we're using no loops and no Schedulers. In fact in RxJS 5, it's not that common for operators to take a Scheduler as an argument. The majority of operators don't because they don't need to schedule anything (such as the `map()` or `filter()` operators) and usually only those that need to work with timers do (basically, all operators containing work "time").

This also implies that we don't need to worry about the different parts of our application is using different even loops. We discussed this topic in Chapter 06, *PHP Streams API and Higher-Order Observables*, and Chapter 07, *Implementing Socket IPC and WebSocket Server/Client*, where we saw that this, left unattended, may cause deadlocks.

We can run this demo and see ever-increasing counters triggering:

```
$ node interval_01.js
#2 Next: 0
#1 Next: 0
#2 Next: 1
#2 Next: 2
#1 Next: 1
#2 Next: 3
```

A good question is why is it so simple in JavaScript and yet needs to be so complicated in PHP?

Node.js and asynchronous events

Node.js is in fact one large event loop based on the libuv library (http://docs.libuv.org/).

Let's consider the following example that demonstrates adding a new callback to the event loop:

```
// node_01.js
console.log('Starting application...');
var num = 5;
```

```
console.log('num =', num);

setTimeout(() => {
    console.log('Inside setTimeout');
    num += 1;
    console.log('num =', num);
});

console.log('After scheduling another callback');
console.log('num =', num);
```

When we run an application in Node.js, it takes our code as a single callback and starts executing it. Somewhere in our code, we're calling the `setTimeout()` function that takes as argument another callback that will be executed after some period of time. However, we called `setTimeout()` without providing any timeout.

This in fact doesn't matter because `setTimeout()` adds the callback to the event loop to be run as the last one after all other callbacks are executed. Using callbacks, we can easily make Node.js run our code asynchronously. It's also typical for Node.js that all system calls are asynchronous and take callbacks as parameters in order to be non-blocking.

The output in the console is as follows:

```
$ node node_01.js
Starting application...
num = 5
After scheduling another callback
num = 5
Inside setTimeout
num = 6
```

We can see that the callback was really called after the outer callback got finished. When there're no more callbacks in the event loop and no callbacks are pending, then Node.js terminates.

Deep inside libuv, there's actually a thread pool that runs in parallel and handles system calls that can be run concurrently. Nonetheless, this has no effect on our code because Node.js will always execute callbacks one after another. This is a huge difference to PHP where none of this exists and the only way to schedule asynchronous calls is using custom event loops just like we did with `StreamSelectLoop`.

Keep in mind that from our point of view, Node.js is always single threaded and strictly sequential. This means that just like in PHP if we write code that is blocking, it's going to block the execution thread as well. Node.js never executes callbacks in parallel. This of course applies to browser JavaScript environments as well.

If we wanted to run code in parallel, we could spawn subprocesses just like we did for example in Chapter 06, *PHP Streams API and Higher-Order Observables*.

Lossy backpressure with the debounceTime() operator

We know what backpressure is already from Chapter 07, *Implementing Socket IPC and WebSocket Server/Client*. A typical use case in RxJS is debounceTime() that takes a value and then waits until the specified timeout expires before re-emitting it further. This is very useful, for example, when creating an autocomplete feature where we want to postpone sending AJAX requests when the user is still typing into an input field (as we saw in Chapter 1, *Introduction to Reactive Programming*).

Let's have a look at its marble diagram:

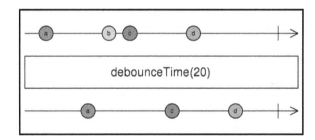

In order to illustrate a practical example of debounceTime(), consider the following example:

```
// debounce_time_01.js
Observable.interval(100)
    .concatMap(val => {
        let obs = Observable.of(val);
        return val % 5 == 0 ? obs.delay(250) : obs;
    })
    .debounceTime(200)
    .subscribe(val => console.log(val));
```

This example emits a value every 100 ms and every fifth value is delayed by 250 ms. That's why most of the values are ignored by debounceTime() because this operator requires an at least 200 ms long period without any emission from the source.

The output is as follows:

```
$ node debounce_time_01.js
4
9
14
```

There's one very nice practical example for `debounceTime()` that makes use of JavaScript's asynchronous callbacks.

In the first chapter, when talking about reactive programming, we mentioned that a common application that we consider "reactive" is Excel. We have multiple cells with equations that define their relations and every change to any cell is propagated to the entire spreadsheet.

Let's consider the following spreadsheet with three input values A, B, and C and the following equations we made on them:

	A	B	C
1	A	B	C
2	1	2	3
3			
4	AB = A + B	BC = B + C	
5	3	5	
6			
7	ABBC = A + B + B + C		
8	8		
9			

Now, how can we create something similar in RxJS? We can represent each cell as `BehaviorSubject` with a default value (we need to use Subjects in order to be able to change cell values later). Then, each equation (for example, A + B) will be held by `combineLatest()`.

The preceding spreadsheet could look like this in RxJS:

```
// excel_01.js
const Rx = require('rxjs/Rx');
const Observable = Rx.Observable;
const BehaviorSubject = Rx.BehaviorSubject;

let A = new BehaviorSubject(1);
let B = new BehaviorSubject(2);
let C = new BehaviorSubject(3);
```

```
let AB = Observable.combineLatest(A, B, (a, b) => a + b)
    .do(x => console.log('A + B = ' + x));

let BC = Observable.combineLatest(B, C, (b, c) => b + c)
    .do(x => console.log('B + C = ' + x));

let ABBC = Observable.combineLatest(AB, BC, (ab, bc) => ab + bc)
    .do(x => console.log('AB + BC = ' + x));

ABBC.subscribe();
```

We're using `combineLatest()` to get notified when any of the source Observables for each equation change. We also have multiple `do()` operators to log what's going on in our Observable chains.

When we run this demo, we'll see the following output:

```
$ node excel_01.js
A + B = 3
B + C = 5
AB + BC = 8
```

This is obviously correct. Each equation was called exactly once.

Now, let's imagine that we change the B cell value to 4 after the default values were propagated. This means that it'll need to recalculate AB, BC, and ABBC. The desired state after updating the B cell should look like the following screenshot:

	A	B	C
1	A	B	C
2	1	4	3
3			
4	AB = A + B	BC = B + C	
5	5	7	
6			
7	ABBC = A + B + B + C		
8	12		
9			

Append these two lines to the source file:

```
...
console.log("Updating B = 4 ...");
B.next(4);
```

Then, rerun the example and pay attention to what equations were evaluated:

```
$ node excel_01.js
A + B = 3
B + C = 5
AB + BC = 8
Updating B = 4 ...
A + B = 5
AB + BC = 10
B + C = 7
AB + BC = 12
```

The first three are alright. Then, we set B = 4, which triggers the recalculation of A + B, and right after that, AB + BC equals 10. Well, this is not correct because we haven't updated also B + C, which comes next. Then, after updating BC, the AB + BC is recalculated again and the correct value is set to ABBC.

We could just ignore this because the result is correct at the end. However, if the number of cells and the number of equations grew, then each redundant update would still cause an update to the page's DOM. As a result, this could make the page laggy and the user might notice the cells blinking.

So how can we avoid this?

We said that when debounceTime() receives a value, it stores it internally and starts a timeout. Then it doesn't re-emit any value until the timeout's callback is evaluated, which re-emits only the last value debounceTime() received. We can use this to our advantage by knowing that we can set 0 timeout, which won't delay the callback but just puts in at the end of Node.js's event loop.

In other words, when we use debounceTime(0), we'll ignore all values that debounceTime() receives until the end of this callback. So, we can use this to calculate AB + BC:

```
let ABBC = Observable.combineLatest(AB, BC, (ab, bc) => ab + bc)
    .debounceTime(0)
    .do(x => console.log('AB + BC = ' + x));
```

Now if we run the code again, we'll see the output we wanted:

```
$ node excel_01.js
A + B = 3
B + C = 5
Updating B = 4 ...
A + B = 5
B + C = 7
AB + BC = 12
```

This is definitely an advanced use case that we won't encounter on a daily basis, but it's nice to see that we can use JavaScript internals to our advantage.

Note that this is something very difficult to do in RxPHP without using an event loop and custom operators, yet relatively simple in JavaScript.

Higher-order Observables in RxJS 5 and RxPHP

When developing browser applications, we very often need to make AJAX calls to fetch data asynchronously. For example, in Angular2, this is very common, and in fact, any AJAX request made using Angular2's HTTP service returns an Observable where we typically chain the `map()` operator to decode JSON and then use `subscribe()` to be notified when the response is ready.

We can simulate such a situation with the following code:

```
// http_mock_01.js
const Rx = require('rxjs/Rx');
let data = '[{"name": "John"},{"name": "Bob"},{"name": "Dan"}]';

Rx.Observable.of(data)
    .map(response => JSON.parse(response))
    .subscribe(value => console.log('Next:', value));
```

Variable data contains a JSON-serialized array of objects that we decode and pass to the observer. The output looks like the following:

```
$ node http_mock_01.js
Next: [ { name: 'John' }, { name: 'Bob' }, { name: 'Dan' } ]
```

Well, it works, but what if we wanted to receive only objects with the `name` property starting with the letter B? Right now, we received the entire array of objects as a single emission.

So, the question is how can we unpack the array and emit every single object separately?

One option that can be used in RxJS and RxPHP in exactly the same way is using `concatMap()` (`mergeMap()` would work as well) and return a new Observable created from an iterable object. In RxJS, this could be as follows:

```
// http_mock_02.js
...
Observable.of(data)
    .map(response => JSON.parse(response))
    .concatMap(array => Observable.from(array))
    .filter(object => object.name[0].toLowerCase() == "b")
    .subscribe(value => console.log('Next:', value));
```

In RxJS 5, `Observable.from()` takes as a parameter any array-like object and emits all its items. In RxPHP, we'd use `Observable::fromArray()` instead.

Now the output is a single item because the rest was skipped thanks to the `filter()` operator:

```
$ node http_mock_02.js
Next: { name: 'Bob' }
```

In RxJS 5, there's also another and quite clever way to achieve the same result.

We've talked about operators that work with higher-order Observables, such as `mergeAll()` or `concatAll()`. These subscribe to an Observable that emits Observables. Due to RxJS 5 inner implementation, we can use a little trick and use operators that normally work with only higher-order Observables to work with arrays as well.

Let's see how `concatAll()` can be used to achieve the same result as `concatMap()` in the preceding example:

```
Observable.of(data)
    .map(data => JSON.parse(data))
    .concatAll()
    .filter(object => object.name[0].toLowerCase() == "b")
    .subscribe(value => console.log('Next:', value));
```

So, this obviously shouldn't work. How can `concatAll()` subscribe to an array?

The answer lies in the way `concatAll()`, and basically, all operators working with higher-order Observables internally subscribe to items emitted by the source Observable. In PHP, we'd expect that all of them have to be other Observables, but this is not the case for RxJS 5.

Some operators in RxJS 5 subscribe to inner Observables via a function named `subscribeToResult()` (it's defined in `src/util/subscribeToResult.ts`). This function has multiple handlers for different types of items. There's of course a handler for Observables, but apart from that, it also knows how to work with Promises as well as JavaScript arrays.

When we used `concatAll()` earlier, the `subscribeToResult()` function just iterated the array and re-emitted all its values. Note that it just iterated the array internally. It didn't create another Observable from it.

So, these were just two, but useful, differences we can encounter when switching from RxPHP to RxJS 5.

Operators specific for RxJS 5

As we said, there are extra operators in RxJS 5 that aren't available in RxPHP right now. There are in fact, quite of few of them, but many are very similar in principle. We mentioned some of them in `Chapter 07`, *Implementing Socket IPC and WebSocket Server/Client*, such as `audit()` or `throttle()`, including all their variations that use timeouts or other Observables to create time windows. Also, all operators derived from `buffer()` aren't so interesting for us.

We'll have a look at the three of them that serve some other interesting purposes.

The expand() operator

The interesting thing about the `expand()` operator is that it works recursively. It takes as a parameter a callback that needs to return another Observable. The callback is then applied to all values emitted by the returned Observable. This goes on as long as the returned Observables emit values.

Consider the following example where we use `expand()` to recursively multiply a value by two as long as the result is less than 32:

```
// expand_01.js
const Rx = require('rxjs/Rx');
const Observable = Rx.Observable;

Observable.of(1)
    .expand(val => {
        if (val > 32) {
            return Observable.empty();
        } else {
            return Observable.of(val * 2);
        }
    })
    .subscribe(val => console.log(val));
```

We stop the recursion by not emitting any value and returning just `Observable.empty()` (which emits just a complete signal).

All intermediate values produced by all the recursive calls are re-emitted by `expand()`, so the output from this example will look as follows:

```
$ node expand_01.js
1
2
4
8
16
32
64
```

The finally() operator

As the name suggests, this operator executes its callback on both the `error` and `complete` signals. It's important to see the difference between `finally()` and just subscribing and using the same callbacks for error and complete signals.

The `finally()` operator doesn't turn cold Observables to hot. So, it's more similar to the `do()` operator than to the `subscribe()` method:

```
// finally_01.js
const Rx = require('rxjs/Rx');
let source = Rx.Observable.create(observer => {
        observer.next(1);
```

```
        observer.error('error message');
        observer.next(3);
        observer.complete();
    });

source
    .finally(() => console.log('#1 Finally callback'))
    .subscribe(
        value => console.log('#1 Next:', value),
        error => console.log('#1 Error:', error),
        () => console.log('#1 Complete')
    );

source
    .onErrorResumeNext()
    .finally(() => console.log('#2 Finally callback'))
    .subscribe(
        value => console.log('#2 Next:', value),
        error => console.log('#2 Error:', error),
        () => console.log('#2 Complete')
    );
```

The first subscription will receive only the first value and then the error signal. Note the order in which we used the `finally()` operator and the `subscribe()` call. Operator `finally()` comes first so it also receives the error signal first.

The second subscription is analogous. Also, this one uses `onErrorResumeNext()` to ignore the error signal (even though it won't receive the last value because it has already unsubscribed). It'll receive just the complete signal. Again, note where the `finally()` operator is used.

When we run this example, we'll get the following output:

```
$ node finally_01.js
#1 Next: 1
#1 Error: error message
#1 Finally callback
#2 Next: 1
#2 Complete
#2 Finally callback
```

Even though both `finally()` operators are used before `subscribe()` (which is obvious because these are operators that need to be somewhere in the chain), their callbacks were executed after the error or complete callbacks from `subscribe()`.

This is the fundamental difference of the `do()` operator and also the reason why `finally()` might come in handy in certain situations.

The withLatestFrom() operator

In `Chapter 07`, *Implementing Socket IPC and WebSocket Server/Client*, and `Chapter 8`, *Multicasting in RxPHP and PHP7 pthreads Extension*, we used the `combineLatest()` operator, and we mentioned that in RxJS 5, there's also a slightly modified variant.

The `combineLatest()` operator takes multiple source Observables and emits their most recent values as an array when any of them emit a value. Then, there's the `withLatestFrom()` operator that takes multiple sources as well, but this operator emits a value only when its direct predecessor in the chain emits a value (its source Observable).

Consider the following example with multiple timers:

```
// with_latest_from_01.js
const Rx = require('rxjs/Rx');
const Observable = Rx.Observable;

let source1 = Observable.interval(150);
let source2 = Observable.interval(250);

Observable.interval(1000)
    .withLatestFrom(source1, source2)
    .subscribe(response => console.log(response));
```

Both `source1` and `source2` emit multiple values every second. However, `withLatestFrom()` re-emits their values only when `Observable.interval(1000)` emits a value.

The output from this demo is as follows:

```
$ node with_latest_from_01.js
[ 0, 5, 2 ]
[ 1, 12, 6 ]
[ 2, 19, 10 ]
[ 3, 25, 14 ]
[ 4, 31, 18 ]
[ 5, 38, 22 ]
[ 6, 45, 26 ]
[ 7, 51, 30 ]
```

Use cases for this operator are very similar to those for `combineLatest()`. We just have a better control of the re-emission, which could be useful, for example, to implement caching mechanisms where the 1-second interval could control when we want to refresh the cache.

While speaking of caching, we will have a look at the last and very nice example in this book.

Caching HTTP requests with publishReplay() and take()

This example is my favorite. I show this demo to people who want to start with RxJS and they're overwhelmed by the complexity and don't see the practical advantage.

A very common use case in frontend development is that we need to cache results from AJAX calls. For example, we might have a server that we want to query once a minute at most. All subsequent calls under one minute won't spawn another AJAX call but receive only the cached data.

This can all be done by leveraging the `publishReplay()` and `take()` operators:

```
// cache_01.js
const Rx = require('rxjs/Rx');
const Observable = Rx.Observable;

var counter = 1;
var updateTrigger = Observable.defer(() => mockDataFetch())
    .publishReplay(1, 1000)
    .refCount();

function mockDataFetch() {
    return Observable.of(counter++).delay(100);
}

function mockHttpCache() {
    return updateTrigger.take(1);
}
```

We're creating mock requests with the `mockDataFetch()` function that increments the counter every time it's called (this is to make sure that we're not making more calls to the server than we think). Then, we delay this Observable to pretend it takes some time.

Every time we want to get current data from a cache or from a fresh AJAX request, we use the `mockHttpCache()` function that returns an Observable.

Let's have a look at how we schedule a couple of calls and then make sure that this really works as we expect from the console output. After this, we can explain why this works:

```
mockHttpCache().toPromise()
    .then(val => console.log("Response from 0:", val));

setTimeout(() => mockHttpCache().toPromise()
    .then(val => console.log("Response from 200:", val))
, 200);

setTimeout(() => mockHttpCache().toPromise()
    .then(val => console.log("Response from 1200:", val))
, 1200);

setTimeout(() => mockHttpCache().toPromise()
    .then(val => console.log("Response from 1500:", val))
, 1500);

setTimeout(() => mockHttpCache().toPromise()
    .then(val => console.log("Response from 3500:", val))
, 3500);
```

We're making five requests in total. The first two should receive the same response. The next two will receive another response, and the last one will have the third response. For illustrational purposes, we're caching responses only for 1 second.

Now, let's see the console output:

```
$ node cache_01.js
Response from 0: 1
Response from 200: 1
Response from 1200: 2
Response from 1500: 2
Response from 3500: 3
```

So, it really works as we want; but how?

The `publishReplay(1, 1000)` operator multicasts responses for 1 second via `ReplaySubject` (see *Chapter 8*, *Multicasting in RxPHP and PHP7 pthreads Extension*, for more info on multicasting). After 1 second, it discards the stored result.

When we call `mockHttpCache()`, one of these situations occur:

- We subscribe to `ReplaySubject` that already has a cached response. In that case, on subscription, it immediately calls `next()` and sends this value to its new subscriber. Since there's `take(1)` operator, it passes the value and the chain completes. The `ReplaySubject` then checks whether the subscriber has stopped after passing it the cached value. Thanks to `take(1)` it does stop, so `ReplaySubject` won't subscribe to the deferred Observable.
- We subscribe to `ReplaySubject`, but it doesn't have any valid response cached and/or it also needs to subscribe to the deferred Observable that triggers a new AJAX request. When the request is ready, it's passed down the chain where `take(1)` re-emits it and completes.

So this was a pretty short and clever way to make already sophisticated functionality that would normally require using at least one `setTimeout()` and at a minimum two state variables to keep the cached response and the time it was created.

Summary

This final chapter was dedicated to RxJS 5 to show that while most principles are the same, there are a couple of differences that we can take advantage of.

After reading this chapter, you should know the differences between RxJS 4 and RxJS 5, what technologies are used to develop and deploy RxJS 5, how Node.js handles asynchronous code, and what operators are present in RxJS 5 already but aren't implemented in RxPHP yet.

Hopefully, you'll take the best out of RxJS and RxPHP and use it to write faster and more readable code yourself.

Index

www.ingramcontent.com/pod-product-compliance
Lightning Source LLC
Chambersburg PA
CBHW062052050326
40690CB00016B/3063